CRISWELL'S GUIDEBOOK FOR PASTORS

W. A. CRISWELL

BROADMAN PRESS Nashville, Tennessee

4225-36
ISBN: 0-8054-2536-5

Dewey Decimal Classification: 253
Subject heading(s): MINISTERS//CHURCH WORK
Library of Congress Catalog Card Number: 79-7735
Printed in the United States of America

DEDICATED
TO
MY FELLOW PASTORS
IN THE FAITH

FOREWORD

There are only two reasons why I should be asked to write a guidebook for ministers and pastors. The first is because I have been a pastor for over fifty years, thirty-six and beyond of those years being with the church here in Dallas. The other reason is because God has so signally blessed the work with the dear people of the Dallas congregation. We are working now toward eight thousand registered every Sunday in Sunday School and toward a giving program of over eight million dollars a year. If we can also baptize more than one thousand souls a year and teach our people the mind of God which was in Christ Jesus, we shall be on our way toward even greater things for our Lord (John 14:12).

My guidebook is for pastors and ministers in churches of all sizes and locations—the open country church, the village church, the town church, and the mammoth metropolitan church. My first church had thirty-five members. Remember that I prayerfully offer these materials as suggestions.

Many things does a pastor learn along the shepherd road of caring for the flock of his Lord. Most of these things he cannot learn in a book. The knowledge comes by hard experience, by hand-to-hand conflict with Satan and all his angels (Eph. 6:10-18). But experience also deepens the life of the pastor as he prays with and for his congregation. It is not all tears and sorrows and conflict. It is also victory and advancement and joy in the Holy Spirit. Leading people to Christ and seeing them grow with the pastor in every Christian grace is a consummation devoutly to be wished and an ineffable gladness.

What is written here cannot take the place of the pastor's personal experience. He has to learn for himself. He has to try for himself. He has to see what works in the blessing of God upon his congregation. But any pastor can profit by the experience of others. It is with this hope that my fellow pastors can be blessed by my long journey down this servant road that these chapters are penned. Maybe there are suggested methods of approach that the pastor can use; maybe there are pitfalls that he can avoid; maybe there are encouragements that will help him to persevere when he is sorely tempted to quit. If in any of these ways the book can be a help, then the effort is well worth the while of writing.

Now may God bless the eyes that look upon these pages and bless the brave-hearted pastor that attempts to place in actual working order the thoughts and suggestions offered in the book. There is so much to do. There is a whole world to win. We are ever only one generation from absolute and utter paganism. We must do our assignment well and with haste. God speed us in the way!

W. A. Criswell
First Baptist Church
Dallas, Texas

About the Author

Dr. W. A. Criswell desires no accolades for himself, even though many have referred to him as the greatest preacher of the twentieth century and one of the greatest in Christian history. He is recognized as one of evangelical Christianity's clarion voices.

He is the first to admit that he is a servant of the King of kings and Lord of lords. The obsession of his life is to perform an acceptable service for his Lord and Savior, Jesus Christ. His preoccupation with souls accounts for the amazing ministry of the First Baptist Church of Dallas, Texas.

He was not in an enviable position in 1944 when he accepted the call of the First Baptist Church, because he had to follow one of the premier pastors and preachers of modern history, Dr. George W. Truett. Almost four decades of ministry with that congregation have demonstrated that Dr. Criswell, through the Holy Spirit, has done remarkably well indeed!

Dr. Criswell is a native of Eldorado, Oklahoma, and grew up in New Mexico. He entered the ministry at the age of seventeen in 1928. He served as a student pastor in college and seminary. He graduated from Baylor University and The Southern Baptist Theological Seminary, Louisville, Kentucky (Ph.D.). He was also given an honorary degree by Baylor University.

He served the maximum term, two years, as president of the Southern Baptist Convention for 1969 and 1970. He has preached the message of redemption through Jesus Christ on every continent in the world.

Dr. Criswell has served his state convention and the Southern Baptist Convention in innumerable capacities. He has given unstintingly of his talent and time to Convention causes. He is virtually a fixture at the annual SBC Pastor's Conference which precedes the Convention. He has preached to multiplied hundreds of evangelistic conferences, state convention sessions, and other gatherings. He preached the annual Convention Sermon at the Southern Baptist Convention in 1947.

Under his Spirit-led leadership the First Baptist Church in the downtown area of Dallas is still growing. The membership has far exceeded 20,000 and continues to increase every week.

Dr. Criswell has published over thirty books, nine with Broadman. His Broadman titles, all in print but the first, are *The Gospel According to Moses, Why I Preach That the Bible Is Literally True, Look, Up, Brother! The Scarlet Thread Through the Bible, What to Do Until Jesus Comes Back, Welcome Back, Jesus! What a Savior! With a Bible in My Hand,* and this book, *Criswell's Guidebook for Pastors.*

CONTENTS

1

The Place of the Pastor-Preacher in Christ's Plan

The Ascension Gifts of Christ

1. The ascension gifts of Christ are in most places in the New Testament endowments, abilities conferred upon men and women to magnify the Lord and to further the ministries of the church. They are sometimes called *ta pneumatica* (1 Cor. 12:1) and sometimes *ta charismata* (1 Cor. 12:4). But in one place the ascension gifts of Christ are called *doma* (Eph. 4:8), a "gift," a "present," and here refers not to endowments but to chosen, elected people. The gifts, bestowed by Christ upon his churches after his ascension into heaven, are based upon his victory over Satan, sin, and the grave. Victorious, he has the right to distribute the spoils and to dispense these marvelous presents. Named in those glorious gifts of Christ to his church is the pastor-teacher. How exalted his calling! How marvelous his election! God calls the pastors and gives them, assigns them to his churches.

2. The call of the preacher is deprecated by many in the secular world.

At the beginning of this century a literary critic in a New York paper, after receiving a book about preachers of the day, including Phillips Brooks, added a derogatory remark that "it was a pity so much ability and labor were spent upon men whose work was entirely aside from the main currents of human interest."

When I gave my life to be a preacher, the remark was made to me, "What a pity to throw your life away!" The judgment of so much of the unbelieving world is that the influence of the pulpit has long since been rejected by thinking people, and that the ministry of the pulpit is irrelevant and insipid.

But in the judgment of God those ascension gifts of Christ are the most valued, the most precious, and (bless his name), the most lasting.

The riches of the churches are not found in monumental buildings and monetary investments but in the people God has called and given to be the ministers of his redeemed.

3. Christ from heaven never fails to bestow upon his churches those ascension gifts.

Through the centuries, and until Jesus comes again, these Christ-chosen, Christ-sent, Christ-given men do and will endow and enrich the churches of our Lord.

In the Apostolic Age were the great preachers of the Lord: Peter, Paul, Stephen, Philip the evangelist, Apollos the orator, Timothy, and Titus.

In the Ante-Nicene, the Nicene, and the Post-Nicene Age were Polycarp of Smyrna, Papias of Hieropolis (across the Lycus River from Laodicea), Ignatius of Antioch, Justin Martyr of Samaria, Irenaeus, Tertullian, Origen, Augustine, Chrysostom, the "golden mouth."

In the Pre-Reformation Age were Peter Waldo, John Wycliffe, Savonarola, John Huss, Thomas Cranmer, Hugh Latimer, Menno Simons, George Fox.

In the Reformation Age were Martin Luther, Melanchthon, Ulrich Zwingli, John Calvin, John Knox, Balthasar Hübmaier, Felix Manz.

In the seventeenth century were John Bunyan, Richard Baxter, Samuel Rutherford, William Guthrie, Roger Williams, William Penn.

In the eighteenth century were John Wesley, George Whitefield, Jonathan Edwards, David Brainerd, William Carey.

In the nineteenth century were Christmas Evans, Charles H. Spurgeon, Joseph Parker, Thomas Chalmers, F. W. Robertson, Alexander Maclaren, Charles G. Finney, Dwight L. Moody, Sam Jones, John A. Broadus, Adoniram Judson, David Livingstone.

In the twentieth century were Robert E. Speer, John R. Mott,

George W. Truett, Lee R. Scarborough, Robert G. Lee, Billy Sunday, and more yet to be added.

Always and in all ages the preacher is there, called of God and proclaiming to the world the truth of heaven.

There is a statue of John Bunyan in Bedford, England. Inscribed on the back panel are the words he wrote·in *The Pilgrim's Progress* as in the Interpreter's House, Christian saw the picture of:

> A very great person hung against the wall;
> and this was the fashion:
> eyes lifted up to heaven,
> the best of books in his hand,
> the law of truth was written upon his lips,
> the world was behind his back;
> he stood as if he pleaded with men;
> a crown of gold did hang above his head.

This is the preacher and he is God's gift to the world. We could not do without him.

Lloyd-George, British prime minister during the First World War, declared, "When the chariot of humanity gets stuck . . . nothing will lift it out except great preaching that goes straight to the mind and heart. There is nothing in this case that will save the world but what was once called, 'the foolishness of preaching.' "

The Divine Assignment of the Pastor-Preacher

The preacher is sent on a heavenly mission. He is to declare the message of God to the world, "whether they will hear, or whether they will forbear" (Ezek. 2:5,7; 3:11).

1. Preaching was recognized as a gift from God in the Old Testament. Noah was "a preacher of righteousness" (2 Pet. 2:5) by whose testimony the antediluvian world was condemned (Heb. 11:7). The psalmist and the prophets delivered their messages of truth in pleading, exhortation, prophecy, and promises from the Lord. The prophets were the preachers of their day and the predecessors of the New Testament heralds of the gospel.

After the Exile the reading and exposition of Scripture were from the beginning the chief feature of the synagogue service, and is frequently mentioned in the New Testament. Jesus, "as his custom was," went to the synagogue service on the sabbath day and there delivered the wonderful message of hope recorded in Luke 4:17-22. In Acts 13:15, "after the reading of the law and the prophets" the rulers of the synagogue invited the two preachers, Paul and Barnabas, to deliver this message of exhortation. In Acts 15:21, James, the pastor of the church at Jerusalem and the presiding officer over the council in Jerusalem, spoke of the fact that "Moses of old time hath in every city them that preach him, being read in the synagogues every sabbath day." Judaism has always had its preachers.

2. The New Testament church, likewise, moves on the feet of those who "preach the gospel of peace and bring glad tidings of good things" (Rom. 10:15). It was Paul who declared that faith in Jesus as Lord will save all who call upon him (v. 9), but "How . . . shall they call on him in whom they have not believed? and how shall they believe in him of whom they have not heard? and how shall they hear without a preacher?" (v. 14).

This preaching of salvation that Paul referred to is the proclamation of the Word of God recorded in the Holy Scriptures and centered in the redemptive work of Christ. It is a summons of men to repentance, faith, and obedience before the Lord Jesus. It is God's appointed means for communicating the gospel of hope to the unbelieving world and for the strengthening of the faith of those who have found refuge in our living Lord.

The apostolic message (*kerygma*), the preaching of the men who first heard the Great Commission of our Lord, consisted of these seven things:

(1) It was a definite body of facts; it was "propositional truth."

(2) It was not speculative philosophy but an announcement (you could say a heralding) of the intervention of God in human history for the salvation of those who would hear, heed, and accept.

(3) It was centered in the redemptive work of Christ, in his cross and atonement, and glorious resurrection.

(4) It was witnessed to and confirmed in the human heart by the Holy Spirit.

(5) It was historically and organically related to the Old Testa-

ment (it was the flower and fruit of which Judaism was the root and stem).

(6) It imposed a stern, ethical demand upon men.

(7) It was a vast eschatological dimension. It looks forward to a triumphant forever in Christ.

The Truth of God Through Human Personality

In God's economy, there is no such thing as the delivery of this glorious message of truth without a preacher. In the elective purpose of God his will and work are made known to us through a living personality. This is the essence of preaching and is the first, primary calling of the pastor.

Phillips Brooks in 1877 in his *Yale Lectures on Preaching* said: "Preaching is the communication of truth by man to men. The truest truth communicated in any other way than through the personality of brother man to men is not preached truth."

Preaching is the truth of God mediated through a man's voice, life, heart, mind, in fact, his whole being. That is why Spurgeon preached from a "rail," not a pulpit desk. He said a man preaches with his whole body and it ought not to be hidden.

The need for that living message is everlasting (Rev. 14:6).

For every congregation, through every continuing generation, the truth of God must be relived, re-presented, reincarnated by the preacher.

An article was published calling for a moratorium on preaching. The day is coming, a prognostication was made, when a half dozen famous ministers would deliver sermons by means of radio (now it would be television) for all the churches and their congregations. Local pastors would only be errand boys for the people. The saints would then listen to the great beacons and the lesser lights would be submerged in the greater glory.

Why did this prophecy miserably fail? No great lover can love for us; no one husband can father all our children. Each generation must experience falling in love, building a home, rearing children. So each congregation must have its living pastor. The truth of God must be made to live again and again. That is the calling of the preacher-pastor.

2

The Pastor in the Pulpit

The Paramount Importance of Preaching

It is still written in the Bible, "It pleased God by the foolishness of preaching to save them that believe" (1 Cor. 1:21). There is no ministry under heaven so worthwhile, so vitally needed, so God-blessed as that of preaching the gospel. In 1950 Dr. Duke K. McCall and I went on a preaching mission around the world. When we came to Manila we were invited by the American ambassador to the Philippines, Myron M. Cowan, to eat lunch with him in the embassy. He said that he wanted to talk to us. What about? I was amazed when he said that the people of the Islands for the most part had a religion they could not understand and that they needed preaching to, that they needed to be taught the Word of God in their own language so they could become a nation of integrity and honesty and Christian nobility. He asked if our denomination would not send one thousand preacher-missionaries to the Islands! When we were in Japan General Douglas MacArthur asked for the same thing.

It is preaching the Word of God that people need. And it is preaching that feeds the souls of Christian converts.

A Lutheran church in Siberia, which had been without a preacher for forty years, was recently visited by a representative of the Lutheran World Federation. After forty years without a pastor, what happened when they finally again saw one? This representative of the Lutheran World Federation, with a collar and a cross around his neck, and official papers certifying his ordination—what happened when after forty years this ordained pastor stood there before them? What did they say?

They said, "Take your Bible and preach to us." He preached for an hour and they wanted another, and he preached for a second, and they would not permit him to leave that makeshift pulpit, and he preached for a third. When his voice gave out he stopped, because clearly they would have wanted a fourth hour. They wanted that because they were hungry, not because, as some might be inclined to suggest, forty years of persecution had turned them into masochists who enjoyed suffering. "Take your Bible and preach to us."

They did not ask him to organize and administer the parish and clean up their parish records which, if they existed, had to be a mess. They knew who was there and who wasn't. They didn't ask him to gather a small group and be an enabler. When there was need, they were able. They didn't say, "See, we have all these personal problems and we want to schedule appointments so you can counsel us and help us deal with them." It seems that, being a supportive, caring community of faith, they did that themselves, perhaps in what Luther called "the mutual consolation of the brethren." They didn't ask him to help them develop a statement of mission; they seem to have known their mission. They didn't ask him to help get a prayer group started; it seems they knew how to pray. And nor did they haul out some carefully hidden communion vessels and a baptismal ewer and ask him to give them the sacraments; they didn't need a priest; they had found ways to do that, too. "Take your Bible and preach to us."

Not that any of the above are wrong. Not that if that pastor from the Lutheran World Federation had been there a year instead of a day they might not have gotten to some of those things. Those things were not the critical ones. Those things were not the central ones, not the one absolute essential. For them, the crisis stripped them down to the one thing, and that was, "Open your Bible and preach to us."

The Pastor and Public Worship

1. Paul wrote about the services of public worship in Corinth, "Let all things be done decently and in order" (1 Cor. 14:40).

That verse concludes his whole, long discussion concerning the disorder that marred the meetings of the Corinthian Christians. The worship of God ought to be worthy of his glorious name. It is not a hoodlum's rally.

What is true worship? The word for worship is used in the Bible in some form or another no fewer than two hundred times. More than twenty times the people of God are explicitly instructed to "worship the Lord." It is important that we know just what worship is.

Probably the most comprehensive definition of worship I have ever heard or read is:

To worship is to quicken the conscience by the holiness of God; to feed the mind with the truth of God; to purge the imagination by the beauty of God; to open up the heart to the love of God; to devote the will to the purpose of God.

The achievement of this purpose is the supreme privilege and opportunity of the pastor. That is why the order of service ought always to be made by him. He also is to lead and direct his people in the worship of God.

2. There are always some mundane considerations that ought to be remembered when people are brought together in the preaching-worshiping service. The preparation of the building is one. The temperature ought to be right. The seating, acoustics (public address system), lighting (no lights ought ever to shine in the eyes of the congregation), cleanliness, everything should be in tip-top, excellent arrangement and condition.

3. There should always be a stated time to begin, and begin a minute or two or three before the announced hour. To begin late is unpardonable. The King's business requireth haste. We are gathered for an important service. It must not be delayed.

4. Let the whole tone and atmosphere of the service be one of joyful triumph. The psalmist sang, "I was glad when they said unto me, Let us go into the house of the Lord" (Ps. 122:1). Again the psalmist admonished: "Serve the Lord with gladness: come before his presence with singing. Enter into his gates with thanksgiving and into his courts with praise: be thankful unto him, and

bless his name'' (Ps. 100:2,4). Let the greeters, ushers, platform personalities, printed programs, everybody and everything reflect that happy, glad spirit.

5. In so many instances, the service of the church is almost wholly led by the pastor. He ought to plan the service, but insofar as is possible it is good for other ministers and laymen to share in the hour. The preacher ought not to do it all by himself; that is a weakness. It is good to have someone else to lead the invocation, another to lead the benediction, still another to lead in the reading of the Scripture, yet another to lead in the prayer of thanksgiving before the offering, and yet another to make the announcements and to greet the guests. The more the people can share in the service, the more they will feel they are a part of it.

6. The music of the worship service ought to make the very angels of heaven envious over the glory and splendor. The praises of earth prepare for the praises of heaven.

God's people in the Old Testament were devoted to the study and practice of music. It is the only art that seems to have been cultivated to any extent in ancient Israel. David invented musical instruments for the high worship of the Lord and taught the four thousand Levitical singers how to glorify God with them (1 Chron. 23:5). In the church we are admonished to praise the Lord ''in psalms and hymns and spiritual songs, singing and making melody in your heart to the Lord'' (Eph. 5:19). One of the psalms those Christians sang goes like this: ''Praise [God] with the sound of the trumpet: praise him with the psaltery and harp. . . . praise him with stringed instruments and organs. . . . praise him upon the high sounding cymbals'' (Ps. 150:3-5). Then the psalmist concludes: ''Let every thing that hath breath praise the Lord. Praise ye the Lord'' [the English translation of the Hebrew ''hallelujah''] (v. 6). Could anything be more fulsomely appropriate and more Christ-honoring? Let every church have a wonderful orchestra and a glorious choir.

The music of the church ought to be church music everlastingly and always. It ought to be reverentially worthy of our Lord, not cheap, jazzy, and secular. In order to attain the high result intended, the music of the faith must be religious. It must be of a worshipful heart. Nothing can really fulfill the idea of religious music which is not the breathing of true love for Jesus. Even the instruments in the orchestra will not play the true notes of power unless the touch of faith is upon them and the breath of holy feeling is in them. This is doubly true of the voice that sings in the choir; the very qualities of sound are inevitably toned by the holy and heavenly urge that moves them.

The song service ought to be in keeping with the message of the hour. It ought to infuse enthusiasm and the spirit of deepening interest on the part of the people. The selection of hymns should go along with the unity of the hour. It is a wonderful thing for the choir to sing a special number while the offering is being taken.

It is a fortunate church that has a gifted, dedicated minister of music, song leader, and choir builder. His place is one of praise and glory.

7. In the reading of the Scriptures in the service the selection ought to be made by the pastor and it should fit the theme of his sermon and his appeal of the hour. It should always further the goal of the preacher in delivering his message.

In keeping with the story of Ezra, the people stood up when the book was open. It is a wonderful thing if the congregation can stand up for the reading of the Scripture and it is fine if the people will read the Scripture with the pastor. That encourages the people to bring their Bibles to church. Before the passage is read, whoever leads the people in reading the Scripture should be very well acquainted with the passage. He should study it before he leads the people in reading it publicly, understand the meaning, convey the sense, pronounce the words correctly, and not drag the reading into a funeral dirge. Let all the people read with interest and with enthusiasm (a Greek word that means "God in you").

8. Cleansing the Temple (Mark 11:17), our Lord quoted Isaiah 56:7, "For mine house shall be called an house of prayer for all people."

In the front of my preaching Bible I have these lines written:

> He stands best but who kneels most.
> He stands strongest who kneels weakest.
> He stands longest who kneels longest.

Every divine service ought to be characterized by earnest, sincere intercession and supplication, not that they are to be lengthy (in private prayer there is no limit to the time of tarrying before the Lord, but public praying ought to be brief), but moving in depths of love and commitment. Public prayer ought to be carefully thought out. It should be something in which the people are blessed. It is not my persuasion that the prayer be written and read, but rather that it ought to be carefully thought through by the one who is to lead it. Extemporaneous prayer does not necessarily mean unpremeditated prayer. The prayer ought to contain, according to Paul in Philippians 4:6, thanksgiving to God for his mercies to us and then the intercessions that we would lay before God's throne of grace. Actually, the prayer ought to be the overflow of the inner life of the one who is praying. There ought to be, also, in the pastoral prayer, heartfelt sympathy with the lives of the people in their temptations, sorrows, dangers, and hopes.

Here are a few things that ought to be avoided in public prayer. The suppliant ought to avoid frequent references to himself. He ought to avoid, for the most part, personalities in his praying. Compliment or criticism in public prayer is to be especially avoided. Admonition and scolding ought to be avoided in prayer. It is not good to have a didactic, doctrinal method in prayer, as though we were assuming to instruct God. The prayer is not a sermon. It is the outflowing of religious emotion and desire toward God. The prayer ought to have a very definite form, from thanksgiving to confession to petition and intercession.

As to the posture of praying in the Bible, the people stood when they prayed, they knelt when they prayed, they lay prostrate before God in their praying. In my humble opinion, kneeling is a beautiful way in which to pray. It seems right that we kneel before God. Our eyes should be closed and our countenance should be natural and serious. The language should be simple, devout, and scriptural. One of the most beautiful things in the world is to hear a man pray who knows the language of the Bible. The tone of the voice in public prayer should be that of the natural expression of supplication.

We have an altar rail (kneeling rail) in our church that has changed the whole spirit and atmosphere of our public services. It came about like this. Several years ago Dr. Grady Cothen, then executive secretary of the Southern Baptist General Convention of California, called me on the telephone, asking me to come there for a retreat. He said: "My preachers are greatly discouraged. I will call them together, pay their expenses in coming, and you preach to them for a week. There will be no promotion; just listening to the word of the Lord and seeking the face of our Savior." I accepted and after traveling by air to San Francisco, was taken to a Nazarene campgrounds called Beulah Park. When I entered the large, open building where the services were held, I saw a mourner's bench (a flat bench without a back) stretching across the entire front of the auditorium, but paid no further attention to it at that time. On Thursday night of the week of preaching, as I drew toward the end of my sermon, a man stood up in the center of the congregation, walked to the aisle, down to the front, fell down at the mourner's bench, and began to weep audibly. As I continued preaching, another man stood up, did the same, came to the front, and began to weep at the mourner's bench. This continued with one man after another until I had to stop preaching. There were several hundred men down there on their knees, crying softly, and making confessions before God. It moved my soul to tears. It was one of the greatest services I have ever been in.

When I returned to Dallas, I received a letter from one of the pastors in California. In it he apologized for interrupting my preaching service at Beulah Park and asked me to forgive him. But he wanted to explain to me what had happened that caused him to do what he did. He wrote that he and his wife, in abysmal discouragement, had resolved the week before to resign the church, quit the ministry, and enter secular employment. The Sunday before he was to make known his decision to leave his calling of God to preach, he received the letter from Dr. Cothen, asking him to come to Beulah Park. The pastor said to his wife: "My expenses are all paid. It will cost me nothing. I will go, then when I return we will leave the church." That Thursday night, he wrote, something happened in his soul. He said he was not a forward person, not one for public demonstrations. But he just found himself standing up, going down to the front, and falling before the Lord on his knees, telling him all about the heartache and sorrows of his work, even telling the Lord of his reconsecration of his life to the task for which the Lord had appointed and ordained him. He concluded by saying that he and his wife were back at the job, working with renewed dedication, that God was blessing, but that he wanted me to forgive him for breaking into my sermon.

I wrote him in reply saying that he had blessed my life more than he could ever know and that I had resolved in my heart to do something if only God would give me courage to do it. I did not tell the pastor in my letter what it was I had resolved to attempt, but it was this: to have a kneeling rail, a mourner's bench, in my church.

At our first deacons' meeting, I attended with the full intention to ask them their permission and blessing upon what I wanted to do. But the meeting gathered, did its work, and was dismissed. Courage had oozed from my fingertips. I could not summon enough bravery to set the proposal before them. Meeting after meeting, month after month, went by and I still could not face the deacons with the request. (As I look back over those days, I am astonished at my timidity.) Finally, it came to pass, with all the fortitude and intrepidity I could command, I talked to the men about my experience at Beulah Park in California, and then asked that we build a mourner's bench (altar rail) in our church. My speech ended in a long, seemingly unending silence. No such thing was seen in our Baptist churches. At long last, an old, white-headed deacon stood up and said, "Brethren, if God has placed it upon the heart of our pastor that we have a mourner's bench in church, I make a motion that we build one." It was seconded. passed. It was built. (I have only one objection to it: they so beautifully it looks like an architectural decoration.) added kneelers at all the pews.

el when we pray. That is where we belong, on our knees

verts come forward at the invitation time we kneel ayer. Nothing has so blessed our service of worship eeling together in intercession.

on is the center of the Christian worship of ding to the Word of God. The Roman centurion, Cornelius, by divine direction from an angel from heaven (Acts 10:3), gathered his household together, presented Peter to them and said, "Now therefore are we all here, present before God, to hear all things that are commanded thee of God" (Acts 10:33). The Scripture then states, "Then Peter opened his mouth" (v. 34) and proceeded to preach the saving message of the Lord Jesus, "To him give all the prophets witness, that through his name whosoever believeth in him shall receive remission of sins" (v. 43). This is worship at its highest; all the faculties of the mind and all the power of the soul are raised to their highest use. It becomes an offering up to God of the truth proclaimed in his name. Ritual is no substitute for reality; ceremony cannot displace consecration. Let us reread Romans 10:17.

Faith cometh by purification?

          by candlelighting?

          by incense burning?

          by liturgy repeating?

No, but by hearing the word of the Lord.

What was central here must always be central, namely, the preaching of the Word of God. John the Baptist preached (Matt. 3:1); Jesus preached (Mark 1:14); Simon Peter preached (Acts 2:14,40); Paul preached (Acts 20:7-11, sometimes until after midnight!); and we ought to preach. The pulpit ought to be in the center of the church where the pastor expounds the immutable and eternal Word of God.

Many things might interestingly occupy an hour: current events, travelogues, book reviews, speculation. But never mind all that. That drivel is hashed and rehashed on radio, television, newspapers, editorials. You can buy the stuff at a magazine rack and read all about it on a sofa at home after dinner if you do not fall asleep. But the preacher is to deliver what God says, how our souls can be saved from hell, and how we can be born to eternal life, here and hereafter.

In the Bible, "Thus saith the Lord" is repeated more than two thousand times. The preacher, with the Word of God, stands in a great, towering fortress. If he stands in his own speculation, he stands in a paper tower his own hands have fashioned. It will burn down or the tempest will blow it away. But the true preacher, preaching with every drop of his lifeblood and with every spark of his understanding of the Word of God, has an unction from heaven itself. His feet may tremble but the rock upon which he stands shall abide forever.

Look at the work of Paul. He was God's preacher. His ministry is outlined in Acts 26:26-18.

We need the burning heart of the true preacher of Christ. We need the spirit of Amos 7:10-15; 3:8; of Jeremiah 20:2,7-9; of Paul, 1 Corinthians 9:16; of John Wesley, who loved to chant:

> Spirit of burning come.
> Refining fire go through my heart.
> Oh, that in me the sacred fire
> Might now begin to glow.

With the sermon the center of the worship service, everything in the hour ought to contribute to its delivery. That is why the pastor ought to plan every part of the meeting. There ought to be a unity of thought and purpose apparent in all that is said and done. This sustaining interest that the preacher is seeking to accomplish will encourage the congregation to respond beautifully and nobly.

The pastor in leading the service of worship needs to be deeply sensitive to pulpit decorum. For one thing, the preacher must always remember that he sets the tone of the public worship service. If he is devout and reverential, the people will be. If he is flippant and careless, the people will also assume that attitude toward the meeting. In the pulpit he ought always to sit with his feet on the floor and his legs never crossed. He ought not to slump in his chair, but to sit up straight. His manner of handling the Bible and the hymnal ought always to be reverential. As far as possible, he ought not to gossip with others on the platform. Only in a matter of dire emergency should he be busy talking to others and changing final arrangements.

10. The sermon of the pastor ought to climax in an appeal for souls. The invitation ought to be pressed in every service and the pastor as well as the congregation ought to pray for, work for, and expect a harvest. It is a sorry spectacle to see a preacher preach with no expectancy and the congregation wait for a hurried benediction as though its pronouncement were an amnesty. That

is what it is all about—getting people to Jesus, saved from the judgment of hell to the joy and glory of heaven. Many times I have seen a preacher announce an invitation hymn then stick his nose down in the hymnal trying to sing it. If someone came forward to accept Jesus as Savior, he would have to jar the preacher out of his musical preoccupation to make public his confession of faith. These must be pastors who believe in the extracanonical beatitude, "Blessed is he that expects nothing, for he shall not be disappointed!" Pastor, preach for a verdict and expect it. God will honor your faith with souls.

His Manner and Appearance in the Pulpit

When you see the man in the pulpit, what do you see? And what do you think of the pastor standing before you? Is he representing to you the greatest cause and mission known to man? Let us judge the pastor by the ten tremendous characteristics great preachers have in common.

1. He has an enormous capacity to identify with people. Call it rapport, empathy, or ability to establish friendly relations, he has it. You know he wants to be friendly. No high-hatism, no show of professionalism. Great preachers are grand, friendly.

2. His personality is pleasing. He is likeable in his manner of dress and grooming. People feel comfortable with him. He is glad to have met them as friends. He has acquired graciousness and poise. He looks at you when you are speaking to him and always responds kindly to your remarks. There is healing in his presence.

3. He possesses masterful preaching techniques: voice, gesture, articulation. He is readily heard. His choice of themes has tremendous appeal. He works not only on his sermon preparation, but also on himself as the instrument of the timely address. The mighty preacher is a mighty, hardworking man. Not just an occasional message, but all of his sermons are outstanding. The great minister sits, stands, and speaks in the pulpit as a professional. He is as a prophet of Israel when he addresses his people. People leave the sanctuary knowing they have heard a wonderful sermon from a man of God.

4. The great preacher is undergirded with influential support. He becomes a part of issues and objectives greater than himself.

His name carries the weight of mighty causes. He aligns himself with issues and causes that are great.

5. He lives in an area of tremendous support on the part of family and congregation; all show absolute integrity.

6. He builds an image of success, good programming, and solid reasoning behind every endeavor.

7. He will be capable of using all of his tools excellently and well, studying, sermonizing, preaching expositorily, and using other methods of preaching. His people are not disappointed because of trivia.

8. He is a prodigious reader. Journals, books, articles, magazines, newspapers are familiar to him.

9. He always presents a positive and constructive outlook and answer. He challenges people to live up to their best. He believes he is on the side of God and therefore cannot lose.

10. He appeals for souls. He builds his church. As he builds sermons he builds congregations, and as he preaches the gospel he wins the lost.

It is important how the pastor looks and works in the pulpit and among his people.

I like for the preacher to look like a preacher, not like a bum. I would expect the head of a state or an ambassador from a mighty nation to look the part. The preacher is ambassador plenipotentiary from the greatest court in the universe, even from the throne of heaven itself. He ought to reflect the garments of glory in his own manner of dress.

He ought to dress immaculately, neat, and clean, whether in the office, in the pulpit, or in making visits.

Pastor, be sure that your nails are clean and use hand lotion if necessary to keep your hands smooth. Keep your hair clean, styled, and combed. Do not neglect your shoes; always have them shining and be sure your heels are not run over. Wear socks the color of your shoes and always wear dark socks on the platform. Always be careful that you have a clean collar and your coat and pants are clean and pressed.

The pastor ought to be dressed appropriately all the time for every occasion. There is a way to dress for a church camp, there is a way to dress at a wedding, there is a way to dress for a party.

Good, common sense will dictate what ought to be worn. Just remember that appropriateness of dress can speak more loudly than your words.

Be wise and cautious in the selection of your clothing. Avoid extremes and unusual dress. Do not seek to be shocking or startling in your wardrobe. Darker colors seem to carry more of a command for respect than lighter ones. Accessories matching the suit can be most impressive.

Change clothing often. Care for your apparel with meticulous diligence. Rotate the wearing of your suits, shoes, and other garments. This gives the clothes time to get back into shape.

Dress beautifully and well and the church will pay for it (gladly and happily will they support a pastor who looks the part). Dress beautifully and then, as you stand before the people, forget about how you look. Before you go out before the people, take a good, earnest look at yourself in the mirror, then dismiss your appearance from your mind. Dress so that the people are not looking at what you have on, but at you.

Do not stuff your pockets full of things. Never let them bulge. Your shirt collar ought to be large enough to give you proper room in which to speak and deliver your message.

In general appearance, look the part of health, happiness, confidence, and assurance. God is with us and the victory is his. In posture, demeanor, and every attitude lift up the spirit of the people. Wear your best clothing with a big, sincere, glowing smile. The world needs it.

Watch your mannerisms. Some of this may be a part of your outgoing personality, but mostly they are little peculiarities that creep upon us unawares and soon become distracting habits. Ask a family member or a trusted friend to point out to you any gesture or grimace that is hurtful. Hands in your pockets, facial distortions and contortions, yanking up your pants, scratching your head or your ear, weaving back and forth, looking always above the heads of the audience, these and a thousand other like provocatives induce unconscious dislike. Look at other preachers and learn from them what to emulate and what to avoid.

Do not take lightly this admonition about mannerisms. They can absolutely ruin the effectiveness of an otherwise gifted pulpiteer. Remember that many idiosyncrasies can creep into a minister's delivery without his ever being aware of it. This is particularly true if he has been preaching for several years. What are some of these peculiarities that can be annoying to an audience and in extreme cases so objectionable that the minister may be asked to leave? One minister I know assumed what might be called a "stained-glass window" tone as soon as he began his sermon and sustained it throughout his speaking. This speech was entirely different from his normal voice and gave an almost sepulchral sound which was irritating to his listeners. A word from a wise critic (his wife) might have helped him to overcome this defect.

Another unpleasant habit is that of "fiddling" with apparel, rattling loose change, taking one's hands constantly in and out of one's pockets, straightening a tie, swinging keys, and all such disturbing activities. He should groom himself (perhaps before a mirror) immediately before coming to the pulpit and rest in the assurance that he looks fine, and leave it at that.

There is not much that one can do about extremely poor English in the pulpit, especially if the minister has been preaching a long time. Habits like this have been acquired in early life, elementary and high school, and in his home environment. But even one who ordinarily speaks good English can fall into the habit of over-working certain words until they lose their meaning and the audience begins to count the number of times each recurring word is used. Superlatives are particularly noticeable, such as "the most tremendous, the grandest, the most exciting, the highest, the most far-reaching."

Let the pastor be the best preacher he possibly can. There is no limit to improvement through careful trial and study, even down to old age. He or she is a friend who helps you do better.

The Sermon He Preaches

Christ is the one great theme of the pulpit and around this all other themes gather as to their center and as to their end. Paul said, "We preach Christ crucified" (1 Cor. 1:23). He states this again in 2 Corinthians 5:18-21, in Galatians 6:14, and in many other passages. When somebody came to Spurgeon and said that all of his sermons sounded alike, he admitted: "That is correct. Wherever I take my text, I make a bee-line to the cross." All true preaching, whatever its range of topics, is the preaching of Christ. No topic is fit for the pulpit which does not lead to him. The themes of the preacher are essentially the same in all ages, for the human heart in its depravity and need does not change with the changing years. God's remedy is the simple gospel and that ever remains the same yesterday, today, and forever.

Effective preaching in all ages adheres to these same great truths. They have differed only in modes of illustrating and applying them, but the subject matter of the minister's message is unchangeable. The sermon, according to John 6:63, is not of words, cold and indifferent, but of soul-changing truth, filled with Spirit and life. The pastor's heart will be ennobled by the study of the Bible and its quickening thoughts of God. But there is more. As the days pass, the preacher will be speaking out of a rich, personal, religious experience.

A mere auditory ministry is a failure. A man ought not be just a pep talker, or just a tightrope walker, afraid of falling off in either direction. He ought to present the whole counsel of God. He ought to avoid a dry, formal, metaphysical method in his message. A sermon is not a theological essay. It is designed to move the heart and the will of the people as well as to instruct them in the way and in the faith. A sermon ought to be like the epistles of Paul. The apostle wrote of great doctrinal truth and teaching, then he closed with wonderful practical application. All of Paul's letters are like that. The first part is doctrinal and the second part is always practical when he applies the truth of the gospel of Christ.

There are many different kinds of preaching, but the heart of it all is to preach the Christ of the Bible, the Word of God incarnate, spoken and written. It is a strange thing that all three are called the Word of God, whether robed in flesh, or committed to a scroll in ink, or reverberating with the voice of God. The Bible and the Christ are inseparable. To minimize the written Word is to dishonor the living Word. To magnify the Book is to glorify Christ.

The Bible and the Christ stand or fall together. The storm centers of Christian theology today, as in centuries past, are the deity of Christ and the infallibility of the Holy Scriptures.

A man and his word may be two different things, but not God and his Word. God's Word is like God himself, the same yesterday, today, and forever (Heb. 13:8; Ps. 119:89). To love the Word is to love God. To receive the Word is to receive God. To believe the Word is to believe God. Spiritually, to know the Word is to know God. We see Christ in the pages of the Bible. Erasmus wrote in the preface to his Greek New Testament, the *Textus Receptus,* the first ever published (1516) and the text that became the basis for the King James Version of the Bible, these words: "These holy pages will summon up the living image of His mind. They will give you Christ Himself, talking, healing, dying, rising, the whole Christ in a word. They will give Him to you in an intimacy so close that He would be less visible to you if He stood before your eyes."

If I could live my life over, going back to my seventeenth year when I began to preach, I would preach the Bible. If I could not get a message out of a verse, I would take a paragraph; if not a message out of a paragraph, then I would take a chapter; if not out of a chapter, then out of a book; if not out of a book, then out of a Testament. But I would preach the Bible.

There is "problem preaching" and "life situation preaching" but this kind of preaching tends to make people problem conscious and savors more of psychology than religion, more of self-help than God's help. We need to forget about ourselves and think more of Jesus and the people for whom Jesus died. Through the preaching of the Word of God, we point men to Jesus.

In preaching the Bible the pastor may follow several different approaches.

One is to preach it expositionally. This is the method of selecting a large portion (a paragraph or more) of the Bible and expounding its meaning and applying the message before the people.

Another is to preach the Bible textually. This is the exposition of a smaller portion of the Scriptures, as one verse or one word.

A third method of preaching is topically. This is the preparation of a message on a subject presented in the Bible, such as assurance, faith, commitment, atonement (they are without number). Dr. George W. Truett was a great topical preacher.

A fourth approach to the message of the Bible is through character studies. This is the simplest, easiest, and, in many instances, the most enjoyable way to preach. To make Bible characters live before the people, with all their faith, faults, and failures, is a most rewarding challenge.

A fifth way to preach is by way of using special occasions to bring a pertinent message from God to the listening congregation. Mother's Day can be a sermon on the home, New Year's Day a sermon on renewed Christian commitment, Easter on our hope of a resurrection, Christmas on the gift of God's love, Thanksgiving on the debt of gratitude we owe the Lord, and on and on.

Concerning the ways of preaching I would like to make three observations.

1. The pastor ought to vary his preaching. We ought to employ every type of sermon. We ought constantly to shift and change our methods, approaches, emphases, and materials. We ought to be like the smart farmer who rotates his crops for fertility and yield. Preach every kind of way.

2. Andrew W. Blackwood, Sr., in his book, *The Preparation of Sermons,* quotes from B. H. Streeter's "Concerning Prayer," these observations: "A connected series on any subject by a man of moderate ability will make for more permanent impressions than an equal number of isolated sermons by a brilliant speaker. The congregation recalls what was said the last time. They look forward expectantly to what will be said next time."

This is so true in my own experience. Besides my expounding the Word of God book by book in the Bible, I work on a special series of sermons all the time. Here are two series I am working on now: My annual pre-Easter services (Dr. Truett started them and I have continued them now in the sixty-fourth year) which are built around the theme, "God Speaks to America."

Monday—"Is War in the Will of God?"
Tuesday—"The Red in Our Flag Is Blood"
Wednesday—"The Cancer That Consumes Us"
Thursday—"Slavery or Freedom?"

Friday—"The Saving of the Nation"

The other concerns a series on the problems that face all humanity, and especially we who are living in the present permissive generation. The messages are built around characters in the Bible and the problems that overwhelmed them. Such subjects as:

Noah: Drugs, Drunkenness, and Nakedness
Lot: Living with Homosexuals
Ishmael: Islam and the Oil Slick
Achan: The Sin We Are Afraid to Confess
Elkanah: Household Heartaches
Eli: Undisciplined Children
David: Sexual Drives
Ahab: Forty Years with the Wrong Woman
Malachi: When a Parent Has No Partner (God and Divorce)

3. My third observation concerning three ways to preach concerns the best method of delivering God's message. It is to preach expositionally. The best of all sermons is an expository sermon. That is, without doubt, the greatest way to build a marvelous congregation, to preach expositorily. There is an advantage in this way of preaching for the preacher himself. He learns, he grows in his heart, and the message that he reads in the Bible becomes flesh and blood in him. There are also advantages to the congregation, world without end. They learn to love the Bible, they learn the message of God, and they become acquainted with the Holy Scriptures. One of the tragedies of our modern day is that the Bible is largely a sealed book to the people. They do not know what it presents. How little of all the wealth of the Scripture is presented in the pulpit! The method of expository preaching is one of the finest in the world.

Avoid in expository sermons a parade of learning and allusion to commentaries or too many references to other people who have studied. Present the message in your own way and in your own self. It costs far more labor to preach an expository sermon than any other, but it is the greatest way to preach. The mightiest pulpit power in the years passed has been in the expository method of preaching such as found in Chrysostom, Augustine, Luther, Calvin, Chalmers, Andrew Fuller, and of course, many modern pulpit giants.

However the method of preaching, remember the people. Preach to the needs of the people, remembering their interests, sorrows, trials. To make God's Word live for the people is an incomparable challenge. Address their wills, conscience, understanding.

The message is for *them,* not for selfish purposes of ostentation, exhibition, or show. The difference between a bore and a good conversationalist is that the bore has not discovered the distinction between what interests him and what interests his hearers. Of a certain scholarly but monotonous preacher it was said, "If he doesn't Greek-root you to death, he will Hebrew-stem you to death." For the sermon to bless the people, it must develop one idea, repeated many times under a few main points, from two to five and never more than seven. The sermon ought to be about thirty to forty minutes in length.

Teach in your preaching. In Ephesians 4:11 the pastor and the preacher are linked together. The Greek is pastor-teacher, the same person. If all the sermon is a pep talk, then twenty minutes for its length may be too long. But if the preacher is teaching the Word and will of the Lord in his message, twenty years is too short. The pastor ought to help carry out the admonition of Simon Peter in 2 Peter 3:18, helping the people to grow in grace and in the knowledge of the Lord Jesus Christ. Teaching through preaching nurtures the faith of the people. They are busy in the secular world. They have set you aside for the purpose to make known to them the Word of God. Find out the marvelous truths of God and reveal them to the congregation (Deut. 29:29). Every sermon ought to make appeal to the lost but it also ought to be a banquet spread for the hungry-hearted people.

The Pastor Speaking His Messages

The tools of the pastor are words. How he speaks them molds and shapes what he is seeking to accomplish just as certainly as does the brush in the hands of the painter creating his picture or a compass and trowel in the hands of a builder erecting a building.

The life of the preacher is in his words (John 5:43,47; 17:20; Prov. 25:11). Words are the vehicles by which the pastor reaches, touches, and blesses the lives of his listening audience.

The pastor ought to stand up squarely, face his congregation fully, open his mouth widely (the larger the cavity, the richer and more pleasant the sound), and speak distinctly, addressing his sentences to the last member who sits on the last pew of the church. When that farthest away fellow can hear, then all who sit between him and the preacher can also hear. The preacher is not preaching to himself; he is preaching to the people and when he speaks he ought to keep them in his eye, in his mind, in his thoughts, and in the loudness of his voice.

There is a saying in preaching that goes like this:

Begin slow, talk low.
Rise higher, take fire.

It is a saying worth remembering. Many speakers start at too high a pitch. By starting too high, there is no further place to go but to strain even more. It is better to find the best, most natural pitch for your voice and then raise or lower it according to the emphasis of your message.

It is interesting to look at sheets given to a homiletics class with which the young theologues were asked to grade the preachers they were to hear. They were to grade them in posture, gesture, vocal contrast, projection, vocal variance, eye contact, humor, vocabulary, diction, attitude, and grammar. I wonder how each of us would come out if we were so graded by these students?

Let me speak a brief word about the last category, grammar. Incorrect grammar and mispronounced words will turn off most any educated person. Men like Dwight L. Moody are an exception to that observation, but the exception only proves the rule. Correct grammar and exact pronunciation can cause an educated person to listen to a message he does not think he wants to hear. The pastor cannot lose in training himself to be careful in his speech. Those who are sensitive to it will respond with gratitude; and those who are unaware of it are not bothered by it since they do not realize the difference.

Here are five rules about the pastor's use of words that are worth the pastor's perusal.

1. The first rule of pulpit oratory is to keep it simple. Excessive verbosity indubitably dissipates desirable semantic lucidity! Use plain ordinary English. The King James Version of the Bible is a powerful witness to simple and forcefully beautiful English.

2. Avoid words that are too familiar or are not familiar or words that are heard too often. Do not confuse or misuse words. Use the dictionary. Look it up.

3. Be terse. It is easier to understand something that is brief. Even legal contracts, traditionally long-winded and difficult to understand, are changing. As their length decreases, their comprehension usually increases.

4. Recognize the connotation of a word as well as its denotation. A word's denotation is what it means precisely; its connotation is what it suggests, its overtones. "Fat" has a different connotation from "plump." Remember Mark Twain's observation? He said, "The difference between the right word and the almost right word is the difference between the lightning and the lightning bug."

5. Seek simplicity. If you can use a one-syllable word in place of a three-syllable word, do it. As it happens, it is usually the Anglo-Saxon words that are short, hard, gritty, and add clarity and strength to speech or writing. Most excellent writers will use six Anglo-Saxon words for every one that comes from Greek or Latin words, even though the dictionary shows that only one word in ten comes from the Anglo-Saxon.

Remember to speak naturally, plainly, simply, fervently. This is the Puritan ideal. The genius of Puritan preaching lay in its simple, unadorned, plain presentation. Jonathan Edwards listed in his book of *Resolutions:* "Never to speak in narrations anything but the pure and simple verity."

The most important textbook of that era was that by William Perkins, Cambridge, England, *The Art of Prophesying,* published in 1592. He wrote: "Human wisdom must be concealed, because the preaching of the Word is the testimony of God and the professing of the knowledge of Christ and not of human skill. The hearers ought not to ascribe their faith to the gifts of men but to the power of God.'' Paul in 1 Corinthians 2:1-5 said the same thing.

Thomas Hooker in his book, *The Soul's Preparation* (1632), wrote: ''I have sometimes admired (wondered) at this: why a company of gentlemen, yeomen, poore women, that are scarcely able to know their A B C's yet have a minister to speak Latine, Greeke, and Hebrew and use the Fathers, when it is certain they know nothing at all. The reason is, because all this stings not; they may sit and sleepe in their sinnes, and goe to hell hood-winckt, never awakened.''

May God deliver us from such a judgment.

When the pastor stands up to speak, let him be himself. You may be a fair imitator of somebody else but you are the best example of you God ever made. However you are, in whatever manner God constructed you, let him glorify himself through your individual personality. Be yourself.

When I was a student at Baylor, seventeen years old, the Volunteer Band came out in a bus to hear me preach under a tabernacle. After the service they said to me: ''It was awful. You preached all over the place. You shouted at the top of your voice. It was terrible. No tall steepled church in any city would ever call the likes of you. You are too loud.'' The criticism cast me down. After humbling inquiry, I was directed to an expression teacher, Miss Martha Folkes Hawn, to learn to mend my boisterous ways. I had had expression lessons since I was eight years old, but I began all over again. One day Miss Hawn asked me to preach a sermon for her. She had her own little theater building, so I took my place and stance, opened my Bible, and preached a sermon for her. She said not a word in response. She just asked me to preach another sermon the next time I came for a lesson. I did so a second time. When I returned for my next lesson, she invited me to sit by her side on the sofa. She wanted to talk to me. This is what she said: ''I have been thinking much about you and your preaching. This week a friend of mine from Kansas City came to visit me. I asked her where she went to church. When she told me, I remarked that she did not belong to that communion, and then I asked why she chose to worship there. The friend replied, 'Because the pastor there really preaches, and when I go to church I like to hear a man stand up and preach.' " Then Miss Hawn added to me, "I am exactly like that. When I attend church, I like to hear a man preach. So you do in your preaching exactly as you feel. If you feel like doubling up your fist, double up your fist. If you feel like shaking your head, shake your head. If you feel like stomping your feet, stomp your feet. I am not saying that everybody will like you, but I am saying that everybody who hears you will listen." Then she added, "This is your last lesson. You do not need to return anymore. Just be yourself, and do not let anyone ever bother you or trouble you about the way you preach."

I went away with the burden of the world lifted from my shoulders. Since that day I have never let any caustic criticism about the way I preach trouble me. I am just being myself.

Let every man be like that—just however God has put him together. Some will be soft and quiet, some loud and uninhibited, some slow and deliberate, some like a machine gun fire. But however we are, God made us that way for the best. He made us to differ. It is like this:

The animals had a school. The curriculum consisted of running, climbing, flying, and swimming. All the animals took all the subjects.

The duck was good in swimming and fair in flying. But he was terrible in running, so he was made to drop his swimming class and stay after school in order to practice his running. He kept this up until he was only average in swimming. But average was acceptable. The others (including the teacher) were no longer threatened by the duck's swimming ability. So everyone felt more comfortable—except the duck.

The eagle was considered a problem student. For instance, in climbing class he beat all others to the top of the tree, but used his own method of getting there. He had to be severely disciplined. Finally, because of noncooperation in swimming, he was expelled for insubordination.

The rabbit started at the top of the class in running, but was obviously inadequate in other areas. Because of so much makeup work in swimming he had a nervous breakdown and had to drop out of school.

Of course, the turtle was a failure in most every course offered. His shell was considered to be the leading cause of his failures, so it was removed. That did help his running a bit, but sadly he became the first casualty when he was stepped on by a horse.

The faculty was quite disappointed. But all in all it was a good school in humility—there were no real successes. None seemed to measure up to the others. But they did concentrate on their weak points and some progress was made.

Maybe the moral is: do not let anyone take off your shell or clip your wings. Just be yourself.

The Pastor Preaching Without Notes

When I began my preaching ministry at seventeen years of age, I got down on my knees and asked God to help me preach without notes. The very thought of doing it terrified me. What if I forgot the next point in the middle of my sermon? Such a thing is so easily possible. But I asked God in faith to help me. That is now fifty-one years ago. And for these fifty-one years God has never failed me or let me down. For a brief moment I may forget in the middle of the sermon, but just keep on talking until the point comes back to mind!

The pragmatic practicalities that enter into the many-faceted efforts of that kind of pulpit ministry go like this: I carefully outline the sermon on a folded piece of typewriter paper that makes four pages. As I preach the sermon, in my mind's eye I go down each page, then turn the page and preach down that one. Then I go over to the next page and preach down that one, and then turn in my mind to the last page and preach down that one. It is my persuasion that in careful preparation for the message and in an absolute dependence on God that the Lord will help you to achieve this most blessed of all ways of delivering the sermon.

Pastor, earnestly and prayerfully attempt to follow this way of preaching. The eloquent Cicero (106-43 BC) who enthralled Rome with his eloquence of speech, had strong convictions about speaking without the impediment of a manuscript. He declared: "In delivery, next to the voice in effectiveness, is the countenance, and this is ruled by the eyes. The expressive power of the human eyes is so great that it determines the expression of the whole countenance.''

Often have I wondered about the preaching of the prophets and the apostles. Did they preach from notes? Did Jesus? Read Luke 4:17-21. With all eyes fastened upon the face of the Lord Jesus, how incongruous if his eyes, in turn, were fastened upon a manuscript as he delivered his message to the townspeople in the synagogue of Nazareth!

John Wesley wrote, ''Look your audience in the face, one after another, as we do in familiar conversation.'' If you were pleading with a man personally, face-to-face, about giving his soul to Christ, would you use notes? Wouldn't you look him directly in the eye? It is no different in pleading with more than one man. One or one thousand, do it all the same.

Looking the man in the eye as you speak means that you are not staring at the wall or looking out a window or studying your shoelaces. If you are engaged in this, listeners are not sure where your remarks are directed. You are talking to your audience; look at *them*.

Harry Simmons, a well-known management consultant, writes about ''Four Looks for Successful Speaking'' (*How to Talk Your Way to Success*, Castle Books).

First, look at your audience. Pay attention to the people, not the ceiling, walls, and windows. Only as you look at your audience will you receive the inspiration that comes from observing their approval.

Second, look at your audience constantly. You must keep the listeners in your gaze so that they will feel that so far as you are concerned, they are important. Give the audience your undivided attention throughout the message.

Third, look at the people in your audience. Address various groups of people individually, moving your head and eyes as you give attention to each section of the congregation. By devoting a few seconds to each segment, you give individuals the feeling that you have been talking personally with them.

Fourth, look at individuals among the people. Look into the eyes of listeners. If you are not accustomed to doing this, it may be hard at first. But stay with it, and your diffidence will soon fade. Such attention to details in delivering the sermon will pay high dividends.

The preacher should be especially careful to maintain eye contact whenever something happens to distract attention. If a noise comes from the outside, don't call further attention to it by looking in that direction. Concentrate on the congregation, and they will focus on you in return.

When there is any kind of a disturbance in the audience (a person is the subject of a heart attack, a baby begins crying, somebody walks into the middle of the aisle), I always look away. I continue preaching in another direction and people follow my eyes. If I look, they look. If I stare, they stare. If I seem disturbed, they are upset. Let the pastor keep his "cool" and go right on with his message.

Looking at the congregation and not at a manuscript or at an outline of notes, the preacher can give himself to the leadership of the Holy Spirit. Some things may need to be changed in the message; something may need to be especially emphasized. Free to follow the leadership of the Spirit, the preacher can doubly be God's messenger with God's message for the hour.

Trust God for the memory of what you have prayed and prepared to say. God will see you through. He will not let you down. It is *his* message. If our souls are saturated with a heavenly purpose, then automatically we will deliver it. We do not memorize our children's names. We just know them. So our sermon, if it is a real part of us, we just know it.

Let me add this note, however. Many of the greatest preachers in Christendom have preached with notes. Some of them have even read their sermons, delivering them with their nose stuck in a manuscript. Such a man was Jonathan Edwards, even reading his powerful, soul-convicting message, *Sinners in the Hands of an Angry God.*

Here is a list of preachers of ancient days and modern days, arranged according to how they delivered their messages.

1. Those who read (preached) from a full manuscript taken into the pulpit: Phillips Brooks, Horace Bushnell, Thomas Chalmers, Jonathan Edwards, Harry Emerson Fosdick, John Henry Jowett, Peter Marshall, John Henry Newman, Paul Rees.

2. Preachers who memorized their sermons: Ernest T. Campbell, Timothy Edwards, Billy Sunday, Alexander Maclaren, J. Vernon McGee, Dwight L. Moody, Wilbur Smith, John Stott, Solomon Stoddard.

3. Preachers who delivered their message without notes: Henry Bast, Charles G. Finney, Harry Ironside, Charles W. Koller, Robert G. Lee, Clarence E. Macartney, George Herbert Morrison, Harold Ockenga, Alan Redpath, T. W. Robertson, Ralph Sockman, Charles H. Spurgeon, George Whitefield.

As can be readily seen, there is no one way to preach. Marvelously successful preachers have used every conceivable approach to get their message across. Let each man be fully persuaded in his own heart how he feels it is best for him to do. In my opinion, however, the man of God is far more effective in the pulpit if he preaches with a Bible in his hand without taking along his study notes.

Emotion in His Sermon

Let not the pastor be afraid of emotion in his preaching. True eloquence flows out of deep feeling. Jonathan Edwards appealed to the emotions. He believed that the passions are the prime movers in life. He was not afraid to appeal to the elementary instincts of fear, love, hope, deliverance, security. He believed that unless a man is moved by some affection he was by nature inactive. He said, "Take away all love and hatred, all hope and fear, all anger, zeal and affectionate desire, and the world would be in a great measure motionless and dead; there would be no such thing as activity among mankind or any earnest pursuit whatsoever."

Jonathan Edwards also wrote, "As the passions are the springs of conduct, vital religion must consist in an exercise of these." He presented the glowing joys of the redeemed, the blessedness of the union with Christ, the felicities of the full knowledge of God. He also presented the horrors and terrors of hell. The early Christians also did this.

The sermon is no essay to read for optional opinion, for the people casually to consider. It is a confrontation with the Almighty God. It is to be delivered with a burning passion, in the authority of the Holy Spirit.

One modern layman wrote: "The present day layman is seeking a stronger emotional spirit in his religion. He is prone to deemphasize the intellectual. It seems that in recent years our younger preachers began to get less emotional and more intellectual. Their sermons were less like a sermon and more like a lecture. The 'We must be born again' kind of religion disappeared. We quit singing, 'There is wonder-working power in the blood' and started singing some new songs with a different kind of message. We became interested in something the people called 'the social gospel.' The laymen listened, approved, then started playing golf on Sunday morning.

"Today laymen want to recapture some of that 'you must be born again' philosophy. They want to be stirred and moved. They want a religion that is strong medicine. In words of the popular song, it has to have 'heart.' "

Again, in an article I read one writer said:

"It worries me that so many of our younger ministers feel that they must preach in a quiet and solemn voice with never a gesture, never a smile, never a change in cadence. It would be a relief if they would hit the pulpit just once."

Abraham Lincoln once said: "I don't like cut and dried sermons. When I hear a man preach, I like to see him act as if he were fighting a swarm of bees."

The word we preach from our pulpits ought to be like the Word of God itself—like a fire and like a hammer that breaketh the rock in pieces (Jer. 23:29).

You cannot read the New Testament without sensing that the preachers were electrified by the power of the gospel and swept off their feet by the wonder of the great revelation which had been committed to their trust. There is something wrong if a man charged with the greatest news in the world can be listless and frigid and dull. Who is going to believe that the glad tidings brought by the preacher means literally more than anything else on earth if they are presented with no verve or fire or attack, and if the man himself is apathetic, uninspired, afflicted with spiritual coma in unsaying by his attitude what he says in words?

John Wesley spoke well when he advised, "Put fire in your sermon, or put your sermon in the fire." How could it ever be that a minister can speak of the tragic condition of the lost, of life and death, hell and heaven, time and eternity with cold, removed, impersonal indifference? The response the pastor seeks to elicit from his people is the most meaningful decision in human experience. Let him plead for it as such, and that with all his soul.

Robert Murray McCheyne, who died at the early age of twenty-nine (he literally burned himself out for God), had a profound effect upon Scotland and upon the religious world. A traveler from afar made the journey to his church in Dundee, Scotland, to discuss the secret of the young man's powerful ministry. When the visitor arrived, to his great sorrow the pastor was away. But the custodian was there. Seeing the disappointment registered on the visitor's face, he asked the stranger why he had come. The reply was to find the secret of the young preacher's power. The janitor replied: "I can show you. Come with me." He took the traveler to the study of the pastor, then said, "See that chair? That is his chair. Sit down in it. Now place your arms upon the desk, bury your face in your hands, and weep." He took the traveler to the pulpit in the sanctuary, then said, "Climb up into the pulpit. Stand behind it. Now bury your face in your hands and weep."

It is not recorded in the Scriptures that Jesus ever laughed or smiled but they do speak of his weeping, this man of sorrows and acquainted with grief. He may never have burst into laughter but he did "burst into tears" (the literal translation of John 11:35). Paul never spoke of his frivolities but he often referred to his tears. For a man to be moved by the great issues of life and death is not to show weakness or maudlin sentimentality, but rather to reveal a soul moved with compassion for the hurts of the people. God bless the pastor who cares enough to cry.

Sometimes I think that the reason the movie house is so popular and the soap operas on television are as universally viewed is because the people can follow the stories of human heartache, weep, and no one is there to shame them for their weakness. But if we can weep over cheap fiction, why would we be critical of the burdened heart that would weep over the destruction of lives, homes, children, souls? It does not make sense.

The other day I picked up a piece of literature a merchandising company was handing out to its salespeople. The things I read in the little bulletin were astonishing. Some of the sentences were these: "Appeal to emotion whenever you can. Logic may provide the reasons for buying something, but emotion supplies the urge (the captions under a drawing of a store window filled with kittens, a sign over it saying, 'We're lonely, aren't you?' and a little boy by the side of his mother carrying the little kittens in his arms, smiling from ear to ear)." Another sentence was: "If logic dictated our buying habits, cigarette companies would be out of business, night clubs would close at 10:00 PM, and women would not wear high heels." Here is another: "A man may need a pair of shoes but want a bottle of whiskey. Until you've succeeded in making him *want* a pair of shoes, all the fine logic as to why your particular shoes are better is completely wasted."

Is not patriotism an emotion? Is not mother love an emotion? Is not true marriage love an emotion? I would hate to think that a fellow who married never knew what it was to "fall in love," but took a girl to the altar only on the basis of cold, impersonal logic. I wonder what kind of kids a computer sires?

Pastor, do not be afraid of being moved in your heart for the people. Jesus was. Paul was. The really great preachers always have been. Here are the wellsprings of life.

The Pastor and Prayer Meeting

There is a wider divergence in the way pastors conduct their midweek prayer services than in any other area of church life. Some men make the gathering one of the mighty, soul-winning convocations of the congregation. They have a full-orbed preaching service with choir, orchestra, sermon, invitation, and all the attendant characteristics of Sunday morning worship hour. Pastors who so lead their people into a midweek experience like that are to be commended. They make of the hour truly "An Hour of Power."

Many pastors simply let the midweek service of prayer find its own level, which for the most part, is extremely low. Someone said that you could go to the sanctuary on Sunday morning and tell how popular the preacher is, go to the church on Sunday night and see how popular the church is, go to the church on Wednesday night and see how popular Christ is. There is truth in that observation. Not many people like to pray, yet prayer is the soul's communion with God and the foundation of all our power in the gospel. O Lord, how we need to pray!

Here are seven things that I think each pastor should try to realize in the service of prayer no matter how the meeting is emphasized (or neglected, God forgive us).

1. The pastor should preside over the service and strive to make it helpful to the people.

2. The parts of the program should be carefully arranged, just as the order of service on Sunday morning.

3. The meeting ought to open and close at an appointed time. (Specially called prayer meetings can have no limit.)

4. For the most part, the divisions of the service ought to be brief.

5. The pastor ought to insist upon brevity from all the sharing people, whether in testimony, intercession, singing, or whatever.

6. The service ought to avoid sameness, repeated uniformity, and monotony. Vary the meetings. Boredom will kill any service.

7. The pastor ought to divest the midweek service of all stiffness, formality, and personal indifference. Let the whole course of the meeting be a homelike gathering of God's children in the Father's house.

From personal experience, I can remind my fellow pastors that the midweek prayer service is a marvelous time to teach the deep truths of the Word of God. The Lord will bless the pastor with a wonderful, eager-hearted audience who will thus pour his soul into the opening of the Holy Scriptures (Luke 24:32).

3

The Pastor in His Study

The Mornings for God

There is a theme in my life that I refer to again and again. Like the motif in Beethoven's *Fifth Symphony* that is sounded over and over and heard in a dozen different parts and variations, so the basic, underlying persuasion of my own pastoral work is this: Keep your mornings for God.

When asked by *The Baptist Program* magazine about my study time, I answered that I keep my mornings for God and I have my study at home. There is a telephone on my desk, but it does not ring. At night in the quietness of the shining stars and of the soft gloom of the evening, I can work and study and prepare. In the morning I can walk into my workshop and there slave at my desk to my heart's content.

I can pray and I can prepare my sermons. I can write books. I can think through the problems that confront us. I can live the life of a king in a castle in my study with its thousands of theological books and with its afforded opportunity to escape from the pressures of the world. Nobody there but God, and he is waiting for my arrival whenever I come.

When I leave the study, I try to be a servant of the church and of the world. I visit. I answer letters. I go to meetings. I preach. I hold funerals and weddings. I administer the affairs of the congregation. I try to help with my denomination. I do a thousand other things. But the time I spend in the study is mine and God's. That has extended my ministry and has blessed my life; it is the secret of the enormous amount of work I am able to do.

When asked about my study, sermon-preparation habits by *Moody Monthly* magazine, I answered that if I had one thing to tell a young preacher, it would be this: "Keep the mornings for God. Shut out the whole world and shut up yourself to the Lord with a Bible in your hand, with your knees bended in the presence of the holiness of the great Almighty."

What will the people say if the pastor is unavailable in the mornings? What would the community think if they are unable to reach him in the mornings? How would the church get along?

My answer comes out of long years of experience. The people will praise God for the pastor who will spend time with an open Bible on his knees before the Judge of all the earth. It may seem strange, but any congregation would rejoice to think that their pastor came before them out of the holy of holies where he had met with the Lord face to face.

I have watched this with my own eyes. On a pastor's first Sunday he announces that he is their servant and shepherd to care for their souls day and night. He then explains that the mornings he keeps for Bible study, for prayer, for intercession, for preparation. In the afternoons he does the work of the church, such as visiting, answering mail, counseling, and doing all the multitudinous administrative details. In the evenings he is free to attend the meetings and the other things that go on in a vibrant church. But in the morning he asks the people to leave him alone that he might stay in the presence of God.

Any church honors a request like that. They will love the pastor for it and will help him to keep those hours sacred. Then, when the preacher comes before his people, he does not preach out of a bare necessity, but out of the overflow of his life. He is enriched in his own soul, and the people glorify God in the marvelous message he brings them from the Lord.

What the Pastor Studies

What does the preacher study in those mornings? I have a very definite, pragmatic answer. Always preach through some book of the Bible. In our First Baptist Church in Dallas I spent seventeen years and eight months preaching from Genesis to Revelation. It was an incomparable blessing to me and to the people, though I would not advise a young minister to do that. It takes too long to get to the Gospels and the Acts and the Epistles. It is better to preach through a book of the Bible. Then follow the exposition of that book with yet another one, alternating between the Old Testament and the New. This is what I am doing now, and I am finding it a precious blessing.

A remarkable thing happens when a pastor preaches through a book of the Bible. Too many preachers walk up and down their studies wringing their hands, crying: "What shall I preach? And where can I get the pertinent material I need for my listening saints?"

I also walk up and down my study, but my cry is altogether different. There is so much to preach, and so much God has said that I am afraid I am going to die before I have delivered the messages that I see in God's Book. Those two attitudes are as different as up and down and light and dark. When the preacher is expounding a Bible book, his text is automatically stated. All he need do is find out what the text says and what it means to us today.

His sermon is then pertinent. Ten thousand times the people are bombarded with what the politician says, what the psychiatrist says, what the psychologist says, what the editor says, what the commentator says, what the man on the street says, what everybody says. But, what we would like to know is: Does God say anything? If God has anything to say, what does God say? That is the assignment of the preacher. And, when he delivers that message faithfully and well, the people are marvelously blessed.

Do you remember the cry of King Zedekiah to the prophet Jeremiah: "Is there any word from the Lord?" Jeremiah replied, "There is" (Jer. 37:17). "Preacher, for God's sake, tell us what God says. That is what we long to hear. What we need to hear. What we want to hear." And if the messenger of the Lord is faithful, that is what the people will hear.

The preacher who does not expound the Word of the Lord is forced to get his sermons from a thousand inconsequential, impertinent sources. I know a preacher who got his sermon like this: He watched a cat gingerly walking on the top of a fence-wall embedded with sharp glass. That was his inspiration. So he preached about the cat walking on the top of that wall in the same kind of way as we have to walk amid all of the sharp things that happen in the world.

I have no quarrel with the preacher and his cat, not even with the height of the wall or the color of the sharp glass; I am just avowing that it is ten thousand times better for him to find the well of his inspiration in the living water of the holy Word of God. He will not fail to have messages that are even more pertinent than those about a cat gingerly walking in the midst of sharp glass!

Preparing the Message

In preparing the sermon, bring to bear in the message all of your understanding and knowledge. If you can read the text in Hebrew or in Greek, that ought to be first. Then study the text through the eyes of great commentators. When you have done this, you will have a thorough understanding of what God is saying.

With a complete and absolute knowledge of the passage, read all of the things that you can find that might be pertinent to it. Use encyclopedias, Bible dictionaries, other sermons, other homiletical material. Find it. Read it, and make notes on it. Remember, everything is grist for the preacher's mill. Draw on anything in history, in literature, or in life to make the passage God has inspired meaningful and pertinent to the people.

After you have studied the passage prayerfully and earnestly, and after you have read all that you can, ask God to form in your soul the message that ought to be delivered. God will not fail you in this. The message will form in your heart as you study. Outline the sermon under two, three, four, or five main headings. Drive toward a final appeal as you write down the main points and the subpoints that follow each heading.

Always have some great, godly direction and purpose. Drive it home with all your force. Stand on the Word of God and on the basis of the Lord's authority and his holy revelations in the Scriptures. Make your appeal. It may be for consecration. It may be for prayer. It may be for salvation. It may be for ministry commitment. But always drive toward that final appeal. The Holy

Spirit will work with you, and the power of God will rest upon you if you do. The Lord has a marvelous reward for us if we will thus give ourselves to the expounding of the Word of God.

The Pastor's Schedule

The pastor, of all people with executive responsibilities in the earth, ought to rigidly program his life and schedule his time. There is so much to do and such few hours in the day to do it. Robert Murray McCheyne on the face of his watch had a setting sun painted and underneath the Western sky the words printed, "The night cometh when no man can work." Let the pastor consider these things:

1. Busy business does not always indicate success or progress. A minister can be overworked operating a mimeograph machine or running small errands for church members or having a poor schedule of daily, monthly, or weekly activities. The quality of a man's work counts more than the quantity.

2. Unless a minister schedules his activities, he will likely sidestep those matters which will do him and the church the most good. A man needs a schedule in order to give first consideration to priorities.

3. Take care of details at specified times. Do your letter writing at a time, your telephoning at a time, your reading the daily paper at a time.

4. Announce your schedule to your people, especially the word that you must keep your mornings for God.

5. Examine the limits you have put upon your ministry and time, and live within those limits. Do not try to do everything yourself. Some work should be delegated to others.

6. Set yourself a few well-defined monthly, semiyearly, or yearly goals. Have project targets and target dates.

7. At the end of each month, have an evaluation session. Ask yourself what you have really accomplished. Check to see how much of your ministry has simply been the spinning of your wheels. Your time as a minister is valuable. Time is the stuff life is made of. Do not waste it. Make that time in your study pay off as you carefully review all your work.

The Pastor as a Student

Paul wrote to pastor Timothy, his son in the ministry, "Till I come, give attendance to reading, to exhortation, to doctrine" (1 Tim. 4:13). Again he wrote in his last letter, "Study to shew thyself approved unto God, a workman that needeth not to be ashamed, rightly dividing the word of truth" (2 Tim. 2:15). Not only among the Greek philosophers who said it, but everywhere, knowledge is power. The pulpit especially requires study because of its demand for sermons that are filled with freshness, originality, and force; and the pastor who does not enter into this with real dedication and hard labor will lose his hold upon his people.

No man can meet the demands of a pulpit who does not constantly and earnestly *study*. There are two possible extremes in a pastor's life. Both extremes are to be avoided. On the one hand, the pastor can be a mere bookworm, secluded, with no practical living contact and sympathy with life around him. On the other hand, a minister may be a mere gossipmonger, going from house to house. He can be a busybody, as Paul calls him in Thessalonians. He can be just a backslapper. The grand object for the preacher is to combine the student and the pastor, to know God's Word, and to know God's people.

The minister ought to be a student everywhere. Everything is grist for the preacher's mill. He ought to make notes of things that come to him as he works in his parish. He ought to have a program definitely worked out for himself. He ought to consecrate a specific part of each day to severe, systematic work in the privacy of his study. A good habit once fixed is an ever-increasing power. The more fixed and long-continued the habit, the more easy, rapid, and powerful the mental processes. Let the pastor announce this program to the people and the congregation will conform to the pastor's plan.

If the preacher does not grow, he will become an increasingly narrower and weaker man. He ought to discipline himself. Nothing will overcome the temptation to dissipate his life but a profound conviction that study—persistent, regular, and lifelong—is the first duty of the man who seeks to stand before God in the pulpit as an instructor of the people. Let other duties have their place, but the first, the most imperative duty of him who teaches others is to teach himself.

What the preacher ought to study for his sermons is the Holy Scriptures *and* everything else. He ought to prepare his sermons from biblical texts, but he will become less versatile in mind, and his sermons will have no freshness in them if he does only that. There ought to be a general study in his effort aside from his studying the holy Scriptures. With the pastor's background in geography, history, literature, and all that goes into the makeup of the Bible, he has an unlimited field in bringing the truth of the Lord to the people.

The Pastor's Refusal to Dissipate His Life with Trifles

Take time for prayer and study and preparation. If the message is of little cost to the preacher, it will be of little value to the congregation.

Avoid like the plague the temptation to squander and dissipate your life in endless engagements and backslapping. Whoever wrote this poem surely knew the modern-day pastor:

> On Monday, he lunched with a Housing Committee,
>   With statistics and stew he was filled;
> Then he dashed to a tea on "Crime in Our City,"
>   And dined with a Church Ladies' Guild.
>
> On Tuesday he went to a Babies' Week Lunch.
>   And a tea on "Good Citizenship";
> At dinner he talked to the Trade Union bunch,
>   (There wasn't a date he dared skip).
>
> On Wednesday he managed two annual dinners,
>   One at noon and the other at night;
> On Thursday a luncheon on "Bootleg Sinners,"
>   And a dinner on "War: Is It Right?"
>
> "World Problems We Face" was his Friday noon date
>   (A luncheon-address, as you guessed);
> And he wielded a fork while a man from New York
>   Spoke that evening on "Social Unrest."

> On Saturday noon he felt in a swoon,
> Missed a talk on the youth of our land . . .
> Poor thing, he was through! He never came to,
> But died with a spoon in his hand.

Fill your calendar with engagements with God in Bible study and prayer. When asked for an invocation to be delivered at the beekeepers association, you have an engagement and an important one; namely, one with the Almighty God.

The reward of prayer, study, and soul-saturation is heavenly. The ordinary preacher becomes a great preacher. Robert G. Lee said, "You cannot live on skim milk during the days of the week and preach cream on Sunday." The preacher must himself be filled with the truth of God.

Charles G. Finney, without organization, depended solely upon preaching, prayer, and inquirers' classes for his great revivals. He prepared himself and depended upon the Holy Spirit to guide him in selection of text and message.

The Need for Strong, Doctrinal Truth in Sermons

A listener to pastors preaching for forty years said, "The modern sermon is empty; it has no doctrinal content." Another observer said, "The modern sermon is light, superficial, and has little or no doctrinal content."

This is one reason why the pastor needs to study. There is no doubt but that most sermons are thin, like soup made with the same soupbone used over and over again for a solid year. The clichés are meaningless. The message is trite. Even the preacher is bored by his own delivery and he has no fire, no enthusiasm, no zeal, no expectancy. Our preaching needs to reach continually new depths in grace and truth and new heights of freshness in thought and content. Without this firm, studious presentation of the teaching of God's Holy Word, our people fall into every kind of error, into every known heresy, and become the dupes of any passing ecclesiastical demagogue. Look at this, for example, to see how far and how easily doctrinal error can penetrate our spiritual world:

Recently I read about a professor at one of our schools who

said, "There is no such thing as a personal devil." When I read that, I felt like the prizefighter whose opponent was beating him about half to death. As he sat on the stool between the rounds, his manager said, "Go get him, Tiger, he hasn't laid a hand on you!" The fighter kind of cleared his head and looked at his manager and said, "Then keep your eye on the referee, because somebody is beating the daylights out of me!"

The interesting observation about this is, if there is no devil, if there is no such thing as a personal devil, then I'd like for that same professor to identify the one who is inflicting such pile driver-like blows on our society!

As we study the new theology, we find that basically it revolves around three points:

First of all, it questions the authority of the Scriptures.

Secondly, it denies the existence of judgment and hell.

Finally, and I suppose this is the most devastating of all, it accepts and teaches a form of humanism which is by all criteria the deification of man himself.

How do we counter such subtle error taught and preached by the seducers of truth? We do it with long study and the zealous, unmoved dedication of our souls and hearts to the mind of God revealed to us in the Scriptures. The preacher *has* to study if his congregation is to survive.

Improvement of Preaching Through Study

Even after Phillips Brooks had attained fame as one of the world's greatest preachers, he continued to take lessons in homiletics. We are to study and to keep on studying.

1. Somewhere the pastor must select a place where he can get to himself with his Bible and with all his other books and spend hours and hours in preparation. He must at all costs eliminate the casual, gossipy, and oftentimes retired visitor. I tried in my first full-time pastorate to have my study at the church. My predecessor who had pastored the church for many years had so chosen to do this and I was counseled to follow his example. It was death to me. A fellow would come just to take a minute to say hello to the young pastor. He would take an hour to say it. I moved out to a bedroom in the parsonage. Here in Dallas the church built a

wing on the house for me and my books. I cannot carry on my work without that secluded, private, protected sanctuary when I meet God and the great minds inspired by his counsel.

Without doubt, and I cannot emphasize the conviction too much, the best place for the pastor's study and library is in a separated room at his home. The preacher who has his study at the church uses his finest morning hours to shave, bathe, comb his hair, tie his shoes, start his car, drive to the church, unlock his door, and look nice for any stranger who may wander in. I do not need my mind to be fresh and rested to comb my hair and tie my shoes. I can do those things when I have studied myself stupid.

When I get up in the morning, I go immediately to my study. By saving those precious morning hours through the years I have added almost a lifetime of wonderful concentration and preparation to my homiletical efforts. Another blessing in having the study at home is that I am able to study at night, making up for hours I have lost because of the exigencies that inevitably arise in a pastorate.

My daily schedule is very simple. In the morning I study, in the afternoon I do the work of the church, and in the evening I attend the meetings of the congregation. When I lose those morning hours because of an exigency, I try to make them up at night. That message I am to deliver to my people is all-important.

2. On my study desk are these books (I write them down as I look at them, writing by longhand this chapter): three Bibles, a Bible dictionary, the Greek New Testament, an analytical Greek lexicon, two dictionaries of the English language, *Strong's Exhaustive Concordance* of the Bible, the church hymnbook, the Hebrew Bible and lexicon, and a few books taken off the shelves that have to do with the particular series of sermons I am now delivering.

To my immediate left in a revolving case is *Ellicott's Bible Commentary, The American Commentary of the New Testament, Commentary on the Whole Bible* by Jamieson, Fausset, and Brown, and *Gray and Adams Bible Commentary.*

On my right just beyond is the collection of books comprising my Greek and Hebrew libraries. Then all around me and in the stack room close by are the thousands of books that are literally mines of gold as I dig in them. There are all the commentaries and volumes on the books of the Bible in their order, beginning with Genesis and continuing through the Revelation. There are the Bible encyclopedias and dictionaries, particularly *The International Standard Bible Encyclopedia,* and *The Zondervan Pictorial Encyclopedia of the Bible.* Here also is the tremendous *New Schaff-Herzog Encyclopedia of Religious Knowledge.* Here is the invaluable *Life and Times of Jesus* by Edersheim and *The Life and Works of Flavius Josephus.*

In the large collection of books on theology there is especially Strong's *Systematic Theology.* In that book we have a good illustration of how a pastor ought to read and study. A. H. Strong was a theistic evolutionist, a position my soul doth loathe. Yet most of his pages of study are incomparable. So let the pastor read as he would eat a fish—when he comes to an unpalatable bone, just eat around it; do not swallow it! There are innumerable books in which there are both good and bad. Choose the good and avoid the bad. You will readily know which is which if you truly believe the infallible Word of God.

Continuing to look at the library, I see in the large section given to secular studies and literature the many volumes of the *Encyclopedia Britannica.* Here is a section on church history with Newman's *Manual of Church History.* Here are many books of biography. Here are also numerous volumes on missions. And here is an extensive library of sermons including Spurgeon's *Treasury of David,* along with his tremendous *Metropolitan Tabernacle Pulpit.* I love to read Spurgeon. This side of the apostles themselves, he was the greatest preacher who ever lived. The Spirit of the living God breathes in his pious life and beautiful message. He was God's man in a great age of preaching.

Effect of the Pastor's Habit to Study

In a few moments I can tell whether or not a pastor is studious. Little things broadcast the news, almost unconscious to him. For example, if he does not use his dictionary, he will burst forth with a loud, "Thus say-eth (saith) the Lord!" The word is pronounced "seth." He will say lambast (long a); the word is lambast (short a).

God revealed himself in the pages of the Bible and his Bible is made up of words. The preacher's tool is words. As a mason uses a trowel, as a carpenter uses a hammer and saw, as a baseball player uses a bat, as a farmer uses a plow, so the instrument of use and communication for the preacher is words. He must study to use them forcefully. They all have overtones that color all we attempt to say.

Words are amazing creations and creatures. An Argentine ambassador was answering his American guest's question concerning the family of the diplomat. Did he have any children? Explaining that his wife could not have a child, the ambassador said, "You see, my wife is impregnable!" Sensing that that was not quite the right word he added, "No; you see my wife is inconceivable!" Again sensing that he had not used the correct descriptive adjective, he finally and triumphantly explained, "You see, my wife is unbearable!" The English language, especially and particularly, is really some vehicle in which to convey the everlasting truth! Be careful how you use it.

Filing Systems

No man can keep in his head all the pertinent information he ought to know. He needs a filing system. A short pencil is better than a long memory. Every pastor's study ought to have plenty of room for filing cabinets. One simple way to file material is this: Start with the number 1 and give to each piece of paper you wish to keep a number, on and on, ad infinitum. Place those pieces in manila folders in succession in the filing cabinets. In a box, put cards arranged alphabetically and write on them all the subjects on which you are gathering the material. On the cards write the number on the paper and whatever you would like to add descriptive-wise. Do the same for a poetry file. This filing can be added to forever, and any subject can be easily and quickly found.

The filing of sermons and addresses can be done in several ways. I first write them down in a large, ruled book, with the text, title, and time and place of delivery. I then file the sermons according to text, beginning at Genesis and going through the Revelation. I also have a file of sermons delivered on special occasions, such as Mother's Day, Father's Day, patriotic messages for first part of July, Thanksgiving Day, Christmas Day, New Year's Day, Easter, Memorial Day, evangelistic conferences, Bible conferences, and so forth.

As the pastor grows older, he increasingly builds up a vast wealth of preaching material that represents his very life. If it is filed correctly, all of it is at his fingertips upon any moment of call.

4

The Pastor in His
Sermon Preparation

A decade ago I was asked by the editor of *Moody Monthly* magazine to write out the delineation of my sermon preparation. I still follow the thoughts and convictions that I held then. As any pastor would, I have learned much in the half century through which I have been preaching, and the learning has probably solidified and crystallized into habits of study and preparation that are now part and parcel of my daily life. These are the persuasions of procedure that I present in this chapter.

The Pastor Moved by the Truth

What is preaching? How does it differ from lecturing? From counseling? From teaching? What sets preaching apart from all other kinds of discourses?

The answer is plain. Preaching is addressed to the will, to the conscience, and its ultimate purpose is to move the soul Godward and heavenward. The preacher does this by literally living out in public utterance the truth of God.

In delivering a sermon I feel as in actual life the subject matter I am presenting. Even in preparation I live through these truths, many times weeping at my desk before the moving revelation of God. No experience is more intense than that of the true preacher who thus unfolds before his people the marvelous vistas of the riches of God in Christ Jesus.

Depth of Doctrinal Truth Needed

Modern times have seen a significant decline in doctrinal preaching. We have become so fair-minded, so dialectical, so ecumenical, so anxious to preach our question marks and intellectual doubts that we are neglecting to teach our people the meaningful, doctrinal truths of the Word of God.

Wherever there is strong doctrinal preaching, there is usually a healthy, virile church. The evangelistic sermons of the New Testament are filled with the mighty doctrines that present and delineate our Lord—the life of Christ, the death of Christ, the resurrection of Christ, the return of Christ, the redemptive power of Christ, the sinfulness of man, his need of a Savior, and the urgent appeal to come to him as Lord and Master.

Our preaching needs depth, force, and doctrinal content, and the only way to get it is by long hours of study and prayer.

The Most Fruitful of Homiletical Discoveries

The most fruitful homiletical discovery I ever made centers about a simple but effective way of indexing my source materials. I have numbered seriatim the books of sermons and other volumes that have come into my hands. Then I have placed by the text in a wide-margin Bible the number of the book and the page on which the discussion of the text is found. This lays open to me a vast range of literature as I preach through the Word of God.

When I began preaching, I thought I had to spin everything out of my own shallow, meager resources. I thought I had to be positively and absolutely original in every thought and every message. No wonder my beginning preaching was as shallow as water disappearing in sand!

For almost two thousand years gifted men of God have been praying, preaching, and writing down their inspired utterances. Use their recorded studies!

Make good use of your library. It would be redundant for me to expatiate upon the need of the true minister to study the Bible with all the help, concordances, commentaries, versions, languages, articles, sermons, experiences, and all the other material that he can assemble. But such study is essential.

Read everything. Anything that touches life concerns the preacher. From the daily newspapers, magazines, radio commentaries, editorials—from all of creation—the preacher has opportunity to bring into his message those enriching events and comments that will help to explain the meaning of the Word of God.

Be an attentive listener. While you are talking you are not learning anything. No one ever had a silver tongue who did not first have a golden ear.

The Pastor Preaching the Bible

To me the best way to preach is to take the Bible book by book, section by section, paragraph by paragraph, verse by verse, and proclaim its meaning to the congregation with an emphatic and convincing "Thus saith the Lord!" One day in Dallas I started preaching at Genesis 1:1 and went through the Bible to the last verse of Revelation. It took me seventeen years and eight months, but it was positively the most rewarding study of my life.

On another occasion, on a New Year's eve, I began preaching at 7:30 with the first verse in Genesis and preached through the whole Bible, closing after midnight. Our auditorium, one of the largest in America, was packed when I began and it was still packed with people standing around the walls, upstairs and down, when I finished after midnight. (Broadman Press published that long sermon under the title, *The Scarlet Thread Through the Bible*.)

Preaching the Bible is incomparably the most marvelous way to preach. Those who come to church want to know if God has anything to say. The preacher is in the pulpit to tell them what God says. He learns the message of God from God's self-revelation and self-disclosure in the Holy Scriptures. The preacher then stands upon a solid rock, preaching the immutable, eternal Word of God.

The Pastor Following the Holy Spirit

Let me illustrate why it is better to follow the mind of the Holy Spirit than to follow any man-made arrangement. In these last several years I have been preaching every Sunday night from the life of Christ. I started the series following the life of our Lord through a harmony of the Gospels. After a few years passed, I was keenly aware that I was spending much time on the beginning ministry of our Lord when I needed to preach his atonement and glorious resurrection.

It then came to me what the Holy Spirit has done in the arrangement of the books of the Bible. There is the story of the life of Christ, then the tremendous presentation of his death and resurrection. After that the Holy Spirit begins the story again and leads up once more to his death and resurrection. The Holy Spirit then does the same thing again. And even then he is not done. For the fourth time he begins the story of Christ and leads up to his death and resurrection.

Seeing this, I corrected my mistake, telling my congregation of the misjudgment I had made in departing from the Holy Scriptures. I announced that I was going to follow the order even as the heavenly Spirit of wisdom has given it to us in the inspired Book. So I am now preaching through the Gospels, one after the other, and, as one man said, "everlastingly bragging on Jesus," bringing them again and again to his cross and to his resurrection.

An Illustration of Sermon Preparation

On Sunday mornings at this writing I am preaching through Ephesians. Recently I preached on Ephesians 4:30. The title of the sermon was "Grieving the Holy Spirit." One Lord's Day I preached on Ephesians 4:32: "And be ye kind one to another, tenderhearted, forgiving one another, even as God for Christ's sake hath forgiven you."

This is how I prepared. First, I read the text in the Greek. If a preacher does not know Greek, he can read the passages in several translations and get a really good idea of the original words. From the Greek I learned that the conclusion of the passage is not at the end of Ephesians 4, but that it continues through the first two verses of Ephesians 5. For the introduction of this sermon, therefore, I presented the text in its context. That is always a good way to begin.

In Ephesians 5:1, Paul avows that we are *tekna agapeta,* "loved children." In 1 John 4:8 John calls God *agape,* "love." We are precious, loved, desired, prayed for children of God. As such, Paul enjoins us to be like our Father. He says, "Be ye therefore followers of God." The word translated "followers" is *mimetai* from which we get our English word *mimic*. We are to be mimics or imitators of our heavenly Father.

If we are to imitate our Father, what is he like and what does he do? How can we imitate him? The "therefore" in 5:1 refers to the verse above. I read 4:32 in order to know what to do to be an imitator of our heavenly Father. What is God like? The beautiful text declares that he is kind, tenderhearted, and forgiving.

The sermon then went on to speak of the kindness of God, the kindness of Christ, and the kindness of his people. Under these three points, following the introduction mentioned above, I searched the Bible for material to illustrate and enforce the message. I found I had enough material for several hours. Thus I had to cut it back, using only the more impressive illustrations and discussions.

On the third point, speaking of the kindness of God's people, I noted the need for encouragement and sympathy. Here I found poignant illustrations in the lives of the poet Sir Walter Scott (encouraged by Bobby Burns) and Gipsy Smith (encouraged by Ira D. Sankey). Then I spoke of how this kindness blesses the church, making it warm, hospitable, and friendly. Lastly, I spoke of how it blesses and wins the lost. They are moved more by kindness, love, and compassionate interest than by cold, correct theology. Then I appealed for the lost for whom we had prayed to give their hearts to Jesus.

As I study the message comes to my soul and the arrangement of the material is easily crystallized under three or four main points. I drive them home to the hearts of my listeners with all the fervor and fire that God gives me.

There is a principle here. If you have something to say, do not worry, you will find a way to say it. If you are moved, the audience will be moved. If the truth of the Lord burns in your heart, it will burn in the hearts of the congregation.

Final Form of the Sermon and Preparation for Delivery

Prayerful study of the Scripture will bring a message to your heart. This will never fail. God will do it for you. In preaching the Bible the pastor will inevitably touch on every pertinent issue of human life and living. Pray and study the Holy Scriptures till the message is born in your heart. Give it a brief, attractive title. Divide it up into three or four or five points. Relate the message to the needs of the people.

In fixing and memorizing the message in your mind and heart, study by intervals. Spread the work throughout the week. Remember, in working too long at the desk you can study yourself stupid.

Finally, when the sermon is finished, go over in your mind the message before going to sleep. Psychologically, your mind will enforce each sermon. It will be a part of you. Just before preaching, go over it if possible; pray over every point. Then stand up, trust God, and go ahead. The Holy Spirit will do the rest.

Suggested Books for Study on Preaching

Here are some books on sermon preparation and preaching that will bless the pastor.

Jay E. Adams, *Studies in Preaching,* Presbyterian and Reformed, 1976

J. Daniel Baumann, *An Introduction to Contemporary Preaching,* Baker, 1972

H. C. Brown, Jr., H. Gordon Clinard, and Jesse J. Northcutt, *Steps to the Sermon,* Broadman, 1963

B. H. Carroll, *The Three Baptisms,* Evangel Press, 1957

E. C. Dargan, *A History of Preaching,* Baker, 1967

Eric W. Hayden, *Preaching Through the Bible,* Zondervan, 1964

Charles Koller, *Expository Preaching Without Notes,* Baker, 1962

Clarence E. Macartney, *Preaching Without Notes,* Abingdon, 1946

G. Campbell Morgan, *Preaching,* Marshall, Morgan, and Scott, 1955

A. T. Robertson, *The Minister and His Greek New Testament,* Baker, 1977

William E. Sangster, *The Craft of Sermon Construction,* Epworth Press, 1964

————, *The Craft of Sermon Illustrations,* Baker, 1973

C. H. Spurgeon, *An Allround Ministry,* Banner of Truth, 1972

V. L. Stanfield, *Effective Evangelistic Preaching,* New Orleans Baptist Theological Seminary, 1965

Merrill F. Unger, *Principles of Expository Preaching,* Zondervan, 1955

Wayne E. Ward, *The Word Comes Alive,* Broadman, 1969

5

The Pastor and His Staff

Staff Relationship Inherent in Organization

If there is an organization, there is concomitantly some kind of a staff to run it, whether paid or not.* If there is a church, it must have a pastor and deacons and other leaders in order to prosper. A meeting of the pastor and these heads of organization would be a meeting of the pastor and his staff. In a small church the entire staff could be the pastor, a Sunday School superintendent (or director), a Church Training director, a WMU director, a Brotherhood director, a song leader, and a chairman of the deacons. In such a situation it might be better to call the group a church cabinet, but whatever it is called, the group represents the motivating and driving force behind the success of the organization.

In a larger church the word *staff* refers to the paid leaders, directors, and employees of the church. In our church we have about three hundred fifty such personnel. They lead the church and work for the church in all its many ministries. The pastor sometimes meets with the entire staff. Most of the time he meets and works with just the heads of departments in the group.

---

*My prayer is that this book will bless ministers and pastors of all Bible-believing, evangelical denominations. I am aware that Baptist terms for pastors (ministers), organizations, and staff members will be different from many other denominations. WMU in Baptist churches is the women's missionary organization. Brotherhood is the men's group.

Size of the Pastor's Ministry and the Staff

Any preacher-pastor can reach and keep just so many people. The size is definitely numbered. When he reaches a certain number, while he adds to it in his work in one area, erosion will subtract from it in another area. It is like covering a barrel with a piece of cloth too small. When he pulls it over to cover one side, he pulls it away and exposes the other side. After he gathers a certain number, he will subsequently lose as many as he wins.

A church grows like a tree trunk, always in the circle on the outside in the annual rings. The tree does not grow in the middle, but always from the outside. At the center will be the pastor, the faithful deacons, and the dedicated families. Then the circle grows, and other families are added. The center stays the same with the same faithful people, but grows toward the outer periphery. If the circle continues to grow, always it will be from the outside, adding to the outer ring.

The opposite is true about the decline and death of a church. It will start the erosion from the outside, losing a family here, losing a family there, until finally the group is back to when it began, with the pastor and the faithful few surrounding him.

How is the church then to continue to grow if the pastor can reach and hold just so many people? The answer lies in the staff. Each staff member added can himself reach and hold a certain number of people. The size of the number depends upon his ability and dedication. Around every staff member will be a cluster of people added to the whole. This can continue on and on almost without end. The tree of life grows and grows until it becomes gigantic.

My predecessor in the First Baptist Church in Dallas was the famed prince of preachers, Dr. George W. Truett. He had been the pastor of the congregation for forty-seven years. When the pulpit committee talked with me about becoming pastor of this great church, I frankly and boldly told them I could not build the church as Dr. Truett had done. He built this church by the powers of his personal magnetism, his magnetic presence, and preaching. He had a small staff, maybe a half dozen or less. I truthfully said to the pulpit committee that I could not build the church on the power of preaching alone; I am no Truett. I asked the men and one woman on the committee if they would look with favor upon my selecting a staff to help me, one chosen by me and responsible to me alone. They readily acquiesced. Then we began and thus we continue after these thirty-six full years. Even the great Truett could reach just so many. The staff we have built reaches and holds many thousands more.

We have never had any real trouble in the church here in Dallas. The only time there was any bare approach to deep difficulty lay in the staff. Some of the superintendents and leaders in the Sunday School had been in their places of leadership for many, many years. When I sought to bring in young staff members, just graduated from seminary to direct the work, these older volunteer officers rebelled furiously. "I was here doing the task before you were born," he or she would belligerently announce to the newly employed staff member. I laid the whole case before the deacons. After discussion, they voted unanimously to stand behind the pastor in his attempt to build the church with those chosen, prepared, and educated-for-the-purpose staff members. The trouble resolved itself. The staff members came, stayed, and increased in number. This was the actual beginning of our vast outreach.

Payment of a Staff Member

How can a church pay the salaries of their employed staff members? I have learned that a good staff leader pays for himself or herself many times over again. All a staff member has to do to pay for his salary and upkeep is to win and to hold twelve new families to the church. That will do it. Ten of the tithing families will pay his salary on whatever economic level the congregation lives (one hundred twenty dollars a year in Uganda, twenty thousand dollars a year in Dallas). The tithes of the other two families will pay the light bill and the janitor bill for his service.

The only problem is finding the staff worker who will visit, pray, witness, testify, cultivate, and love the lost into the saving relationship with Christ and his church. It would seem to me that every God-called, vocational servant of God would and could do that—win twelve families in a whole year. If he will, the pastor has it made.

That is why a lazy, indifferent staff member is a drag on all the other workers. Not paying his own way, someone else has to make up for his dereliction. That is a heavy burden to bear, and an increase in the work of the good staff member that he ought not have to assume. An unproductive staff member is a liability in the kingdom of God. Sometimes the tree needs pruning in order for it to bear fruit.

When President Jimmy Carter delivered the eulogy at the memorial service for Senator Hubert Humphrey in St. Paul, Minnesota, he read this: "Mahatma Gandhi once wrote that there were seven sins in the world, wealth without work, pleasure without conscience, knowledge without character, commerce without morality, science without humanity, worship without sacrifice, and politics without principle."

These words of wisdom by the wise former prime minister of India apply to everybody, and in fact to all civilization. But they especially apply to Christian people, and most especially to those of us who work vocationally in the vineyard of the Lord. We ought to labor (not take advantage of our type of ministry in order to shirk and avoid our responsibilities) and we ought to live those principles before the people. "Like priest like people." Our labors of love ought to be clearly manifest and our devotion to Christian ideals ought ever to be seen. Such devoted consecration in a staff member makes him worth his weight in diamonds. What an open, unbounded ministry is open to such a servant of the Lord!

The Pastor Selecting the Staff

When the pastor is able to begin building the church with the selection of a paid staff, where should he begin? I think he should first choose a combination person who can direct the educational program and be also a minister of music. This leader can literally be the right-hand man of the pastor. The two are seen together in the pulpit, at funerals, at all public services, and they make a perfect team in emphasizing and directing the work of the church. Next to the pastor himself, this man is the most valuable.

The next staff member I would select is a children's worker. Jesus said to Simon Peter, "Feed my lambs," before he said,

"Feed my sheep" (John 21:15-17). Adults are not coming unless there is something good planned for the children. There must be a place for the baby if the parents are to attend the services.

All the while, the business affairs of the church must be carefully administered. Volunteer help can do this if the church remains small, but if the congregation grows, there must be someone to direct all the efforts for maintenance, upkeep, and janitorial services, beside the counting of the tithes, gifts, and the payment of the salaries and bills.

After these beginning staff members are added to the list of vocational workers, the remainder can be added as they are needed. As I have suggested, there is no limit to the expansion if the staff member will work faithfully in winning people to Christ.

The qualifications of a good staff member are what they would be in the secular world of teaching, administration, education, business, public relations, personality, appeal, and all the rest, with this one additional accompaniment—the staff member ought to feel a real affinity for the work of the Lord, "called" of God to do the task if at all possible. This work is not just another job. It is not punching a clock at 9:00 AM and punching it again at 4:00 PM. It is a dedication either in praying or planning or laboring at the task all the waking hours of the day and night.

Let us take, for example, the choice of a minister of recreation to look at the qualifications of a staff member. Years ago when we first proposed to build a recreational building we sent men all over America to talk with other churches who had such buildings and such programs. This is what we found: where the church had a paid recreational director and staff to direct the use of the facility, it was a help in the ministry of the Lord. Where the church could not or did not have a paid recreational director, the gymnasium was a headache, a burden, and sometimes a disaster. The searching men reported that all over the country they found gymnasium areas closed or diverted to other uses because of the insoluble problems encountered. We, therefore, first had a discussion concerning whether we would be willing to pay a recreational director on a continuing, permanent basis. Having decided in the affirmative, we built the building (ultimately two buildings), hired the director, and have been blessed by the program ever since.

In the published qualifications of the recreational director, the manual goes like this:

1. The director should have experienced salvation and be a mature Christian. He should be a member of a Baptist church.
2. He should have experienced a sense of God's leadership into church-related vocations generally, and recreation specifically.
3. He should be professionally trained in recreation or some related area, and should have training in religious education or equivalent experience.
4. He should possess no questionable habits that would tend to lessen his influence.

Other desirable characteristics are:

(1) Broad vision (ability to look ahead and plan according to people's needs)
(2) Deep-rooted belief in people
(3) Sense of humor
(4) Enthusiasm
(5) A desire to share
(6) Resourcefulness
(7) Humility
(8) Friendliness
(9) (And a great singer, as in our director, if possible!)

The published duties of the director go like this:

1. Administration of the recreation facility
2. Planning, coordinating, and promoting the total program of recreation
3. Enlisting and training of leadership
4. Relationship to community

The time allotted to each of these differs with the situation and the individual. Each category may be broken down further as follows:

1. *Administration*
    (1) See that the facility is in serviceable conditions at all
        times.

(2) Keep necessary records for the proper functioning of the program.

(3) Supervise proper maintenance on all equipment.

(4) Keep accurate calendar of coming events.

(5) Purchase such equipment as needed for the recreation program (does not include major maintenance items).

2. *Program*

(1) Work with the recreation committee in providing opportunities for all members of the congregation to participate in the program.

(2) Provide regularly for each of the age groups represented in the church (RA's, GA's, SA).

(3) Maintain a proper balance of activities throughout the year.

(4) Coordinate the various meetings of the interest groups with the total program of the church to avoid conflicts.

(5) Maintain a master calendar for scheduling purposes.

(6) Use interest groups to undergird the total program of the church.

(7) Promote and plan recreation activities using the existing organizations when possible.

(8) Use every proper existing means of promoting the program plus a weekly mimeographed schedule so everyone will become informed of the program.

(9) Develop one major means of communication in the church such as the bulletin, newspaper, news sheet, etc.

3. *Leadership training and enlistment*

(1) The director will establish definite programs of leadership training for both paid and volunteer staff.

(2) He will enlist adequate numbers of volunteers to maintain a high level of supervision and program.

(3) In-service training will be emphasized, including regular staff meetings and personal evaluations of work being done.

(4) Definite efforts should be made to send volunteers to Conference Center recreation weeks.

To find such a man like this, God must call him and prepare

him. But happy is the church who is blessed with such a useful staff member.

It would be impossible for me to emphasize too much the care that ought to be taken in the choice of a staff member. It is a lot easier to secure a staff member than to go through the tearful trauma of dismissing one. The dismissal of a member of the vocational church leadership is without doubt one of the saddest and heaviest assignments the pastor ever faces. The pastor can work through review committees, but ultimately the responsibility is his. He is finally chargeable for it all, both in the eyes of the people and in the actual structure of the church life.

Whenever a staff member is removed, close friends and their families are inevitable involved. I have never gone through it but that we have lost families from the church, no matter how unworthy the staff worker. We sent away a staff member years ago who was later indicted for molesting little boys, who, rather than face trial, went to a cemetery and committed suicide. Yet when he left us several families took their letters out of the church in bitter reprisal. Again, I say, it is far better and much wiser to pray through the careful selection of a staff member than to hurt the fellowship of the assembly of saints by firing him.

The Best Kind of a Staff Organization

Many years ago when I began the expansion of the church, the staff organization always followed a perpendicular plan. They were organizational up and down, with a leader for the Sunday School, a leader for the Training Union, and a leader for the other groups in the church. I turned the organizational chart over and made it horizontal, with a leader for the age group responsible for his section Sunday morning, *many* in Sunday School, Sunday evening in Training Union, and throughout all the activities of the work. This makes for an excellent program, full-rounded, in every age. Instead of the ministry of the church to a child, a youth, or an adult being chopped up by different leaders who are furthering their own programs, we have one leader over it all for the age who plans the work throughout the days of the week. This kind of an approach has to be supplemented with special people who are gifted in certain areas, such as the choir program for children, but outside these specialties, the plan is sound and good and workable.

The Pastor's Relationship with the Staff

If the pastor can look upon the staff as he would his own family, he will already be on the way toward eminent success. His love for them will be reflected back again upon every occasion. He will meet his own gracious attitude at every turn of the road. Remember staff birthdays and anniversaries with a note, a card, or a letter of appreciation. Most church workers salaries are low—and a word of praise can surely make the worker feel that their pastor knows how hard they work and appreciates their efforts. On a five-year cycle it would be excellent to make special mention of these employees. A little bit of encouragement goes a long way.

Let the pastor look upon his staff not only as a family, but also as peers, yokefellows, fellow workers. They are not menial slaves for him to look down upon. They are God-called vocational leaders who are adept and gifted in their areas of work. Let him toil with them as equals, treating them as he would want to be treated by them (our Lord's Golden Rule; it is amazing how the principles initiated by our Savior will work!).

Let the pastor take that dedicated group into his confidence. They will help achieve his every goal and work with him to bring his every dream to realization. This means planning sessions throughout the year. An annual staff meeting of at least two days will set aside times and seasons in the church calendar for the big events. A weekly staff meeting can implement the remaining details. Every facet of the church program ought to be considered and reconsidered, discussed and rediscussed by the staff. Good planning makes for assured and certain results that please the Lord and bless the people.

It does not hurt for the pastor and the staff not only to pray together but also to play together. For them to share the happy moments of life is no less pleasing to God than to share the sad moments of disappointment and frustration. The big thing is to be *together* in heart, mind, and spirit. Pentecost was like that: the disciples were all together in one place on one certain day (Acts 2:1) *and* in one accord.

The work of the pastor in the vineyard of the Lord can be almost limitless if he is able to further his prayerful hopes and plans and visions through a dedicated staff. If he tries to do all the work himself he can do just so much, then strength for the task wanes. But through a body of assistants he can reach for the last lost, needy soul in the world. A pastor friend of mine was thus seeking to do all the labor in his field by himself. He had been a baseball pitcher, and a man who knew him in those days said to him: "Matty, do you remember when the coach one day said to you, 'Matty, don't try to strike them all out; let the shortstop help you, the outfielder, and all the rest! ' Do you remember when you took his advice and pitched a much better game? Well, the same is true about your church. Don't try to do it all. Let these other people help you." My preacher friend took the second advice, and his congregation was noticeably blessed by it.

Let the pastor delegate responsibilities to staff members then give them freedom to do the task. They will bring to bear upon the situations ways and means the pastor never thought of.

The preacher is an organizer. He is a general who rides up and down watching how his officers and troops are doing. He is the corporate executive who is responsible for the growth and extension of the company. With and through his staff he can study his people and utilize their special aptitudes and gifts. Paul likened the church to a human body. Every member is different but every member has a vital place in it. Some can teach, some can lead neighborhood prayer meetings, some are good at finances, some are good at planning social gatherings and parties, some may be even good lay preachers. But whatever, it is the staff that can give the pastor the means to use all his people.

Let me write of an extreme example of how certain people can be reached by a staff member who otherwise would be unreached by the pastor. In our city, as in every city, there are many deaf people. If would be an unusual pastor who could reach these in his own abilities. We secured the help of a preacher who could deliver Christ's message in sign language, set out to enlist all the deaf in the city, and now we have a Silent Friend's Chapel with all the organization of a teaching, preaching, soul-winning church in and around it. This led to an oral deaf ministry that is an extension of the first ministry.

We now are seeking out the blind in the city, to create with them a ministry to those who cannot see with their human eyes but who can behold the glories of Jesus with their spiritual eyes. We are persuaded the dear Lord will bless us in this staff-led effort as much as he has blessed us with the deaf.

That All-Important Staff Meeting

Any moving, growing, going, glowing company ought to set goals for itself. The striving for their realization is a part of the motivation that leads to pristine success. The same is true for the church. The church ought to set goals for itself. That means the staff must pray, think, survey, and set the goals within reach of the people.

A report of progress is always in order at staff meetings. If the work is going well, then give opportunity for the pastor to compliment and commend their efforts. If the work is not going well, report time gives the pastor fresh cause to review it all and ascertain what can be done to bring about success. Goal-setting and periodic checkups are essential in a growing organization. The reporting and accounting process creates a sense of responsibility. The staff member has something tangible to do, and taking a two-fisted hold on it, he is thus encouraged to get it done.

What about a striving after goals and numbers? Is this ungodly? The editor of a Christian journal wrote that he was not interested in numbers, only in quality. (We are *the* people!) I heard the pastor of a splendid church boast of his few baptisms, for they were silk-stocking converts from the gold coast. Theological fads lead us to forget the masses and concentrate on the quality few.

What about that? The politician knows different. We elect a President of the United States by counting noses. We elect our state governors, our senators and representatives, and all the rest of the officials the same way. "But pastor, you don't understand. These are *quality* votes! " The thundering reply is heard from the Supreme Court, "The law of the land is one man, one vote." The humblest and the poorest count for as much as the richest and the greatest.

The Roman Catholic Church knows differently. There are cities and areas in the United States that once were solidly Puritan and Baptist that are now solidly Catholic (like Rhode Island). Why? They got the families, the children, the immigrants, the people, and whoever gets the people gets the legislature, the judiciary, the schools, the present, and the future.

The Holy Scriptures know different. In Acts 2:41 over three thousand were added to the church (they were counted!). In Acts 4:4 there were over five thousand *andron* counted, men in contradistinction to women. The whole group by then numbered at least fifteen thousand. How it grew in numbers! In Acts 19:10 "all . . . Asia heard" the wonderful, good news of the Lord Jesus. Truly, truly, had the movement of Jesus remained a small sect, it would have been buried beneath the tumbling walls of Jerusalem in AD 70. But it grew instead to cover the whole civilized world.

Jesus reacted different to the multitudes. He did not say, "We are just interested in the quality few." His heart in loving compassion went out to everybody, the poor, the sick, the lost, the rich, the needy. He said he came "to seek and to save that which was lost," *all* of them (Luke 19:10). He said, "Come unto me, *all* ye that labor and are heavy laden" (Matt. 11:28). He did not say, "Take away these wretches, the flotsam and jetsam of human life." He said, "Feed them, heal them, preach the saving gospel to them." And he did it. "He healed them all" (Matt. 12:15). The Scriptures record the reaction of the people to Jesus. "And the common people heard him gladly" (Mark 12:37). Matthew 28:20 speaks of *all* nations in *all* things . . . *all* the days."

The verdict of the great judgment day is no different. Who would boast of the quality few in heaven and the disdained masses in hell? We need the lesson of Luke 14:21-23:

So the servant came, and shewed his lord these things. Then the master of the house being angry said to his servant, Go out quickly into the streets and lanes of the city, and bring in hither the poor, and the maimed, and the halt, and the blind.

And the servant said, Lord, it is done as thou hast commanded, and yet there is room.

And the lord said unto the servant, Go out into the highways and hedges, and compel them to come in, that my house may be filled.

Everybody is somebody in the kingdom of God. The Christian faith is the religion of the one lost sheep, the one lost coin, and the one lost boy.

Is there a way to reach these people for Christ? Then may the pastor and his staff devote their highest efforts toward reaching them.

At the center of the activities of the staff meeting and the work it reviews is the church calendar. On it should be placed *every* activity of the church, the place, the facilities needed, the hours, and everything and everybody involved. This will elminate ten thousand conflicts and confrontations. It is *the way* to run a many-faceted program.

Many fine churches have regular cabinet (or council) meetings. This is an organization presided over by the pastor and includes the heads of all the organized units in the church—director of Sunday School, director of Church Training, director of WMU, director of Brotherhood, chairman of deacons, and leaders of the various groups headed by the staff, such as business administrator, minister of music, minister of outreach, and anybody else the pastor would like to include. Nothing but good could come from meetings that include people like that. The inclusion of lay-elected leaders in this cabinet groups makes it all the more effective.

Compensation for Staff Members

The church should do right by its employees. "The labourer is worthy of his hire" (Luke 10:7). The salary should be commensurate with the responsibility and the work assumed. A house allowance should be provided, along with car expense. A retirement program should be carefully worked out for each employee through the Annuity Board (pension board of the denomination). Each employee should be enrolled in some kind of health insurance program. Vacation time should be arranged, the time allowed given according to the number of years of service. Professional growth should be remembered, with the staff member attending conferences and seminars that concern his or her particular field of work. These expenses would be provided for by the church. And if the staff member is invited to lead those conferences of advancement in leadership skills, the church should allow it for reasonable lengths of time (say up to two or three weeks).

All these things will contribute toward a happy, producing, growing, effective staff member.

The Place of Women in the Work

On our staff are many women, leaders in their areas of educational, missionary, and ministering work. What about that?

Some of our people have strange ideas about woman's work in the church. They have come to me saying, "The Bible says the woman is to keep silence in the church; it is not permitted for her to speak in the church" (1 Cor. 14:34-35). Now that is a strange thing to tell me. In 1 Corinthians 11 Paul had just written how a woman ought to dress when she prayed and prophesied (to speak out for the Lord; the idea of foretelling is a much later, post-biblical idea added to the Word) in the church. Now in chapter 14 he turns around and says it is a shame for her to do what he has just written about her acceptability in doing? No, not at all. Chapter 14 in 1 Corinthians is about speaking in tongues, and Paul writes in the middle of the chapter that a woman is not to do it. (And by the way, stop the women in tongues-speaking and the whole movement will die overnight). The apostle says that the woman is to pray and to prophesy (speak out for Christ) in the church. She has a worthy place of honor in the household of God's redeemed.

Others will come up to me and say, "Pastor, read this passage." Then they will have me read 1 Timothy 2:11-15, which says:

Let the woman learn in silence with all subjection.
But I suffer not a woman to teach, nor to usurp authority over the man, but to be in silence.
For Adam was first formed, then Eve.
And Adam was not deceived, but the woman being deceived was in the transgression.
Notwithstanding she shall be saved in childbearing, if they continue in faith and charity and holiness with sobriety.

Well, what about that? Let us remember that when Paul wrote his letter, he wrote then as we do today—line after line, sentence after sentence, paragraph after paragraph. The divisions into verses and chapters came hundreds of years later. So let us put a bracket around the whole passage Paul is talking about. The section of the subject begins in 1 Timothy 2:8 and concludes with 3:16. In the heart of the passage is the subject of it all clearly delineated—the bishop (pastor, elder) and the deacon. The woman is not to be the teaching-preaching elder of the church. That belongs to the ordained man. In every area of church life she can work to her heart's content: missions, Sunday School, music, staff, visitation, departmental director, everything only the Scriptures say she is not to be the pastor or the deacon. She is not "to usurp authority over the man."

May God wonderfully bless, as only he can, the Marys and the Marthas and the Elizabeths and the Dorcases and the Phoebes and the Priscillas and the Loises and the Eunices in the church. We need them desperately, God knows, and we would woefully fail without them.

6

The Organization
of a New Church

The Meaning of the Word *Church*

In the New Testament the word *church* is a translation of *ekklesia,* which is derived from *ek kaleo,* a preposition *ek* and a verb *kaleo,* signifying "to call forth." Hence, it denotes an assembly summoned or called out, a select body separated from the mass of the people. In classic usage in Greek custom, the word referred to an assembly of the citizens summoned by the town crier. It sometimes referred to a legislative assembly. It was a common term for a meeting of elected officials to discuss the affairs of a free state. It was a term to describe the lawful assembly in a free Greek city of all those possessed of the right of citizenship for the transaction of public affairs.

The word does not denote, except in rare figurative usage, a miscellaneous, unofficial assembly. Thus we find its usage in the New Testament.

Ekklesia is used in the New Testament one hundred fifteen times. Of these instances, two relate to the Hebrew congregation of the Lord, three to the Greek assembly, and one hundred ten to the Christian church. Its ordinary use in the New Testament is to designate a specific, local assembly of Christians, organized for the maintenance of the worship, the doctrines, the ordinances, the discipline of the gospel, and united in a special covenant with Christ and one another to proclaim the gospel to the world. The word occurs in this local sense in ninety-two instances in the New Testament.

The word can also denote the entire body of the elect in heaven and on earth. Here the word is used figuratively. In Ephesians 5:25-27 the church is conceived as the bride of Christ, the Lamb's wife. Other instances of this use of the word to refer to the church universal are in Ephesians 3:10,21; Colossians 1:18,24; Hebrews 12:23. This is a designation of the church referring to all of the redeemed and refers to the invisible church because it has no visible earthly organization. When the word is used to refer to the universal, invisible church, it has no officers, no laws, no ordinances, and no discipline.

The only church with which we have to do is the local visible congregation. These are the churches of the New Testament and of Christendom with their ordinances, officers, commissions, and daily witness to the world. In the New Testament we read constantly of "the churches of Judaea," "the churches of Macedonia," "the churches of Galatia," "the Seven Churches of Asia," and we read letters of the apostles addressed to these local congregations. If we belong to a church, it will be a local, down-to-earth congregation, made up of human beings.

A Real, New Testament Church

1. A church is valid, that is, it is a real, true church only as it conforms to God's Word. It must follow in character, doctrine, practice, and organization the constitution given to us in the Holy Scriptures. This is the only form authorized by Christ.

2. A church being an institution within the kingdom of Christ is properly composed only of subjects of that kingdom. Its membership is made up of baptized believers.

3. The church in its organizational form is plainly delineated in the New Testament. The divine constitution of the church in the New Testament is always congregational. All members of a church, as a life related to Christ, have equal rights.

It is the local church in the New Testament that has the power of receiving, disciplining, and excluding its members (Matt. 18:17; 1 Cor. 5:1-5; and 2 Cor. 2:4-5). The church receives its members in like manner as Peter turned to the brethren and asked about those being received for baptism in Acts 10:47. The church excludes members as seen in Romans 16:17; 2 Thessalonians 3:6; and in 1 Corinthians 5:1-13.

4. The ordained officers of a church are two. First bishops (elders, pastors) and second, deacons (Phil. 1:1; 1 Tim. 3:1-11). These officers are always elected by the church. This is seen in the election of the apostle Matthias in Acts 1:15-26. It is seen in the election of the seven in Acts 6:1-6. It is seen in the election of delegates to accompany the apostles, 1 Corinthians 16:3. It is seen in the election of the elders of the church, Acts 14:23. Here Paul and Barnabas, retracing their way to Antioch on their first missionary journey, "ordained them elders in every church." Here the word rendered "ordained" is the same as that rendered "chosen" in other passages denoting primarily the vote with uplifted hand. Alford comments on this passage in Acts 14:23: "There is no reason for departing from the usual meaning of electing by show of hands. The apostles admitted to ordination those whom the church elected," as in Acts 6:5-6.

5. The external relations of the church are vividly presented in the New Testament. Each church is complete in itself. Its decisions are subject to reversal or revising by no ecclesiastical tribunal on earth. Each church is independent and is accountable alone to Christ as its sovereign head.

Yet the churches of the New Testament were also interdependent and cooperated with each other to promote the cause of Christ (Acts 11:22,23; 1 Cor. 16:1; 2 Cor. 8:1 to 9:5).

The external relations of churches with sister churches are maintained through associations, state conventions, and national conventions. The association is the foundational, primary, and fundamental association with other like bodies.

Procedure in Organizing a New Testament Church

After holding revival meetings in places where there were no churches, I have been called upon to organize a church for the converts and their families. This is the way I have done it.

1. During the meeting (usually at the close of the revival) we asked all who were interested to attend a convocation to discuss the possibility of organizing a church.

2. At this mass meeting, we adopted a resolution stating our purpose to organize a church, inviting pastors and two or more of their members to form a council for the purpose of organizing the same.

3. At the meeting of this council, we elected a moderator to preside over it and a clerk to keep the minutes.

4. Different persons appeared before the council to state the reasons why a church ought to be organized in that place. The council then voted to accept with favor the reasons for the new church (or to reject the reasons and vote not to form the new congregation). Since the vote was affirmative, the church adopted a resolution that the new church be born, and the clerk read the names of those preparing to become charter members, reading either the church letters of those who had already received them from their former churches, or reading the names of those who were becoming charter members on promise of a letter.

5. We then discussed the church covenant and read it out loud together. We then voted to adopt it as our church covenant. I then read the articles of faith one by one; we adopted them one by one as each was read. A covering resolution was then adopted by all the charter members accepting the covenant and the articles of faith, and all of them signed the resolution.

6. We then elected what permanent officers we could, such as a church moderator, church clerk, church treasurer, and appointed a pulpit committee and a deacon ordination committee. We also chose a church name at this time.

7. The council then gave the right hand of fellowship to the charter members of the new church, and the members thus in love shook hands with each other, following one another down the line.

8. The doors of the new church were opened to all who were led by the Holy Spirit to join. In a meeting like this in New Mexico, I remember that we received on that occasion sixteen by baptism.

9. In a benedictory prayer we besought God's blessings upon the growth and Christian excellence of the new church. And God answers prayer.

The Church Covenant

This is the long-established and much-used church covenant that we read together in organizing the new church.

Church Covenant

Having been led, as we believe, by the Spirit of God, to receive the Lord Jesus Christ as our Saviour and on the profession of our faith, having been baptized in the name of the Father, and of the Son, and of the Holy Ghost, we do now, in the presence of God, angels, and this assembly, most solemnly and joyfully enter into covenant with one another, as one body in Christ.

We engage, therefore, by the aid of the Holy Spirit, to walk together in Christian love; to strive for the advancement of this church, in its prosperity and spirituality; to sustain its worship, ordinances, discipline, and doctrines; to contribute cheerfully and regularly to the support of the ministry, the expenses of the church, the relief of the poor, and the spread of the gospel through all nations.

We also engage to maintain family and secret devotion; to religiously educate our children; to seek the salvation of our kindred and acquaintances; to walk circumspectly in the world; to be just in our dealings, faithful in our engagements, and exemplary in our deportment; to avoid all tattling, backbiting, and excessive anger; to abstain from the sale and use of intoxicating drinks as a beverage, and to be zealous in our efforts to advance the kingdom of our Saviour.

We further engage to watch over one another in brotherly love; to remember each other in prayer; to aid each other in sickness and distress; to cultivate Christian sympathy in feeling and courtesy in speech; to be slow to take offense, but always ready for reconciliation, and, mindful of the rules of our Saviour, to secure it without delay.

We moreover engage, that when we remove from this place we will, as soon as possible, unite with some other church, where we can carry out the spirit of this Covenant, and the principles of God's word.

Closing Prayer

Now the God of Peace, who brought again from the dead our Lord Jesus Christ, that great shepherd of the sheep, through the blood of the everlasting Covenant, make us perfect in every good work to do His will; working in us that which is well pleasing in His sight, through Jesus Christ, to whom be glory for ever and ever. Amen.

The Declaration of Faith We Accepted
Article by Article

Baptists do not believe in "Creeds of the Faith" but they have everlastingly believed in "Confessions of the Faith." To me they are the same with the only difference being that the word *creed* carries with it an overture of an authoritative body (either state or ecclesiastical) able to enforce the system of doctrine. For example, *The Heritage Dictionary of the English Language,* published by Houghton Mifflin Company in 1970, defines "creed" as "a formal statement of religious belief; a confession of faith." The same dictionary defines "confession" as "an avowal of belief in the doctrines of a particular faith"; "a group of worshipers adhering to a particular creed." Whether "creed" or "confession," there has to be some kind of doctrinal similarity to make any church or denomination what it is and what it is not.

The Articles of Faith that I read in days past in organizing churches was "The New Hampshire Declaration of Faith," published in 1833. In 1925 the Southern Baptist Convention adopted a revision of the New Hampshire Declaration called, "The Baptist Faith and Message." This again was revised by the Convention in 1963 and published by the same name, *The Baptist Faith and Message.* In 1970 our First Baptist Church in Dallas adopted "The Articles of Faith, First Baptist Church, Dallas," which was also adopted by the new school, "The Center of Biblical Studies." The latter confession is the same as "The Baptist Faith and Message" with the exception of varying revision in Article I (The Scriptures), Article X (Last Things), Article XIII (Stewardship), and Article XV (The Christian and the Social Order).

With this introductory statement we publish herewith the Articles of Faith of the First Baptist Church in Dallas.

I. The Scriptures

The Holy Bible was written by men divinely inspired and is the record of God's revelation of Himself to man. It is a perfect treasure of divine instruction. It has God for its author, salvation for its end, and truth, without any mixture of error, for its matter. It is inerrant and infallible in its original manuscript which is to be taken as verbally inspired. It reveals the principles by which God judges us; and therefore is, and will remain to the end of the world, the true center of Christian union, and the supreme standard by which all human conduct, creeds, and religious opinions should be tried. The criterion by which the Bible is to be interpreted is Jesus Christ.

II. God

There is one and only one living and true God. He is an intelligent, spiritual, and personal Being, the Creator, Redeemer, Preserver, and Ruler of the universe. God is infinite in holiness and all other perfections. To Him we owe the highest love, reverence, and obedience. The eternal God reveals Himself to us as Father, Son, and Holy Spirit, with distinct personal attributes, but without division of nature, essence, or being.

A. God the Father

God as Father reigns with providential care over His universe, His creatures, and the flow of the stream of human history according to the purposes of His grace. He is all powerful, all loving, and all wise. God is Father in truth to those who become children of God through faith in Jesus Christ. He is fatherly in His attitude toward all men.

B. God the Son

Christ is the eternal Son of God. In His incarnation as Jesus Christ He was conceived of the Holy Spirit and born of the virgin

Mary. Jesus perfectly revealed and did the will of God, taking upon Himself the demands and necessities of human nature and identifying Himself completely with mankind yet without sin. He honored the divine law by His personal obedience, and in His death on the cross He made provision for the redemption of men from sin. He was raised from the dead with a glorified body and appeared to His disciples as the person who was with them before His crucifixion. He ascended into heaven and is now exalted at the right hand of God where He is the One Mediator, partaking of the nature of God and of man, and in whose Person is effected the reconciliation between God and man. He will return in power and glory to judge the world and to consummate His redemptive mission. He now dwells in all believers as the living and ever present Lord.

C. God the Holy Spirit

The Holy Spirit is the Spirit of God. He inspired holy men of old to write the Scriptures. Through illumination He enables men to understand truth. He exalts Christ. He convicts of sin, of righteousness, and of judgment. He calls men to the Saviour, and effects regeneration. He cultivates Christian character, comforts believers, and bestows the spiritual gifts by which they serve God through His church. He seals the believer unto the day of final redemption. His presence in the Christian is the assurance of God to bring the believer into the fulness of the stature of Christ. He enlightens and empowers the believer and the church in worship, evangelism, and service.

III. Man

Man was created by the special act of God, in His own image, and is the crowning work of His creation. In the beginning man was innocent of sin and was endowed by his Creator with freedom of choice. By his free choice man sinned against God and brought sin into the human race. Through the temptation of Satan man transgressed the command of God, and fell from his original innocence; whereby his posterity inherit a nature and an environment inclined toward sin, and as soon as they are capable of moral action become transgressors and are under condemnation. Only the grace of God can bring man into His holy fellowship and enable man to fulfill the creative purpose of God. The sacredness of human personality is evident in that God created man in His own image, and in that Christ died for man; therefore every man possesses dignity and is worthy of respect and Christian love.

IV. Salvation

Salvation involves the redemption of the whole man, and is offered freely to all who accept Jesus Christ as Lord and Saviour, who by His own blood obtained eternal redemption for the believer. In its broadest sense salvation includes regeneration, sanctification, and glorification.

A. Regeneration, or the new birth, is a work of God's grace whereby believers become new creatures in Christ Jesus. It is a change of heart wrought by the Holy Spirit through conviction of sin, to which the sinner responds in repentance toward God and faith in the Lord Jesus Christ.

Repentance and faith are inseparable experiences of grace. Repentance is a genuine turning from sin toward God. Faith is the acceptance of Jesus Christ and commitment of the entire personality to Him as Lord and Saviour. Justification is God's gracious and full acquittal upon principles of His righteousness of all sinners who repent and believe in Christ. Justification brings the believer into a relationship of peace and favor with God.

B. Sanctification is the experience, beginning in regeneration, by which the believer is set apart to God's purposes, and is enabled to progress toward moral and spiritual perfection through the presence and power of the Holy Spirit dwelling in him. Growth in grace should continue throughout the regenerate person's life.

C. Glorification is the culmination of salvation and is the final blessed and abiding state of the redeemed.

V. God's Purpose of Grace

Election is the gracious purpose of God, according to which He regenerates, sanctifies, and glorifies sinners. It is consistent with the free agency of man, and comprehends all the means in connection with the end. It is a glorious display of God's sovereign goodness, and is infinitely wise, holy, and unchangeable. It excludes boasting and promotes humility.

All true believers endure to the end. Those whom God has accepted in Christ, and sanctified by His Spirit, will never fall away from the state of grace, but shall persevere to the end. Believers may fall into sin through neglect and temptation, whereby they grieve the Spirit, impair their graces and comforts, bring reproach on the cause of Christ, and temporal judgments on themselves, yet they shall be kept by the power of God through faith unto salvation.

VI. The Church

A New Testament church of the Lord Jesus Christ is a local body of baptized believers who are associated by covenant in the faith and fellowship of the gospel, observing the two ordinances of Christ, committed to His teachings, exercising the gifts, rights, and privileges invested in them by His word, and seeking to extend the gospel to the ends of the earth.

This church is an autonomous body, operating through democratic processes under the Lordship of Jesus Christ. In such a congregation members are equally responsible. Its Scriptural officers are pastors and deacons.

The New Testament speaks also of the church as the body of Christ which includes all of the redeemed of all the ages.

VII. Baptism and the Lord's Supper

Christian baptism is the immersion of a believer in water in the name of the Father, the Son, and the Holy Spirit. It is an act of obedience symbolizing the believer's faith in a crucified, buried, and risen Saviour, the believer's death to sin, the burial of the old life, and the resurrection to walk in newness of life in Christ Jesus. It is a testimony to his faith in the final resurrection of the dead. Being a church ordinance, it is prerequisite to the privileges of church membership and to the Lord's Supper.

The Lord's Supper is a symbolic act of obedience whereby members of the church, through partaking of the bread and the fruit of the vine, memorialize the death of the Redeemer and anticipate His second coming.

VIII. The Lord's Day

The first day of the week is the Lord's Day. It is a Christian institution for regular observance. It commemorates the resurrection of Christ from the dead and should be employed in exercises of worship and spiritual devotion, both public and private, and by refraining from worldly amusements, and resting from secular employments, work of necessity and mercy only being excepted.

IX. The Kingdom

The Kingdom of God includes both His general sovereignty over the universe and His particular kingship over men who willfully acknowledge Him as King. Particularly the Kingdom is the realm of salvation into which men enter by trustful, childlike commitment to Jesus Christ. Christians ought to pray and to labor that the Kingdom may come and God's will be done on earth. The full consummation of the Kingdom awaits the return of Jesus Christ and the end of this age.

X. Last Things

According to His promise Jesus Christ will return personally and visibly in glory to the earth.

The dead in Christ will rise first, then we who are alive and remain until the coming of the Lord shall be caught up together with them in the clouds to meet the Lord in the air. After the judgments of God upon this sinful world in the Great Tribulation, Jesus our Lord will come with His saints to establish His millennial kingdom.

Christ will judge all men in righteousness. The redeemed of Christ in their resurrected and glorified bodies will receive their rewards and will dwell in heaven forever with their Saviour. The unsaved will be separated from the kingdom of God and will be consigned forever to a place of everlasting perdition.

XI. Evangelism and Missions

It is the duty and privilege of every follower of Christ and of every church of the Lord Jesus Christ to endeavor to make disciples of all nations. The new birth of man's spirit by God's Holy Spirit means the birth of love for others. Missionary efforts on the part of all rests thus upon a spiritual necessity of the regenerate life, and is expressly and repeatedly commanded in the teachings of Christ. It is the duty of every child of God to seek constantly to win the lost to Christ by personal effort and by all other methods in harmony with the gospel of Christ.

XII. Education

The cause of education in the Kingdom of Christ is co-ordinate with the causes of missions and general benevolence, and should receive along with these the liberal support of the churches. An adequate system of Christian schools is necessary to a complete spiritual program for Christ's people.

In Christian education there should be a proper balance between academic freedom and academic responsibility. Freedom in any orderly relationship of human life is always limited and never absolute. The freedom of a teacher in a Christian school, college, or seminary is limited by the pre-eminence of Jesus Christ, by the authoritative nature of the Scriptures, and by the distinct purpose for which the school exists.

XIII. Stewardship

God is the source of all blessings, temporal and spiritual; all that we have and are we owe to Him. Christians have a spiritual debtorship to the whole world, a holy trusteeship in the Gospel, and a binding stewardship in their possessions. They are therefore under obligation to serve Him with their time, talents, and material possessions; and should recognize all these as entrusted to them to use for the glory of God and for helping others. According to the Scriptures, Christians should contribute of their means cheerfully, regularly, systematically, proportionately, and liberally for the advancement of the Redeemer's cause on earth. The tithe is to be considered the starting place of Christian Stewardship.

XIV. Cooperation

Christ's people should, as occasion requires, organize such associations and conventions as may best secure cooperation for the great objects of the Kingdom of God. Such organizations have no authority over one another or over the churches. They are voluntary and advisory bodies designed to elicit, combine, and direct the energies of our people in the most effective manner. Members of New Testament churches should cooperate with one another in carrying forward the missionary, educational, and benevolent ministries for the extension of Christ's Kingdom. Christian unity in the New Testament sense is spiritual harmony and voluntary cooperation for common ends by various groups of Christ's people. Cooperation is desirable between the various Christian denominations, when the end to be attained is itself justified, and when such cooperation involves no violation of conscience or compromise of loyalty to Christ and His Word as revealed in the New Testament.

XV. The Christian and the Social Order

Every Christian is under obligation to seek to make the will of Christ supreme in his own life and in human society. Means and methods used for the improvement of society and the establishment of righteousness among men can be truly and permanently helpful only when they are rooted in the regeneration of the individual by the saving grace of God in Christ Jesus. The Christian should oppose in the spirit of Christ every form of greed, selfishness, and vice. He should work to provide for the orphaned, the needy, the aged, the helpless, and the sick. Every Christian should seek to bring industry, government, and society as a whole under the sway of the principles of righteousness, truth, and brotherly love. In order to promote these ends Christians should be ready to work with all men of good will in any good cause, always being careful to act in the spirit of love without compromising their loyalty to Christ and His truth. It should be realized that social change must be the result of changed hearts. Therefore, the greatest contribution the Church can make to social betterment is to bring individual men to a heartchanging encounter with Jesus Christ.

XVI. Peace and War

It is the duty of Christians to seek peace with all men on principles of righteousness. In accordance with the spirit and teachings of Christ they should do all in their power to put an end to war.

The true remedy for the war spirit is the Gospel of our Lord. The supreme need of the world is the acceptance of His teachings in all the affairs of men and nations, and the practical application of His law of love.

XVII. Religious Liberty

God alone is Lord of the conscience, and He has left it free from the doctrines and commandments of men which are contrary to His Word or not contained in it. Church and state should be separate. The state owes to every church protection and full freedom in the pursuit of its spiritual ends. In providing for such freedom no ecclesiastical group or denomination should be favored by the state more than others. Civil government being ordained of God, it is the duty of Christians to render loyal obedience thereto in all things not contrary to the revealed will of God. The church should not resort to the civil power to carry on its work. The gospel of Christ contemplates spiritual means alone for the pursuit of its ends. The state has no right to impose penalties for religious opinions of any kind. The state has no right to impose taxes for the support of any form of religion. A free church in a free state is the Christian ideal, and this implies the right of free and unhindered access to God on the part of all men, and the right to form and propagate opinions in the sphere of religion without interference by the civil power.

Importance of the Confession of Faith

Jude admonished us that we "should earnestly contend for the faith once [for all] delivered to the saints" (v. 3). A strong doctrinal preacher will build a strong church. A weak doctrinal preacher will build a weak church. It is the truth of doctrine that forms the backbone, the spine, the skeleton of the congregation. Without it the church is spineless, soft, flabby, formless, amorphous, without marching, converting, driving power. I would suppose that the one dominant characteristic that makes a jellyfish a jellyfish is that it has no spine, no backbone, no bone structure. Too many preachers and too many churches are like that.

A woman came up to me recently and exclaimed: "Oh, we have formed the most wonderful church. It is perfect. It is delightful. My husband and I have just joined it and we are so happy in it. You do not have to believe anything to belong to our church. Anybody can join it." But I thought in my heart, *What a conglomerate of nothing!* Even a country club or a civic organization or a lodge or a PTA would demand a little something of its members. But the church that believes nothing and expects nothing, therefore does nothing in creating in its membership the mind and heart of Christ.

True doctrine is the truth of God. The truth of God is found fully and marvelously revealed on the pages of the Holy Scriptures. Preach it! Do so fearlessly, courageously, powerfully, zealously, with deep conviction. Paul said it like this:

All scripture is given by inspiration of God, and is profitable for doctrine, for reproof, for correction, for instruction in righteousness:

That the man of God may be perfect, thoroughly furnished unto all good works.

I charge thee therefore before God, and the Lord Jesus Christ, who shall judge the quick and the dead at his appearing and his kingdom;

Preach the word; be instant in season, out of season; reprove, rebuke, exhort with all longsuffering and doctrine.

For the time will come when they will not endure sound doctrine; but after their own lusts shall they heap to themselves teachers, having itching ears;

And they shall turn away their ears from the truth, and shall be turned unto fables.

But watch thou in all things, endure afflictions, do the work of an evangelist, make full proof of thy ministry" (2 Tim. 3:16 to 4:5).

Till I come, give attendance to reading, to exhortation, to doctrine.

Neglect not the gift that is in thee, which was given thee by prophecy, with the laying on of the hands of the presbytery.

Meditate upon these things; give thyself wholly to them; that thy profiting may appear to all.

Take heed unto thyself, and unto the doctrine; continue in them: for in doing this thou shalt both save thyself, and them that hear thee (1 Tim. 4:13-16).

7

The Pastor Structures
the Church

The Necessity for Organization

Often in the Scriptures the Christian life and witness are likened to a warfare. Paul wrote to Timothy, "This charge I commit unto thee, son Timothy, according to the prophecies which went before on thee, that thou by them mightest war a good warfare; Holding faith" (1 Tim. 1:18-19). The apostle in Ephesians 6:11-17 describes the panoply of the Christian soldier in minute detail. Evidently Paul was experientially aware of the onslaughts of the enemies of God. He himself had fought many a good fight for the Lord (2 Tim. 4:7). When Jesus met bitter opposition to his saving ministry, he called out, ordained, and organized a group that he called the twelve apostles to be taught the light and truth that are able to overcome the evil attacks of the devil. These twelve apostles with Spirit-called missionaries like Barnabas and Paul founded and organized churches all over the Roman Empire. Without those organized groups (churches) the faith would have drowned in a sea of secularism.

If the Christian life is likened in the Bible to a warfare, then the army of Christ's soldiers must be powerfully structured, from the leading bishop (pastor) down to the humblest servant in the platoons of faith. We all have a marching, patriotic part, loving and defending the kingdom of God, the commonwealth to which we belong (Eph. 2:12). Scripturally and well do the redeemed of our Lord sing the words written by Sabine Baring-Gould:

113

Onward, Christian soldiers,
   Marching as to war,
With the cross of Jesus
   Going on before!
Christ, the royal Master,
   Leads against the foe;
Forward into battle,
   See his banner go!

Like a mighty army
   Moves the church of God;
Brothers, we are treading
   Where the saints have trod;
We are not divided;
   All one body we,
One in hope and doctrine,
   One in charity.

The true church of commanding and victorious power is just like that, not divided but marching as one mighty host under the banner of the Lord.

But an army, if it is to be at all like an army, must be brilliantly and effectively organized. It is no army without organization. It is a conglomerate mass of uninducted, unrestrained humanity until it is structured along carefully thought-out and predetermined patterns. The church is no different. It, also, must be thoughtfully, prayerfully organized if we are to have any hope for victory.

The Basic Structure of a Church

In my own ministry I have organized the church in seven main areas of labor:

1. The pastoral office and ministry
2. The educational office and ministry
3. The music office and ministry
4. The mission-outreach office and ministry
5. The business office and ministry
6. The recreational office and ministry
7. The two schools in their offices and ministries

Each of these is presided over by the most capable leader I can find, and each has a staff under him according to the growth, need, and necessity of the assignment.

The few comments I make about these areas of work will be by no means exhaustive but rather a few observations that might help the pastor in his planning procedures.

1. Everything heads up in the pastoral office. Here lies the ultimate responsibility for all the church—everything about it. The care of all the people, the smooth running of all the interrelated parts, the services of public worship. In fact, everything that pertains to the church is in the charge and keeping of the pastor and his pastoral staff.

2. The educational office encompasses all the teaching ministries of the church, Sunday School, Church Training, Vacation Bible School, and a multitude of other like ministries. He is a wise pastor who will take time to work enthusiastically and unwearingly with the group. For example, I do not know of a tremendous church that does not have a tremendous Sunday School.

3. The music office enlists the talents of the whole congregation to praise the Lord in melody, in lyric, in special programs, and in beautiful presentations too numerous to mention.

4. The mission-outreach office is largely our ministry to our Jerusalem, the city of Dallas. It is discussed in chapter 10, "The Many Ministries of the Church."

5. The business office is responsible for the entire physical plant, the financial procedures, the reports to the deacons and the church concerning our church records, and all the other matters that pertain to the church as a terrestrial organization with its feet planted on the earth. The custodians, the dining facilities and food services, the monthly and annual reports of the work of the congregation, the payment of loans and mortgages, the personal records of the tithing and giving of our members are dependent upon that office. It must be run well, above reproach, industriously honest in the sight of God and of men.

6. The recreational office is also discussed in chapter 10, "The Many Ministries of the Church."

7. The seventh great area of church administration lies in our two schools, The First Baptist Church Academy, and the Center of Biblical Studies. Each of these is under the direction of twelve

trustees who are elected by the church. These trustees, in turn, elect all the leaders and teachers of the institutions and are responsible for all their financial affairs. They have a heavy assignment and must do exceedingly well for the schools to succeed in their work.

In many churches, and at one time in the church here in Dallas, whole services were taken up with business sessions. That may be acceptable, but visitors are usually bored by it. If a matter really needs to be discussed, there is no turn or inclination or doubtless intimate knowledge on the part of an average congregation of men, women, and children to enter into it. In my judgment it is far better to discuss the matters in the sessions of the fellowship of deacons who can appoint committees to inquire into every facet of the situation, report back, and recommendations be made thereafter to the church. Then at church, mimeograph the reports, adopt them (or refuse them), and get on with the praying and the preaching and the soul winning we ought always to be doing. The men in the fellowship of deacons and their friends will love taking care of all these things. Let them do it. It is their contribution to the extension of the kingdom of God.

The Church Constitution and Bylaws

Every church ought to have a constitution and bylaws. It is a part of a well-kept house and the best well-kept house ought to be the Lord's. Everything ought to be run beautifully and competently. This is the constitution and bylaws of our church here in Dallas. According to the wise choice of any congregation they can be changed and modified to please any local congregation. This is a suggested pattern to go by.

BY-LAWS
FIRST BAPTIST CHURCH
OF DALLAS, TEXAS

ARTICLE I
MEMBERSHIP

A. *THE MEMBERSHIP.* The membership of the First Baptist Church of Dallas, Texas referred to herein as the "Church," shall consist of all persons whose names appear on the Church Membership Roll.

All authority not herein vested in The Deacons or in any officer pursuant to these By-Laws is reserved in and to the Church and the Church reserves the right at any time to amend, supplement or revoke, in whole or in part, these By-Laws.

B. *ADMISSION TO MEMBERSHIP.* Applications for membership shall be voted on at any regular preaching service of the Church on any Sunday, any regular mid-week prayer service of the Church, or any publicly and previously announced preaching service of the Church or at any like meeting held by any Mission of the Church. Membership shall become effective:

1. After a public profession of faith in Christ as personal Saviour, and upon baptism by immersion in water as authorized by the Church; or
2. Upon receipt of a Church letter of dismissal and recommendation from some other Baptist Church of like faith and order; or
3. By statement, acceptable to the Church, of previous membership after baptism in a Baptist Church of like faith and order.

C. *TERMINATION OF MEMBERSHIP.* Membership may be terminated only in the following manner:

1. Upon the death of the member; or
2. Upon issuance of a Church letter of dismissal and recommendation for membership in some other Baptist Church; or
3. Upon a member's joining a Church of another faith; or
4. Upon withdrawal of fellowship by the Church from a member as provided by the Holy Scriptures and more particularly in Matthew 18:15-17 and in 1 Corinthians 5.

D. *VOTING OF MEMBERS.* On any matter coming before the Church for its determination, each member present shall be entitled to one vote which shall be exercised in person and not by proxy; and all such matters shall be determined at a regular or special conference meeting of the Church held in accordance with these Bylaws by the vote of a majority of the members present and voting.

E.   *MEETINGS OF MEMBERS.*

1. Worship Services. Public services for worship shall be held on Sunday morning, Sunday evening, and Wednesday evening of each week. Other public services for worship may be held at such other occasions as are deemed best for the advancement of the cause of Christ by direction of the Pastor or the Deacons or as determined by the action of a majority of the membership of the Church present and voting at any regular or special conference meeting of the Church.

2. Regular Conference Meetings. Regular Conference meetings of the members for the transaction of the business and affairs of the Church shall be held at the first Wednesday midweek prayer service in each month and notice thereof to members shall not be required.

3. Special Conference Meetings.

(a) The Church may be called into conference for the handling of its business and affairs by oral announcement and without prior notice at any regular scheduled Sunday service or mid-week prayer service by the Pastor, the President, the Deacons, the Chairman of the Deacons or a majority of the members present at any such meeting.

(b) Special conference meetings of the Church may be called at any time other than that hereinbefore provided by the Pastor, the President, the Deacons, the Chairman of the Deacons, or by members having not less than one-tenth of the votes entitled to be cast at such Special Conference Meeting. Any Special Conference Meeting called in accordance with this sub-paragraph (b) shall be held at any time after ten (10) days notice thereof has been mailed to each member at his address as shown on the records of the Church or the notice of the Special Conference Meeting has been published in the "First Baptist Reminder" or its successor publication and so mailed to members specifying the time and place at which such meeting is to be held and stating the nature of the business or other matters to be considered.

4. Place of Meetings and Rights of Members of a Mission. The Regular or Special Conference meetings of the Church or any other meeting of the Church at which the vote of the

Church is sought on any matter, shall be held at some location within the Church properties located on Ervay, Patterson, St. Paul, or San Jacinto Streets in Dallas, Texas, unless otherwise specified in connection with a Special Conference meeting called in accordance with sub-paragraph E3(b) of this Article I.

The meetings at which the Church may be called into conference pursuant to sub-paragraph E3(a) of this Article I shall be such a meeting regularly held by the Church at the aforementioned location. No meeting of the members of a Mission or Missions of the Church shall ever constitute either a Regular or Special Conference meeting of the Church for any purpose. No vote on any matter pertaining to any of the affairs of the Church shall ever be taken at any meeting of the members of a Mission or Missions of the Church other than their vote on the admission of a member to the Church as hereinbefore provided. A member of a Mission of the Church, being a member of the church, shall have the right to attend and vote at any Regular or Special conference held by the Church in accordance with these Bylaws.

5. Quorum of Members. The members present at any regularly scheduled worship service on Sunday or mid-week prayer and worship service on Wednesday of each week shall constitute a quorum. The members present at a Special Conference Meeting, after notice thereof shall have been given in accordance with sub-paragraph E3(b) of this Article I, shall constitute a quorum.

ARTICLE II
THE DEACONS

A. *THE DEACONS.* The business and secular affairs of the Church shall be administered by the Deacons (herein collectively referred to as "The Deacons") in accordance with these Bylaws. Although referred to herein as "The Deacons," The Deacons shall constitute the Board of Directors of the Church as required by Article 2.14 of the Texas Non-Profit Corporation Act (Chapter 162, Laws 1959 Regular Session, 56th,

Legislature of the State of Texas); and a Deacon shall be considered as a Director as required in such act.

B. *MEMBERSHIP OF THE DEACONS.* The deacons shall consist of the present Deacons as shown by the records of the Church and of such additional Deacons as the Church may hereafter elect as such. Each member, herein referred to as a "Deacon," shall serve until his term of office terminates as herein provided.

C. *QUALIFICATIONS OF A DEACON.* A Deacon shall be a man who is a member of the Church in good standing and who has the qualifications for a Deacon as set forth in Acts 6:3 and 1 Timothy 3:8-13 inc., and such other qualifications as the Church may from time to time prescribe.

D. *TERM OF OFFICE OF A DEACON.*

1. Term. The term of office of a Deacon shall terminate upon:

(a) his death,

(b) his resignation,

(c) termination of his membership in the Church,

(d) his removal from such office by the Church, or

(e) the action of The Deacons hereinafter provided for.

2. Resignations and unexcused absences. On behalf of the Church and without additional Church action, The Deacons may accept the resignation of any Deacon and may drop from its membership any Deacon who is absent during the previous calendar year for more than five regular meetings of The Deacons without excuses deemed valid by The Deacons after investigation by the hereinafter mentioned reviewing committee of The Deacons as hereinafter provided.

3. Reviewing Committee. The Chairman of The Deacons shall, in January of each year or as soon thereafter as practicable, appoint a reviewing committee from the membership of The Deacons to serve for one calendar year and whose duties shall be to investigate upon instruction of The Deacons:

(a) any request from any Deacon for voluntary withdrawal of membership from The Deacons

(b) improper conduct on the part of any Deacon

(c)   the failure on the part of any Deacon to observe any rules or regulations heretofore or hereafter adopted by The Deacons

(d)   the unexcused absence of any Deacon from regular meetings during the preceding calendar year when such unexcused absences exceed five in number in any such year.

The Committee's findings in each of the above instances will be reported to The Deacons. If the report to The Deacons concerns matters described in sub-paragraphs D3 (a) and D3 (d) of this Article II, The Deacons shall have the power to act pursuant to the provisions of paragraph D2 of this Article II; but, if such report concerns matters described in sub-paragraphs D3 (b) and D3 (c) of this Article II, The Deacons shall make such recommendations as they may deem proper to the Church.

E.   *NUMBER AND ELECTION OF DEACONS.*

1. Number. The number of Deacons shall never be less than three. Subject to that limitation, the number of Deacons as required by these Bylaws shall, at any specific time, be the number thereof who at that time are Deacons in accordance with these Bylaws as shown by the records of the Church. Such number may be increased or decreased at any time by the Church either by the election of additional Deacons or failing to fill vacancies occasioned by the termination of Deacons' terms of office as herein provided.

2. Elections. Deacons may be elected at any time and from time to time by the Church either to fill a vacancy within The Deacons or to increase the number of Deacons. Such Deacons shall be elected by the Church at either a Regular Conference Meeting of the Church or a Special Conference Meeting thereof held and conducted as provided in paragraph D of Article I and sub-paragraphs E2 or E3 or Article I.

F.   *MEETINGS AND QUORUM.* The Deacons shall meet regularly at such time and place as they may determine. Special meetings may be called by the Chairman of The Deacons, the Pastor, or a majority of The Deacons by giving notice thereof to each Deacon. A majority of The Deacons shall constitute a quorum and a majority vote of The Deacons present at any meeting held in accordance herewith (and at which a quorum is present) shall be sufficient to decide on any matter regularly before The Deacons for consideration.

G. *RESPONSIBILITIES OF THE DEACONS.* Except as hereinafter provided and subject to the provisions of paragraph A of Article III pertaining to the Pastor's power to hire employees, The Deacons shall (a) recommend to the Church in conference such policies, practices, and procedures as shall be voted by the Church in conference; and (c) as herein authorized by the Church, shall administer the business and secular affairs of the Church; and, to the extent provided for in these By-Laws and vested in them by the Church, The Deacons shall have full authority to do and perform all things reasonably necessary in connection therewith.

The annual budget for each calendar year shall be adopted by the Church. Prior to the end of each calendar year, The Deacons shall cause to be prepared and submitted to the Church for adoption by the Church a budget for the ensuing calendar year. The budget shall include estimates as to the anticipated liabilities, costs, and expenses of conducting the affairs of the Church during such year and an estimate of the total amount of the anticipated gifts of the Church during each year for denominational or other causes. Expenditures or commitments of any kind during any calendar year which are not included within the budget for that year shall require approval of The Deacons.

The Deacons shall not have the power to borrow money or to sell or encumber any real estate belonging to the Church unless such transaction is authorized by the Church in accordance with these By-Laws.

H. *COMPENSATIONS.* Deacons shall receive no salary or compensation for their services as Deacons.

I. *DEACONS' OFFICERS.* As provided in sub-paragraph B5 of Article III, The Deacons annually shall elect a Chairman of The Deacons, a Vice-Chairman of The Deacons, and a Secretary of The Deacons, and a Secretary of The Deacons, each of which shall be a Deacon, to serve for the term provided for in such sub-paragraph B5 of Article III. As Chairman of The Deacons, such Chairman shall preside at all meetings of The Deacons and shall perform such other duties as The Deacons may authorize consistent with these By-Laws. As Vice-Chairman of The Deacons, such Vice-Chairman shall perform the duties of the Chairman of The Deacons upon the death, absence, or resignation of the Chairman or upon his inability to perform the duties of his office.

ARTICLE III
THE CHURCH OFFICERS

A. *PASTOR.* The Pastor shall be the spiritual leader of the Church. The Church and The Deacons shall support the Pastor with their prayers and finances in such manner as to allow him the greatest time for evangelism and the preaching of the Gospel. It shall be the duty of the Pastor to preach to the Church, to administer or cause to be administered the ordinances of the Gospel, to act as moderator at the conferences when present, and to perform the various other duties incumbent on his office. The Pastor shall be elected by the Church and shall continue as Pastor until his service is terminated by his death, resignation, or by vote of the Church. Without limiting the general powers of The Deacons as herein provided, the Pastor, with the counsel and advice of The Deacons, shall have full power and authority to employ such employees as are necessary to carry on the work of the Church.

Any Associate Pastor or any Assistant Pastor shall, under the supervision of the Pastor, assist the Pastor and perform such other duties as the Pastor may assign to him.

DEACONS. The Deacons are the officers of the Church as provided in Article II of these By-Laws.

CLERK. The Clerk shall keep an accurate record of the proceedings of each business meeting of the Church and shall prepare the annual Church Letter to the Dallas Baptist Association, or any successor agency or other denominational agency with whom such letter should be filed, and shall keep and maintain the membership roll of the church with such other duties as the Church, the Pastor, or The Deacons may prescribe. The Clerk shall be elected by the Church which shall fix his term of office. If the term of office of the Clerk is not fixed at the time of his election or re-election, such term of office shall continue until extended, renewed, or terminated by vote of the Church.

THE CORPORATE OFFICERS

B. *THE CORPORATE OFFICERS.* In compliance with the Texas Non-Profit Corporation Act heretofore referred to, the Church shall have the following Corporate Officers:

1. President. The offices of President and Chairman of The Deacons shall be held by the same person. In addition to his duties as Chairman of The Deacons, the President's only other authority in the capacity of President shall be the power to execute in behalf of the Church instruments requiring execution by the Church when the execution thereof has been authorized as provided in these By-Laws.

2. Vice-President. The offices of Vice-President and Vice-Chairman of the Deacons, the Vice-President's only other authority in the capacity of Vice-President shall be the power to perform the duties of the President upon the death, absence, or resignation of the President or upon his inability to perform the duties of his office.

3. Secretary. The Secretary is authorized to perform the functions of a Secretary. He may or may not be a Deacon but must be a member of the Church.

4. Treasurer. The Treasurer is authorized to perform the functions of a Treasurer. He may or may not be a Deacon but must be a member of the Church.

5. Election of Officers. All officers provided for in this paragraph B of Article III, including the Chairman and the Vice-Chairman of The Deacons and a Secretary of The Deacons, shall be elected for a term of one year annually by The Deacons at its first meeting held in December of the preceding year. Unless an officer's term of office is terminated as provided in paragraph B7 of this Article III, each officer so elected shall continue in office until a successor shall have

been elected as herein provided and shall have assumed the responsibilities of the office. The offices of Secretary and Treasurer may be held by the same person who may be the Business Administrator or someone else, if so decided by The Deacons. A vacancy in any office may be filled by The Deacons at any regular or special meeting of The Deacons.

6. Other Duties and Officers. The Deacons at their discretion, may impose upon the officers referred to in sub-paragraphs 1, 2, 3, and 4 or paragraph B of Article III, such other duties as The Deacons may designate consistent with these By-Laws. The Deacons may also at their discretion elect such other officers and assistant officers as they may deem necessary. Any such additional officer or assistant officer may or may not be a Deacon but must be a member of the Church.

7. Removal of Officers. Any such officer so elected by The Deacons may be removed by The Deacons at any time whenever in their judgment the best interests of the Church will thereby be served. Any office shall become vacant when the holder thereof dies, resigns, or is no longer a member of the Church.

8. Compensation. Unless expressly authorized by the Deacons, the officers provided for in paragraph B of Article III, shall receive no salary or compensation for their services as officers.

ARTICLE IV
CONVEYANCES AND OTHER INSTRUMENTS

The Church may sell, convey, mortgage, encumber, or otherwise deal with or dispose of real or personal property owned by the Church and may evidence any such transaction by deed, bill of sale, mortgage, deed of trust, contract, or other appropriate instrument, with or without the seal of the Church, signed by the President or Vice-President or other officers of the Church when such transaction is authorized by appropriate resolutions of The Deacons adopted in accordance with these Bylaws; provided that any such transaction involving real property shall be authorized by the Church.

ARTICLE V
EFFECTIVE DATE

These By-Laws shall become effective as of the first day of the calendar month immediately following their adoption by the Church, and shall supersede and take effect in lieu of the Constitution and By-Laws in effect prior to that time.

ARTICLE VI
COMMITTEES OF THE CHURCH

The Church reserves the right at any time and in such manner as it may determine to appoint any committee, which shall be considered a Church Committee, which the Church may deem necessary or advisable. Each such committee shall be elected by the Church and shall have the duties and responsibilities imposed upon it by the Church. The membership of each such committee and the term of office of the committee members shall be determined by the Church.

ARTICLE VII
AMENDMENTS

These By-Laws may be amended, supplemented, or superseded at any time by action of the Church taken in the manner provided therefor in these By-Laws.

A Manual of Personnel Policies and Procedures

In order that every employee of the church may understand his relationship with the Church, we have a manual called "Personnel Policies and Procedures." Here it is to be looked upon as a suggested form or model.

PERSONNEL POLICIES AND PROCEDURES
FIRST BAPTIST CHURCH
DALLAS, TEXAS

The policies and procedures contained herein are intended as guidelines for equitable treatment of all employees (any person employed by the Church including ministerial staff employees except where otherwise specifically referred to herein) of the First Baptist Church of Dallas, Texas. These policies and procedures are not intended as minimal standards but it is expected that the policies and procedures will be applied to all employees in an equitable manner.

This manual was prepared by the Personnel Committee and approved by the Pastor, Associate Pastor, and Board of Deacons.

Each employee of the Church is expected to live in such a manner that his or her Christian conduct cannot be questioned. It is not intended that the merits of whether an employee of the Church should be expected to conduct himself differently than others even be discussed. It is a fact that the activities of the Church employees are subject to very critical and close scrutiny by the Church members and members of the public. Violations of basic rules of Christian conduct will not be tolerated and could result in severance of employment.

Any question regarding the interpretation of the policies and procedures contained in this manual should be referred to the Personnel Committee for clarification.

It is important that all new employees be fully informed immediately upon reporting to work regarding the policies contained herein. It shall be the responsibility of the immediate supervisor to carry out this assignment in each case.

1. EMPLOYMENT

A. *Procedure*—As vacancies occur on the staff, the Department Head will counsel with the Personnel Committee with respect to filling such vacancies. The "action" responsibility is assigned to the Department Head concerned.

B. *Conditions*—Conditions of employment should be agreed upon by the new employee and the responsible Department Head.

C. *Completion*—Employment and personnel actions are not completed until notification of all concerned is carried out.

2. EMPLOYEE ABSENCES

Absences from the normal work schedule will be governed by the following, and each absence must be cleared in advance with the supervisor concerned. An appropriate record of all absences will be maintained by the supervisor and forwarded to the business office at the close of each calendar quarter.

A. *Absence due to death in immediate family or household*—In case of death of a member of the immediate family or household, the employee may be paid for the absence from scheduled work for a period not to exceed one week.

B. *Absence due to death of relative other than the immediate family*—in case of death of relative other than the immediate family, the employee may be paid for up to three days with the approval of the immediate supervisor.

C. *Jury and Witness Duty*—an employee is paid for the time absent on such duty and is entitled to retain all compensation received therefrom. If an employee's service as a juror or witness is not required for the entire day, he is expected to report to the Church for the remainder of the day.

D. *Personal Business*—such absences must be approved by the Department Head concerned.

E. *Personal Illness*—illness requiring absence from regular assigned duties should be reported and recorded by 8:30 AM on the first day of illness and each succeeding day thereafter. In reporting, please give best possible information concerning date of expected return. After the third day of absence, a doctor's statement may be required. Under certain conditions as determined by the immediate supervisor, serious illness in the immediate family may be classified as a personal illness.

F. *Leaves of Absence*—such absences should be recommended by the Department Head concerned to the Personnel Committee and approval must be secured from the Pastor.

3. GROUP INSURANCE

The Church provides a free group hospitalization and life insurance program for eligible employees. The employee may elect to include certain eligible dependents. A booklet describing this insurance is available from the business office.

4. HOLIDAYS

All employees of the Church except part-time and temporary employees are eligible to receive pay for the following holidays.

New Year's Day
Memorial Day
Independence Day
Labor Day

Thanksgiving Day
Friday after Thanksgiving Day
Christmas Eve Day
Christmas Day

If a holiday falls on a Saturday, the holiday will be observed on the last working day before the holiday. If a holiday falls on a Sunday, the holiday will be observed on the first working day after the holiday.

5. NIGHT USE OF BUILDING

It is not considered a good practice for.an employee to work alone in a church building at night. If this cannot be avoided, great care should be taken to lock all entrances upon entering and leaving the building.

6. OFFICE AND WORKING HOURS

The offices of the Church are open Monday through Friday from 8:15 AM to 5:00 PM and on Sunday from 9:00 to 10:45 AM and 5:30 to 7:30 PM. Employees will normally be scheduled to work forty hours each week. Office employees will normally be scheduled Monday through Friday 8:15 AM to 5:00 PM with a 45 minute lunch period. However, certain employees will be scheduled differently to provide coverage for the Sunday hours. Employees in other church functions such as kitchen, dining rooms, building maintenance, and schools will be scheduled as necessary. However, under no circumstance will a classified (eligible for overtime) employee be scheduled for more than 40 hours of work at straight time pay in any 168 consecutive hour period.

7. OVERTIME PAY

Overtime pay is defined as one and one-half times the base rate of pay and will be paid to eligible employees for all time worked in excess of 40 hours in any specific work week.

8. PARKING

Employees' automobiles may be parked free of charge in or on Church parking facilities as authorized by the Minister of Business Administration.

9. PART-TIME AND TEMPORARY EMPLOYEES

Part-time (those who work less than 40 hours a week) or

temporary employees are not eligible for vacation pay, holiday pay, hospital or life insurance, or other benefits afforded regular full-time employees.

10. PUBLICITY

No employee will originate or release news which is concerned with the policies, doctrines, procedures, convictions, or activities of the Church for use in newspapers, radio, or television. All such inquiries must be referred to the Minister of Public Media.

11. RETIREMENT PROGRAM

The Church provides and contributes to an excellent Retirement Program through the Annuity Board Plan for all full-time employees. Literature describing this program can be obtained at the business office.

Normal retirement shall be age 65 as provided in the Southern Baptist Protection Plan. Deferred retirement allowed by the Church enables an employee to remain on active service on a year-to-year basis after reaching age 65 upon approval by the Personnel Committee. Compulsory retirement shall be age 70.

Except as otherwise provided herein, no employee shall be entitled to either withdraw or borrow, pledge, or otherwise encumber contributions to the retirement program made by the Church until such employee qualifies for such retirement benefits pursuant to the Southern Baptist Protection Plan in which such employee has participated through the Church. The restrictions and limitations set forth herein shall be applicable to employees participating in Southern Baptist Protective Program Age Security Series C-003 only to the extent of contributions made by the Church to the retirement program after the effective date of this manual.

Vesting under the Retirement Plan shall be as follows:

1. Employees participating in Plan A of the Southern Baptist Protective Program shall be vested immediately.

2. Participation in all other plans of the Southern Baptist Protective Program shall commence at the beginning of the second year of employment and vesting shall commence at the beginning of the third year of participation in such program at the rate of 12.5% per year.

Investment under the Retirement Plan shall be as follows:

Contributions made by the Church shall be invested in Plan A or Plan B, as applicable, with investment in Plan C limited to 25% of the Church contributions, if the employee selects to participate in Plan C.

12. SALARY ADJUSTMENTS

At least once each year the progress and compensation of each employee is carefully reviewed and discussed by the Personnel Committee, Budget Control Committee, and the responsible Department Head.

13. SERVICE ALLOWANCE ELIGIBILITY

A regular employee released from payroll for reasons other than proven dishonesty or immorality or conduct prejudicial to the best interests of the Church may be eligible to receive a service allowance based upon his length of continued service. This will be the responsibility of the Department Head subject to the review of the Personnel Committee. In no event shall this allowance exceed one month's pay.   ·

Employees who resign are not ordinarily paid a service allowance. They receive pay up through the last day worked and for any vacation earned.

14. SICK LEAVE

Employees of the Church who are ill receive illness benefits within any twelve month period as follows:

A. Employees with less than three months of continuous service will not receive illness benefits.

B. At the discretion of the responsible Department Head, employees with between three months and two years of continuous service may receive full pay for each day of absence due to illness up to a maximum of three weeks.

C. At the discretion of the supervisor, employees with two to five years of continuous service may receive full pay for each day of absence due to illness up to a maximum of six weeks.

D. At the discretion of the responsible Department Head, employees with up to five or more years of continuous service may receive full pay for each day of absence due to illness up to a maximum of twelve weeks and an additional ten weeks at one-half pay so long as illness continues.

After maximum illness benefits have been paid, any vacation earned may be applied to cover additional illnesses. However, after the maximum illness benefits have been paid, payments on any earned vacation allowance will be made only at the employee's request.

15. MINISTERIAL STAFF MEMBERS ABSENT ON CHURCH BUSINESS

The staff members are permitted up to two weeks absence each year in relation to church business at the discretion of the responsible Department Head.

16. VACATION POLICIES

In the first twelve months of service, regular full-time employees will be eligible for vacation according to the following schedule: (wherever mention is made of vacation days the interpretation to be made is working days exclusive of Saturday or Sunday).

Length of Continuous Service	Vacation
One month	0
Two months	0
Three months	1 day
Four months	2 days
Five months	3 days
Six months	4 days
Seven months	5 days
Eight months	6 days
Nine months	7 days
Ten months	8 days
Eleven months	9 days
Twelve months	10 days

To receive vacation credit for a particular month, an employee must report for work on or before the 15th of the month.

However, no vacation can be taken until the employee has completed six months of continuous service. In each succeeding calendar year thereafter, through nine years of service, employees will be eligible to receive ten days vacation. Employees will be eligible for 15 days vacation annually in the tenth year of service through the 19th year of service and for 20 days vacation annually in the 20th year of service and each full year of service thereafter.

Vacation schedules should be arranged as early as possible each year with the responsible supervisor or Department Head. Every effort should be made to allow longer service employees first choice of vacation time and vacations should be scheduled to adequately staff the offices and other functions during periods of vacation. Employees cannot carry over vacation from one year to the next.

Under no circumstance will employees be allowed vacation in excess of that shown. An employee cannot remain on the job and receive vacation pay.

17. The effective date of this manual shall be January 1, 1974.

Use of Committees

If the organizational work of the church is to be done clearly, intelligently, and carefully, it must be done through committees. In an open meeting of the church, there is not time or opportunity to probe and to search out all the facts and facets of a problem. Sometimes it takes weeks, months, and in some instances years, to ascertain what ought to be done. This can be the assignment of gifted and dedicated men. Again, the whole church cannot look after a task of preparation, say, for the Lord's Supper. Committees do that excellently. It is not too broad a statement to say that our entire church is run by the Pastor, Staff, and the Committees who work with them.

The main working, responsible groups in the church in its business office is the Fellowship of Deacons. They work through and with the following committees: Auditing, Budget, Christian Life, Recreation, Church By-Laws, Church Manual, Committee on Committees (the deacon nominating committee), Concern (prayer and visitation for the fellow-deacons and their families), Bible College Trustee, Nominating, Dining Room, Evangelism (leading the deacons in soul-winning efforts), Executive (made up of former Chairmen of the Fellowship of Deacons), Academy Trustee Nominating, Investment Advisory (concerned mostly with the investment and use of money and properties especially given to the church), Greeting and Ushering, Insurance, Jewish Fellowship, Yokefellows Nominating (a group of younger men who help us in so many of the ways we seek to make our people glad they came to our church), Library-Audio-Visual, Long-Range Planning, Lord's Supper and Collection (the men who serve the Lord's Supper and take up the offering at the worship services), Music, Outreach-Mission, Parking, Personnel, Preparation-Lord's Supper, Property Maintenance, Property Management (taking care of properties willed or given to us), Public Relations, Religious Education (nominating the officers and teachers of the Sunday School, Training Union, etc.), River Ministry (our mission work in the Rio Grande Valley), Social, Stewardship, Systems (the care of all the computer—filing—reporting work in the church), Technical Services (the electronic equipment in radio, television, public address systems), Transportation (caring for the many vehicles the church owns and otherwise uses), Vocational Guidance (seeking to find employment for worthy members), Wills and Trusts. The work of all these committees is carefully spelled out in a booklet called "Church and Deacon Committees Manual."

Besides these above-named Deacon committees, the fellowship also has Licensing Committees for each education age group in the Sunday School and Educational Program. These Licensing Committees are appointed to help the staff members and leadership in those separate age groups to build up their work and witness for the Lord. There is a Day Nursery Liaison Committee, one appointed for the Cradle Roll, Nursery, Beginner, Primary, Junior, Teen, Youth, College and Career, Single Adults, Young Married, Young Adult, Median Adult, Meridian Adult, Adult, Extension, WMU, and Special Education. [Terms for various age groups will vary.]

In addition to the Deacon's Committees there are also church committees recommended for election to the church by a church appointed committee on committees. These are: Assistant Church Clerks (they help the new members who come forward at the worship services to fill out their decision cards), Baptismal Robing (helping the candidates at their baptismal service), British Intern (taking care of the preacher who comes to us each year from Spurgeon's College in London), Flower (receiving requests from those who place flowers in the sanctuary in honor of and in memory of loved ones), Historical (caring for all the historical memorabilia of the church), Hospitality (taking care of our guests), Yokefellow Selection (nominating members of the group for election by the church), License, Ordination (any God-called preacher to be licensed or ordained is exercised by these committees and thus recommended to the church, New Deacons (this all-important committee nominates men to be added to the Fellowship of Deacons), and finally, Wedding Arrangement.

If all these committees functioned vigorously, the church would be unbelievably alive and vibrant. Our problem is not having a place for everybody to serve. Our problem lies in the lethargy and indifference of the membership. That is why the preacher needs to preach and the deacon needs to "deak," to stir up God's people to shine for the Lord.

Use of Deacon Leadership

He is a wise and Spirit-led pastor who seeks out deacon leadership for the church that will bless the families of the flock and be actively engaged in visitation—soul-winning. In order for the pastor to see the possibilities of leading deacons into a vigorous visitation effort, there is herewith presented "Operation Obedience—Deacon's Visitation Program," a work that we prayerfully seek to further in our church. Here it is:

I. *Purpose*
The purpose of the deacon visitation will be fourfold:

1. To act in obedience to the Lord's command to "go into the world and make disciples of all the nations . . ." (Matthew 28:19).
2. To follow in support of our shepherd's desire to see the Gospel of Christ taken to everyone in our city.
3. To visit all prospects identified by the church staff as being in need of encouragement to join the church and/or Sunday School.
4. To provide all *church visitors* with an opportunity to personally meet with an official representative of the deacon body and to be ministered to by them.

Our deacons are to be ministers of reconciliation and equipped to minister to the spiritual needs of people with whom they come in contact. A church visitor has been led by the Lord to visit the church through some means, either curiosity, brought by a friend, dropped in, or searching for the Lord. A deacon should be equipped on this call to go over a salvation message, assurance of salvation, or an understanding of how to walk in the power of the Holy Spirit with the person.

This visitation will consist of all church and Sunday School visitors, including those who do not express an interest in joining either the Sunday School or church. In other words, many people do not indicate an interest in joining the church due to shyness or fear of confrontation. These are probably the most likely candidates for a salvation presentation.

The purpose of the special assignment calls will be to handle any problem calls that have been given to them by the staff or the Sunday School departments. These calls would be made on members of the church who have specific problems about which they need to talk to a ministering deacon. These could also be evangelistic appointment calls that have been arranged in advance by the concerned parties.

5. To provide all new members with the opportunity of being visited by a deacon.

This is the discipleship end of the deacon's visitation. These new members many times have not been counseled at the altar and are still struggling with assurance of salvation, the ministry of the Holy Spirit, the deity of Christ, marital problems, child-rearing problems, and other areas that are keeping them defeated in their Christian walk. These calls by the deacons should be for the purpose of welcoming them into the church, identifying any spiritual needs, and attempting to meet them out of the Scriptures.

II. *Visitation Program*

A. *Sunday visitation:* Sunday visitation will consist of calling on all *church and Sunday School visitors* who have attended the worship service that Sunday. Distribution of leads will be handled in the following way:

1. All leads will be picked up from the deacon visitation secretary in the business office following the second service on Sunday

morning. All of these leads will be in regional boxes and will be picked up by the regional minister or his assistant.

2. These cards will be taken to the regional minister's home where he will call the appropriate deacons who have committed themselves to visitation on that Sunday afternoon (one designated Sunday per month). This keeps the visitation on a regional basis and enables the deacons to spend less time driving back and forth to the church.

3. Following the calls in the afternoon, the cards will be returned to the regional minister who will then turn them over to the visitation secretary on Sunday evening prior to the service.

4. The visitation secretary will then match these leads up with her control copy and turn them in to the church office where it will be noted that a deacon visitation has been made.

5. For people not at home, the deacon will have one week to make the call and must return the card the next Sunday evening.

6. Sunday night leads will be mailed to the regional ministers to be disbursed to their equipped deacons for follow-up calls.

B. *Saturday visitation:* Saturday visitation will be mainly for calling on *new members* who have joined the church and/or Sunday School the previous Sunday and for the visiting of any prospects who have been identified by the church staff as being in need of more encouragement to join the church and/or Sunday School.

*NOTE: Deacons are encouraged to accompany prospects or to meet them at church: to walk the aisle with them or to meet them at the altar; to pray with them and to introduce them.

These calls will be made by the equipped deacons who commit themselves to Saturday visitation. This visitation will not be done on a regional basis but will initiate from the church.

The purpose of the new member calls will be threefold:

1. To officially greet those who have joined the church and warmly welcome them to the fellowship of the First Baptist Church.

2. To identify through conversation any spiritual needs that can be determined and to meet these needs on this call (i.e., marriage difficulties, child difficulties, assurance of salvation, walking in the Spirit, baptism, etc.).

3. To encourage those who have not as yet been baptized to do

so and to encourage them to join the Bible study ministry of our Sunday School departments if they have not already done so.

III. Leadership Development

If we are going to be obedient to the command of our Lord Jesus to be ministers of reconciliation and to be actively engaged in the fulfillment of his Great Commission, it is imperative that the entire deacon body ultimately be involved in visitation and evangelistic activities. It is the scriptural role of the deacon to be a helper to the pastor and move with all vigor to accomplish what God has told him to accomplish. This will never occur, however, apart from personal discipleship among the ministering deacons. Wherever there is a nucleus of trained and equipped deacons, they can, if they catch the vision for discipleship, ultimately lead the entire deacon board into functioning as the spiritual body that is in accordance with God's plan.

A church is to meet the spiritual needs of its people and to develop men and women who are capable in leading others in discipleship. As Robert E. Coleman said in his great book *Master Plan of Evangelism,* "Christ did not come to develop programs to reach the masses, He came to develop men whom the masses would follow."

Every regional minister will have at his disposal those deacons who have signed up for visitation in addition to a list of all the remaining deacons who live in his regional area. It will be the responsibility of the regional minister and those deacons committed to visitation to involve the other deacons who live in their area in the visitation activity of the church. Once these deacons begin to catch the vision for discipleship from their on-the-job experience, it will further motivate them to become equipped for their work of ministry to which they have been called by God.

The results of this equipping will be that "we all reach unity in the faith and in the knowledge of the Son of God and become mature, attaining the full measure of perfection found in Christ. Then we will no longer be infants, tossed back and forth by the waves, and blown here and there by every wind of teaching and by the cunning and craftiness of men in their deceitful scheming. Instead, speaking the truth in love, we will in all things grow up into

Him who is the Head, that is, Christ. From Him the whole body, joined and held together by every supporting ligament grows and builds itself up in love, as each part does its work." (Ephesians 4:13-16, NIV)

The flow of the work takes this form:

1. Visitation secretary prepares NCR cards for regional pick-up.

a. The deacon visitation secretary will be in the church office during the second worship service. This will enable her to begin to transfer the visitation cards from the first service onto NCR cards. By the time she is finished with the morning service cards, she should have Sunday School classification slips and the second service cards which will enable her to finish them up prior to the close of the service.

b. She will then disburse these leads into their appropriate regional boxes where the regional ministers would then pick them up following the second service.

2. Regional minister picks up cards and calls appropriate deacon visitor.

a. These NCR cards which will be taken in triplicate should be signed by the regional minister. He then takes the top two copies and leaves the pink copy with the deacon visitation secretary.

b. The regional minister will take the top two copies to his home and when it is picked up by one of the deacon workers both copies are signed by the worker so that the regional minister knows who has the assignment and can follow up accordingly.

3. Deacons make visit and return cards to Regional Minister. When these calls are completed the original copy will be returned to the Regional Minister.

4. Regional minister collects cards and information and returns them to visitation secretary.

The regional minister will attach them to his control copies and turn them back into the visitation secretary who will attach the two copies to her pink control copy and the transaction will have been completed.

5. Visitation secretary completes NCR forms and returns to church office for posting.

She will then turn all three copies over to the church office where they will be able to disburse those copies to the Sunday

School department and staff as well as keep a copy for the control board in the church office.

The card which the deacons fill out saying they will help goes like this:

DEACON VISITATION PROGRAM
COMMITMENT CARD

NAME_____ADDRESS_____
PHONE_____(HOME) CITY_____ZIP CODE_____
_____(OFFICE) MAPSCO NO._____

As a deacon, I commit myself to becoming:
( ) A regional minister
( ) An assistant regional minister
( ) A visitation deacon
( ) I also commit myself to ongoing training that will further equip me to minister to the spiritual needs of our people.
. . . .

My preference for visitation is: Sunday afternoon_____
                                     Saturday morning_____

(Signed)_____

MAY GOD BLESS YOU FOR YOUR COMMITMENT TO HIM.

The Pastor and the News Media

Would you like to fill up your church to overflowing so that you cannot find room for another person? Have a great throng to which to preach the gospel? Publicity will do it. It will never fail to do it. The problem is we do not have pastors and media directors who know how to go about accomplishing it. Here are some suggestions that may help.

1. Make the area of communications a part of the structure of the church. Along with the work of deacons and educational direction and business administration have a media office and pro-

gram. Let this group seek to place the services of the church on television, radio, public announcements, billboards, circulars, streamers, bumper stickers, spot television and radio announcements, newspaper stories, anything, and everything to get the church and what it is doing before the people. Cultivate the friendship of those who run the newspapers and radio and television stations and see what they will do to help you and open doors for you. Especially is this true in making a friend out of the editor of the newspaper. Buying ads in the paper will help along the way.

2. Newspaper publicity that can get on the sports page, the front news page, the feature section, and on any prime feature location is worth a lot to the church. How do you go about making these acceptable stories? Do something newsworthy, then write a good story about it. Something unusual, interesting, different. Many things can be turned into a good story. Seek them out and write about them. Every pastor has someone in his congregation who will love the opportunity to do such a work for our Lord.

Just remember these things:

(1) Write for the general public, something that will interest the general readers, not only the deacons.

(2) Identify the article with the name of the church, phone number, and anything else by which the editor can get in touch with you.

(3) Give it a heading.

(4) Type the story double-spaced.

(5) Clip a good black-and-white photograph to it. Correctly identify the people in the photo from left to right.

(6) Make it newsworthy. Newspapers thrive on facts. Cram your article full of them. Names, addresses, dates, numbers, locations, times, are all needed. Be specific, avoid generalities and long, involved sentences with repetitious words and phrases. Give details about people. See that the first line says something potent and pertinent. Keep the facts moving to the last period.

(7) Keep it neat.

(8) Thank the editor for being kind and helpful to you. If you do not succeed with the first story, keep on writing. Do not hide your witness under a bushel. Write about your church for the

news and if you do not give up, it will get there with a flourish.

3. The public media office and staff of the church can assume the responsibility of securing good literature for every member and for every family. This would include good religious magazines, especially the denominational periodicals. This office ought frequently to call attention to what is going on in the library. This office ought to see that tracts are placed in racks around the church where people can easily pick them up. These little winged angels are most valuable auxiliaries to the pastor's work of witnessing.

4. Most any church with a mimeograph machine can produce materials that will greatly enhance the services of public worship and further the activities of the organizations of the congregation. If the church is large enough, a weekly paper can be published with a column written by the pastor. Such a paper is of enormous value to the people. It keeps the whole church aware of every program. This is worthwhile if it did nothing other than to ask the praying people to remember the efforts in their intercession.

5. In our church we have a media-communication manual of twenty-one pages. We have a large print shop that is busy about twenty-four hours of the day. We have a cassette ministry that is manned by several staff members sending the messages about Christ to the ends of the earth.

We are in the business of proclamation, of spreading abroad the good news of salvation.

8
Financing the Church

Need to Provide the Financial Requirements of the Church

Any institution that has its feet on the earth has a financial problem that must be solved, a financial necessity that must be met. If a bank does not solve its financial problem, it will go bankrupt. If a store does not solve its financial problem, it will "go to the wall." If a married couple do not solve their financial problem, they face disaster, no matter how much they say they love each other. Many marital counselors say that money is the number one cause of divorce. Even a government (and that includes the richest nation in the world, the United States) that does not solve its financial problems faces ultimate economic chaos. If the institution is mundane, terrestrial down here in this earth, it has a financial problem. That includes the church. Some day we shall be the church triumphant, we shall be in heaven where the very streets we walk on are paved with pure gold. But down here we are the church militant with our feet on the sod and, like everybody else, we have a financial problem.

How do we solve it? How do we finance the needs of the church?

Every approach conceivable and imaginable has been made to solve the problem of church financing. One time I preached a sermon on the ways churches had employed through the centuries to meet their monetary requirements, including turning the church into a bingo gambling house. The message, broadcast over television, made the station manager furious. I answered his scorching letter with the observation that it is hard to know what to do with truth, and changed television stations.

Surely, surely God has some way to take care of his church. It is not spiritually reasonable that he would leave it with a vast, mighty, worldwide evangelizing, discipling, teaching commission and forget to outline a plan for us to implement it. Does God, therefore, say anything about money and finance and paying debts and paying expenses and taking care of the house of the Lord?

He does! He speaks again and again. The Almighty speaks emphatically, positively, clearly, and with a directive addressed to every member of his church family. God has a way to provide for all the needs of his people. If we follow the way, we have the infinite blessing of God individually and collectively. If we turn aside from the way, we inevitably fall into discord, disunion, and anemic weakness.

We can never improve upon the wisdom of God. We can think and cogitate and ruminate and ponder and devise and contrive until the sky falls down, but we will never improve upon the plan of God. Committees can meet forever, church councils can discuss every conceivable possibility, the pastor can read all the books ever written suggesting how to get blood out of a turnip, but none of them will come forward with a method that supersedes the plain, workable wisdom of God in financing his work in the earth.

God's Financial Plan—Tithes and Offerings

We can teach our people to tithe and to give God an offering of love over and above and thus be blessed and successful in our work, or we can turn aside to our own human devices and fail both in our spiritual blessings and in our church finances. It is that simple; it is that plain; it is that certain. We can plan to succeed with God or we can plan to fail with the means of men. Why not go with God? He never fails. We do but *he* does not. God's ways always work.

The pastor—preacher should follow a program of unapologetic exposition of the biblical basis for tithing—stewardship. Timidity here is like weakness in any other department of Christian life: it leads to compromise and eventual failure. If God says it, we believe it and that settles it. One pastor said: "In my early ministry I made the mistake of emphasizing tithing—stewardship only at budget time. Now I see that the development of church members as Christian stewards is a year-round task, not just a seasonal emphasis tied to budget time." Stewardship—tithing comes from preaching the Bible. The Holy Spirit drives the message home to the heart when the Word of God is faithfully delivered.

What God Says About the Tithe

The tithe is the Lord's. It belongs to him. God says so in many places.

And all the tithe of the land, whether of the seed of the land, or of the fruit of the tree, is the Lord's: it is holy unto the Lord.

And if a man will at all redeem aught of his tithes, he shall add thereto the fifth part thereof.

And concerning the tithe of the herd, or of the flock, even of whatsoever passeth under the rod, the tenth shall be holy unto the Lord (Lev. 27:30-32).

Bring ye all the tithes into the storehouse, that there may be meat in mine house, and prove me now herewith, saith the Lord of hosts, if I will not open you the windows of heaven, and pour you out a blessing, that there shall not be room enough to receive it (Mal. 3:10).

And here men that die receive tithes; but there he receiveth them, of whom it is witnessed that he liveth (Heb. 7:8).

I can either give it to him in a deeply spiritual act of worship, or he can collect it. In either case, God gets his own. A pastor was asked, "How many church members do you have?" He answered, "One hundred fifty." The pastor was further asked, "How many of them are tithers?" The pastor replied, "One hundred fifty." In astonishment the inquirer exclaimed, "What? All one hundred fifty, the entire church, are tithers?" "Yes, indeed," said the pastor. "About fifty of them bring the tithe to the storehouse, and God collects it from the rest." We do not cheat God.

When God gits His
And I gits mine
Then everything
Will be just fine.

But if I gits mine
And keep God's, too,
What do you reckon
God will do?

I believe He will collect,
Don't you?

The unlettered hillbilly who said that was speaking God's truth.

The New Testament Plan of Church Finance

The mighty principles of Christian faith, practice, and doctrine are found in the Holy Scriptures and particularly in the New Testament. For example, the great principle of Christian living is found in a passage such as 1 Corinthians 8:13: "Wherefore, if meat make my brother to offend, I will eat no flesh while the world standeth, lest I make my brother to offend." A true Christian ought not to drink, because some (many, actually one out of nine) are led into disaster through the use of liquor. Our example ought to lead to life not death. It is thus with the principle of giving. The plain directive is set forth in 1 Corinthians 16:1-2:

Now concerning the collection for the saints, as I have given order to the churches of Galatia, even so do ye.

Upon the first day of the week let every one of you lay by him in store, as God hath prospered him, that there be no gatherings when I come.

We are to bring our monetary gift to the church on Sunday, the first day of the week. We are to come before the Lord with an offering in our hands. "Give unto the Lord the glory due unto his name: bring an offering and come into his courts" (Ps. 96:8), our spiritual worship expressed in tangible and loving praise.

Everyone of us is to appear before the Lord in the congregation of the redeemed with an offering in his hands. Does the Scripture really mean that? "Every one?" Does the Scripture say what it means? "Every one?" Then that includes us all, every member of the family. Is the little boy a member of the family? Is he "one"? Is the little girl a member of the family? Is she "one"? Is the baby a member of the family? Is the little child "one"? Did Paul mean "everyone"? He did, and he wrote by divine inspiration and wisdom.

The State Fair of Texas is in Dallas. In the fall is the annual state fair. In the fair is an extensive midway. On a Saturday evening a father takes his little boy and girl to the fair and to the midway. The merry-go-round ride is fifty cents. The roller coaster is seventy-five cents. Popcorn is fifty cents. Peanuts are a quarter. When the evening of fun is over the little boy has spent ten dollars and the little girl a like amount.

Next morning is Sunday and time to go to Sunday School and church. The father reaches down in his pocket and says to the boy, "Here Son, is a dime for Sunday School." He does the same for the little girl. "Here, Honey, is a dime for church." The father does not need to say anything more. The children have learned the lesson early and well. Popcorn is big business. That is fifty cents. Peanuts are a big business. They're a quarter. The midway is a big business. That is ten dollars. But God's business is little business. That is ten cents. The children have learned it well.

Why not do as God says, "Let *every one* of you"? But someone observes: "Only the father's name is on the paycheck. He alone has an income." It all depends upon how you look upon the family. Is not the wife a part? Does she not work at housekeeping, sewing, cooking, cleaning, and a thousand other things? Are not the children a part of the family? Do they not contribute? The family is one, and all are a part, no matter whose name is on the pay-check. If we do according to God's Word, this is what is done: "Son, this is your part," and the father places in the hands of the boy a worthy offering for God. "Sweet daughter, this is your part," and the parents place a worthy offering in the hands of the daughter. "And little baby, *you* are a part of the family. Our home would be empty without you." And the father pins a worthy gift for God on the baby to be brought to the house of the Lord! Then the father and the mother divide up the difference, each bringing to God a worthy part of the weekly increase. God's way works!

But what is this proportion that Paul mentions in 1 Corinthians 16:2, "As God hath prospered him?" What proportion? I know of only one in the Bible; namely, a tithe that belongs to the Lord (Heb. 7:8) and an offering of love above and beyond. If a man preaches the Bible, that is what he will preach.

Teaching the Tithe

1. World without end I hear that we are under grace, not under law. Then follows the inevitable deduction, tithing is law, not grace, therefore we are under no necessity or compulsion to tithe. (Forgetting that Abraham and Jacob tithed under grace hundreds of years before there was any Mosaic law.) These antinomians are unforgivably and grossly inconsistent. Paul wrote in Galatians 5:13, "For, brethren, ye have been called unto liberty; only use not liberty for an occasion to the flesh, but by love serve one another," a passage that referred to old-time antinomians.

Paul was plagued in his day by would-be philosophers and teachers who took his doctrine of liberty and carried it to scandalous extremes. The apostle to the Gentiles avowed that the true Christian was not under law but rather was liberated from the bondage of Sinai and called into the marvelous freedom of Christ. "Well and good," said these old-time antinomians, "we have done with law, we shall live in liberty to the indulgence of every lust we possess." They created havoc with their morals but they had this one virtue—they were consistent. They threw away law as an outworn garment and readily gave themselves to license.

The true gospel preacher is confronted today by a new-time antinomian. He is plagued by would-be interpreters of the Bible who set forth their antinomianism in a diluted form. They read the Old Testament and find therein a great deal about the sabbath, so as Christians they readily agree we should have one day of seven especially dedicated for worship. "Splendid! Let us observe the Lord's Day and keep it holy." They read Genesis and find in it much about marriage and eagerly proclaim monogamy as from the beginning. "Wonderful! Let us live by the ethic of the first moral law." Then they read the Old Covenant and, though finding much about the tithe, the terrible cry is raised, "Let us not return to the law. To tithe is to go back to Sinai, to bondage, to salvation by works." Where stewardship of money is concerned they are antinomians; elsewhere they are satisfied to preach the moral code of Jehovah. "Consistency, thou art a jewel! "

What about the grace of the Lord Jesus and the doctrine of the antinomians (abrogation of law)?

Antinomianism has no place in any code of conduct and least of all in the teachings of Jesus. Did Jesus ever take a piece of Old Testament legislation and lower the plane upon which its morality was to operate? "Think not that I am come to destroy the law, or the prophets: I am not come to destroy, but to fulfil" (Matt. 5:17). Jesus went beyond and above anything the law ever demanded. If the tithe is to be an exception to this and is to be lessened, then it is the first and only instance wherein Jesus fell below the Old Testament standard.

Jesus did not abrogate what God already had done. Jesus came to raise our moral living from obedience to an impersonal commandment to the infinite height of love for a personal Savior. Jesus showed us that if prayer can be taken from pretense, if the sabbath can be taken from sacrilege, if the tithe can be taken from tedium, if all three can be born again into the spiritual and the heavenly, then they can bless us all to the end of time. If Jesus has not done this for his people, he has signally failed.

When Paul asked the people to give "as God hath prospered him," what proportion did they know? None other than the proportion taught in the Old Testament, the only Bible they possessed; the proportion commanded by Jesus and accepted by every soul who knew the ways of God. Only an inconsistent antinomian will fail to do likewise.

2. Whether under the grace of God known to the first patriarchs (like Abraham, Isaac, and Jacob) or under the law of Moses, or under the blessing of the gospel of Christ, tithing has never changed through the ages.

Tithing is as old as the race. As far as we have any records, there is evidence that man was instructed in giving unto God, as an offering, at least a tithe of his income.

Abraham, while living under grace, not under law, gave to Christ (as Melchisedec, who was possibly a preincarnation appearance of Christ) the tenth of all, as is abundantly shown in

Hebrews 7: 1-17. Here is the account of the father of the faithful of all nations, living directly under grace, never under law at any time, giving unto the Lord Jesus, either in type or person, the tenth of all.

Jacob made his first response to God, so far as the records show, by promising him a tithe of all that he might acquire in his journey to Mesopotamia. Note Genesis 28:22, "And this stone, which I have set for a pillar, shall be God's house: and of all that thou shalt give me I will surely give the tenth unto thee."

Moses was God's chosen instrument for revealing the plan which God had for Israel, and when the law was being written for man to use as a guide in all matters of service and worship under the Levitical covenant, the tithe was incorporated in the law, although it had long been a basis for man's expression of stewardship, well-understood long before the children of Israel even went into Egypt. In the law it is recorded, because it was as fundamental as the matters included in the law concerning morals.

The last of the Old Testament prophets, as they are arranged in the canon of the Scriptures, Malachi, after speaking of the coming of the Lord Jesus Christ as "the messenger of the covenant" (3:1), places an emphasis upon the tithes and offerings which is beyond doubt or question, saying, "Bring ye all the tithes [plural] into the storehouse [and that is the New Testament church], that there may be meat in mine house, and prove me now herewith, saith the Lord of hosts, if I will not open you the windows of heaven, and pour you out a blessing, that there shall not be room enough to receive it" (Mal. 3:10). Then if you will read on through the twelfth verse, you will find many other strong and blessed promises connected with faithful stewardship in the tithes and offerings.

And yet there are some dear Christians who are hiding behind the fact that the law included the tithe, and they therefore cannot do it, lest they should be legalists. At the same time, they are strong on not allowing the right hand to know what the left hand is doing, and it may be that they do not let one hand know what the other is bringing into the house of the Lord because they are so utterly ashamed of the proportion. If we as Christians living under grace, not under law, do not do better than the Jews did under law, it is forever a shame to our understanding of Calvary.

Did the tithe originate with the law?

Certainly not. Neither did it end when the ceremonial law was fulfilled. Murder, adultery, swearing, etc., were included in the law, because these things are out of harmony with God's moral character and are eternally wrong, hence they are still wrong, and to commit them is a sin under grace. The tithe was right before the law, during the law, and long after the law as God's manner of dealing with mankind in covenant relationship, surviving throughout the age of grace as a means of helping mankind to know what is the basis of true stewardship.

Does the New Testament have anything to say about the tithe?

Jesus commended the Jews for their careful tithing (Matt. 23:23).

Paul commanded the Corinthians to "lay by him in store, as God had prospered" them, and that means in proportion as they had prospered (1 Cor. 16:2). Abraham and Melchisedec are introduced into the New Covenant relationship, as is shown in Hebrews 7, and there is no escape from the fact that tithing was essentially a part of the revelation here. And since Melchisedec was either a preincarnation appearance of Jesus Christ, or a special revelation showing Christ in type, it is most certain that Abraham had some understanding of who he was, and with that understanding he gave to Jesus Christ a tithe of all. Now remember that Abraham lived under grace, never under the law. He was a Christian, for in Galatians 3, we read, "And the scripture, foreseeing that God would justify the heathen [nations] through faith, preached before the gospel unto Abraham" (v. 8). "Abraham believed God, and it was accounted unto him for righteousness" (v. 6). Then what was it that he believed? There can be no evasion of the fact that Abraham believed the gospel message. That is what makes Christians now, as well as then. Abraham, acting as a Christian, not as a legalist, gave a tithe.

Another aspect of the Abraham and Melchisedec story is the fact that Abraham was able by giving a tithe to Melchisedec to bind his seed to a tithing program, "And as I may so say, Levi also, who receiveth tithes, payed tithes in Abraham" (Heb. 7:9). Now if it is true that Levi and all of his tribe were involved in the tithing program when Abraham tithed, thus making tithing an essential part of the obligations of Abraham's descendants, how about the spiritual descendants of Abraham? Are they less obligated? Note what the Word says about us in connection with our descent from Abraham, "Even as Abraham believed God, and it was accounted to him for righteousness. Know ye therefore that they which are of faith, the same are the children of Abraham" (Gal. 3:6-7).

Our Lord Jesus Christ said, "Render therefore unto Caesar the things which are Caesar's; and [render] unto God the things that are God's" (Matt. 22:21). We often use the first part of this statement to show that a Christian owes an obligation to the state, and no one objects; also to show that Jesus made a clear distinction between the church and the state. But it is not always made as clear that the Christian owes an obligation to God as well as unto Caesar. The tithe is holy unto the Lord. It never is ours, either first or last. We cannot give the tithe. It already belongs to God, and the only thing we can do with it is to bring it into his storehouse for the uses which he has ordained.

But if our giving never goes beyond a cold, legalistic, materialistic submission to the law, the whole meaning of blessed stewardship under God is totally missed, likewise the blessings associated herewith are never experienced. On the other hand, if we live as unto God doing all things as unto him, rejoicing in the glorious privilege of participation with him in his plan of worldwide ministry of the Word, then we are partners with all that divine grace has revealed. Could love withhold anything? Could the children of grace forbear to share in the blessed work of the gospel? Certainly not, unless they are unyielded to his will. All who go on beyond the tithe as a matter of obligation and make offerings of love unto our Lord and Savior who hath redeemed us, will be happy and useful in all relationships.

We have often overlooked another side of this important business with the Lord. Malachi tells the people of his day, "Ye are cursed with a curse: for ye have robbed me, even this whole nation." Thus we are reminded that God not only blesses them who would honor him with their firstfruits, but that he has the very opposite thing for them who will not honor him with their substance—"cursed with a curse." These are awful words, but who among us has not witnessed someone who seemingly had plenty of things, yet his things never brought anything but bitterness of life and defeat of soul. There is a sure curse in the wrong handling of money by Christians. If we rob God, our blessings turn into a curse. Our material prosperity blights us. Our gold and silver become cankered. Our light turns to darkness, especially in spiritual matters. When God is truly honored in our material possessions, honored in our hearts with sincere devotion of the whole life and honored with an unsullied testimony, all the outcome of that life will be a blessing. We are not saying that all the experiences of that kind of life will be without testings, sorrows, and sufferings, for that would not be correct; but we are saying that the outcome will be blessed, both here and hereafter. But let us always keep in mind that the very same God who brings blessings when our hearts are right can also bring a curse when our hearts are wrong, and that applies in material things, too. Let us resolve before God to honor him with our substance, and with the firstfruits of all our increase.

3. The spiritual rewards of tithing to the individual soul and to the church are immense. God has a heavenly purpose in it all.

Tithing is not a money-raising scheme. It is a soul-growing, character-developing program. The purpose of tithing is to secure not the tithe but the tither, not the possessions but the possessor, not your money, but *you,* for God. When a preacher fails to develop his church in giving, he is grievously sinning against his people. When I visit a pastor on his field and watch him approach the money question apologetically and fearfully, I know he has never conceived the bigger and greater program of God's plan.

If tithing is only a scheme to get money, why not get a real money-raising scheme? Let people gamble or draw numbers, and you will raise big money for a while. Tithing is not a scheme of preachers, prophets, or seers, but a plan and program of God to enrich character, develop souls, and enlarge vision. There is nothing normally or spiritually elevating in buying a bowl of oyster soup with a lone oyster for a dollar in order to help a church. But to bring one's tithe into the storehouse and place it on God's altar, thus honoring God with your substance, is worship—a concrete expression of your love to God. It is opening up the depths of your compassion and keeping the stream of benevolence flowing from your heart. This is the means, and the end is a greater soul, a richer character, and abundant blessings of God. God wants us to be like himself—great givers. This is his purpose supreme.

J. L. Kraft, head of the Kraft Cheese Corporation, who had given approximately 25 percent of his enormous income to Christian causes for many years, said, "The only investments I ever made which have paid constantly increasing dividends, is the money I have given to the Lord. Pastors will do their greatest service in leading their men to understand the truth of God concerning the stewardship of time and money."

John D. Rockefeller explained a great principle when he said: "I never would have been able to tithe the first million dollars I ever made if I had not tithed my first salary, which was $1.50 a week."

Money is a good servant but a poor master. The lure for gold is stronger than the human will, and with many a man it stands between his soul and his God. Someday it will be discovered that the bars that shut many out of the kingdom of heaven are forged of silver and gold.

There are notable exceptions. Says Fritz Kreisler, the world's distinguised violinist: "I never look upon the money I earn as my own. It is public money. It is only a fund entrusted to my care for proper disbursement. I am constantly endeavoring to reduce my needs to the minimum . . . . In all these years of my so-called success in music, we have not built a home for ourselves. Between it and us stand all the homeless in the world."

From the beginning of his business career, John Wanamaker, merchant prince of Philadelphia, is said to have dedicated one tenth of his increase to the Lord. Likewise, William Colgate, the great soap and perfume manufacturer, rose to fame and wealth while consistantly paying a tithe of his earnings into the gospel treasury. This he recognized as the minimum requirement designated by divine wisdom; and year by year as God prospered his efforts and multiplied his wealth, Mr. Colgate gladly gave far more than a tenth. Today a great Christian university stands as a monument to his fidelity and generosity.

Throughout his life Robert Hamilton, multimillionaire lumber-man, loyally rendered a tithe to his Maker; and in his last will and testament he counseled all his heirs to dedicate at least one tenth of their total income each year to the Lord.

Thousands of others who conscientiously dedicate a tithe of their income to God find rich rewards in both temporal and spiritual prosperity. Yet none should misunderstand. If a man pays the tithe because he hopes it will increase his income, if he does it to receive the praise of men, if he does it grudgingly for fear of God's displeasure, or if he does it from any other ulterior motive, he cannot expect much spiritual blessing or uplift.

Tithe-paying is not a substitute for heart service, neither is it a gift to our Maker. It is a debt. It is not a tribute exacted by the Deity from those who travel the Christian highway, nor is it the entrance fee to the city of God, for reserved seats in the kingdom are not on sale for cash. All the benefits and privileges from our Father above are absolutely free gifts of his infinite love.

The possession of goods or wealth is not a sin; it is "the love of money" which "is the root of all evil." With the fully surrendered life, money is no longer king. Said Christ: "Ye cannot serve God and mammon"; yet the Christian may serve God with mammon.

It is well to remember that in the Gospels of Matthew, Mark, and Luke, one verse in every six deals with the money question; while of the twenty-nine parables narrated by Christ, sixteen speak of the Christian and his money. The Master does not ask, "How much money do you have?" but "What are you doing with it?" He came to lift us out of our own sordid selfishness and to guide our steps along the path of faith to the mount of blessing.

"I seek not yours but you," rings the heavenly appeal. If you have been remiss in your duty, pay up the arrears; for, in the language of another: "The more you give, the more you will have, and the day will come when all you have will be just what you have given."

There's No Pocket in a Shroud

Use your money while you're living,
Do not hoard it to be proud:

> You can never take it with you,
> There's no pocket in a shroud.
>
> Gold can help you on no farther
> Than the graveyard where you lie,
> And tho' you are rich while living
> You're a pauper when you die.
>
> Use it then some lives to brighten
> As through life they weary plod;
> Place your bank account in heaven,
> And grow rich towards your God.
>
> —AUTHOR UNKNOWN

4. Do not tithe unless you want to be blessed. Tithing carries with it a remembrance from heaven. The spirit that makes a tithe is the spirit that builds for a beautiful life and for a superlative workman. Just according to the measure of the blessings you seek, so give to the kingdom causes of our Lord.

An ambitious young man called on his pastor and promised to tithe, and so together they knelt in prayer to make the promise and to ask God's blessings on the young fellow's career. He was only making forty dollars a week at the time, and therefore tithed four dollars. But before many years his income leaped into higher brackets and he was tithing as much as $500 a week! He decided he had better call on the minister and see if he could not somehow be released from his tithing promise—it was getting much too costly. He told the pastor, "It was no problem when I was only tithing four dollars a week— but now it is up to five hundred dollars—and I simply cannot afford that." The old pastor said: "I do not see how you can be released from your promise. But I tell you what we can do. We can kneel down now and ask God to cut your income back to about forty dollars, then it will make it easy for you to tithe four dollars."

An Annual Stewardship Revival in the Church

Fall in our church is revival time because it is stewardship time. We pour the energies of our congregation into that financial appeal and God blesses with a tremendous victory year after year.

We have never failed to oversubscribe our budget. The giving program of the church has grown from one hundred thousand dollars a year to eight million dollars a year, and it is still growing. God blesses a people who pray and try and work and give.

The program of stewardship follows an order like this.

1. The deacons work on the budget for the coming year from the first of June to the last of August. They carefully consider and screen all the causes of Christ represented by the different organizations of the church.

2. In September the budget is presented to the church for adoption.

3. On successive Sundays the church at the worship services elects a stewardship leader nominated by the deacons, selects a theme, picks out a victory date (many times the Sunday before Thanksgiving), and prepare the people for a tremendous stewardship triumph.

4. Some of the stewardship themes we have used during the years are:

> Tithing—Life's Surest Investment
> Tithing Measures Your Love
> My Church—The Heart of My Giving
> Tithing Is Love in Action
> Tithing Is Giving Thanks to God
> Tithing Is God's Blueprint for Giving
> Tithing Shares Freedom in Christ
> Everybody Tithe
> Everybody Tithe—And More
> Everybody Tithe—And Then Some

5. The Sunday School is the organization we use to get everybody to respond to the stewardship appeal. I think the Sunday School is a gift from God to help the church confront this fast-moving world with the claims of Christ. It is the best organization known to the believing congregation. No group of men or women, no committee in session, no pastor in his study, can think up an organization comparable to the Sunday School. Use it. The Sunday School can reach everybody.

6. The Sunday School drives for a goal of 100 percent pledging, with everybody turning in a pledge card. The monetary goal will take care of itself if all the people pledge.

7. The pledge card ought to be a tithing card. If some do not tithe, they can fill in a monetary amount by the week, month, or year. But the card ought to be true to the Scriptures—a tithe by the week (1 Cor. 16:2). "Upon the first day of the week."

Sometimes a commitment card can read like this:

My church needs my help. I will help.
The Bible shows a way. I will follow it.
"The tithe . . . is holy unto the Lord" (Lev. 27:30). I will give.
I estimate my tithe to be $_____ each week.

Sometimes a commitment card can read like this:

I now covenant with God to start tithing _____.
I am already a tither and will contribute _____.
I will give regularly and systematically _____.
I estimate my weekly contribution to be $_____.

In my humble opinion the pastor and the deacons ought to make up a distinctive card that fits and pleases them. The card can be changed a little in format each year, even the color and type.

What About Pledging?

At stewardship time many church members offer the lame excuse that they do not believe in pledging, in signing a commitment card. Yet all of life is put together by the willingness of people to pledge, to commit themselves.

"I pledge allegiance to the flag . . . ," "On my honor I . . . ," "I do." "To tell the truth, the whole truth and . . . . " Each of these phrases suggests a commitment, a dedication, a pledge to a worthy cause.

The man who refuses to pledge is a man without God, country, wife, home, charge accounts, utilities, job, voting rights, driver's license. Yet some men and women find it within their hearts to refuse to give positive support to their church and its ministries around the world. Definite support is withdrawn through the use of this simple statement, "I don't believe in pledging." To refuse to pledge is to refuse the promises of the Lord as recorded in Psalms and Proverbs.

To refuse to pledge is to go without a telephone (you must promise to pay the telephone company so much a month for the phone), to go without water and electricity (you must promise to pay the water company and the electric company what you use each month), and in many instances to forego the buying of a house and a car because these are many times secured through monthly payments. The bold, blunt, naked truth is this: the man who says he does not believe in pledging is being dishonest.

One time I saw a cartoon that was drawn in a series of four frames. The first frame went like this: A man selling a car says: "You're getting a real buy here. Nothing down, thirty-six months to pay, and almost no interest—just 12 percent." The man buying responds in these words, "Where do I sign? Where are the keys?"

The second frame: A man selling a refrigerator says, "We'll even give you five years to pay for it, what could be more fair?" The same man buying responds, "Nothing! Where do I sign?"

The third frame: A man selling a house says: "Isn't it beautiful? And just think, no down payment—thirty years to pay! We'll even put the closing costs and the insurance in your payments!" The same man responds, "All we ask is, where do we sign? ! "

The last frame: A pastor says to the same man, "Now about our expanded church program. It will require the support of every one of us. How about $_____ per week for 52 weeks from you? " The man in horror replies, "What? Tie myself down for 52 weeks from you? " No, Sir, not me! I never pledge! No, sir! That's suicide! The future's too insecure! No, Sir, not me! "

What do you think of that? Maybe he needs converting, to be regenerated, to be saved. His heart is not right with God.

The Books of the Church

If the church wishes to keep confidential what each one gives, that is right and just. But the bookkeeping of the church must always be above reproach. Honesty ought to be observed to a fault. Accurate and faithful accounting procedures are basic if the congregation is to have any confidence in the financial program of the church. Every penny is accounted for. Every designation is sent to its intended destination. The church treasurer makes detailed reports to the deacons and they to the church at stated conferences. All the monetary involvement of the church is to be open and aboveboard. Let honesty begin at the house of the Lord.

Estate Planning and Stewardship

The blessing of estate planning is forever.

Out of a century of experience as under shepherd of our First Baptist Church in Dallas, I could write a veritable volume on the multitudinous blessings that accrue to a congregation that has in it dedicated Christians who will remember the Lord in their wills, in their insurance policies, and in other ways by which they can carry on a work for Jesus here in this earth after they themselves have been translated to heaven.

When you come to our church to visit, you will see a tremendous building that was made possible by a bequest on the part of one of our dear members. As you look into the program of our church you will find a whole area of ministry which continues because of the loving remembrance of a precious member of our assembly.

All over the church and throughout its many organizations you will find facilities and endowments that bless and help in a work that is too large for us to carry on by ourselves but which work is furthered and blessed by the infinite goodness of those who made possible a glorious support through their remembrances of us in gifts of property and money.

We face a tremendous enlargement of our church facilities. The cost of these expanded programs and enlarged buildings will come to millions of dollars. Will our local budget provide the necessary funds for such an operation? No. The budget cannot carry an answer to that capital needs program.

Our only hope, ultimately and finally, of achieving this expanded ministry lies in the estate planning of our members. It is our prayer that our people by the thousands will remember our church in their wills, in their insurance policies, and in other ways whereby they can make possible a gift to help us in this great assignment.

What we expect from our people in our First Baptist Church in Dallas can be duplicated by any congregation anywhere in the earth. All of us have an open door to support the work of the Lord while we are alive and to continue that support even when we are translated to heaven. This can be done through our estate stewardship.

The pastor ought to encourage everyone to make a will. No matter how little or how much we possess, every member of the church ought to have a will.

The American Institute of Public Opinion reports that seven out of every ten people over fifty years of age leave no will.

A large university recently sent out more than 60,000 questionnaires to their alumni. The replies showed that approximately 50 percent had not made a will.

What is a will?

A will is a legal document to take effect after your death in which you tell how you want your property to be distributed. A will is one of the most important documents which you will ever write and is less trouble to fill out than a tax form.

Why make a will?

1. A will ensures that your estate will be distributed exactly as you desire. Otherwise, your estate will be distributed according to state laws.

2. A will prevents possible misunderstanding among heirs.

3. A will permits you to say who will have charge of the handling of your estate.

4. A will often reduces the expenses of probating the estate and usually reduces the state tax.

Two important steps

1. Make an inventory of your possessions
2. See your lawyer

Whatever the provisions of your will, it must be precisely drawn and executed in order to be valid, and only a lawyer is qualified to do this work for you. Avoid the temptation to copy legal phrases out of books. Your lawyer's fee will be the most economical bill you ever paid.

God bless you as you help to carry forward the work of our Lord through his church until Jesus comes again, whether we rise to meet him in the air or come back to earth with him from heaven.

rials are available to support the programs of church training, music, missions, administration, recreation, pastoral ministries, stewardship, evangelism, Vacation Bible School, summer camps, and many other emphases.

Careful attention is given to the acquisition of materials which will meet special needs, such as the Bible in Braille and talking books for the blind, large print for those with limited vision, easy-to-read books, and recordings for language groups and aids for the deaf.

Attempts are made to reach those people who need extension services. Cassette tape recordings are very helpful in this effort. At times the recorder or playback is provided in order to meet a special need.

The church library provides such services for the church, not only by supplying materials, but by promoting them and by consultation in their use. For instance, instructions must be given in the handling of special equipment, such as projectors, tape recorders, and so forth.

7. Some special services provided by the library staff.

The library staff prepares mediagraphies, book talks, and special displays; provides orientation for new members; teaches the use of reference materials; instructs in the use of audiovisuals; assists with some reading problems; plans reading clubs; gives telephone service; maintains extension libraries on the children's floors; sells books written by the pastor and by the professors; keeps the library open through the day in order to serve lunch-hour patrons and adds hours during the school year; cooperates with other libraries; participates in the local Associational Church Library Organization and the State Church Library Convention and attends other library workshops; preserves historical materials; and cooperates with faculty and students of both the First Baptist Church Academy and the Criswell Center for Biblical Studies.

Praise God for our library and its capable staff.

Our First Baptist Academy, Our Christian Day School

Years ago many denominational leaders were dead set against the Christian day school. I used to hear them speak against it again and again. I listened as they tried to convince me against building one. Through all the years I have felt and believed they were wrong in their attitude. Thank God, in these recent years the attitude of many leaders is changing. We are now seeing our own Sunday School Board staff promote the schools. Wise people they are, indeed.

From the beginning of my ministry here in Dallas I have wanted and worked for an academy, teaching the Christian value system from the nursery day school through the kindergarten to the twelfth graduating grade in high school. It took me a full thirty years to achieve the goal, but blessed be the name of the Lord, we have one, an excellent one, a growing one.

I am not alone in this earnest desire to have a Christian day school. While public school enrollment has been dropping since 1970, the number of Christian schools and their enrolled students have risen dramatically.

The Association of Christian Schools International (ACSI) estimates that about 800,000 students now attend approximately 4,500 Christian schools in the United States. Two new schools sprout up every day, according to ACSI administrators. Why?

Disturbing to many Christian parents is the rising tide of anti-Christian philosophies taught in public classrooms. Evolution, for instance, is often taught as truth rather than theory. And secular humanism undermines Christian values based on God's Word.

Any school system which intentionally leaves God out can only move in the direction of humanism. Christian parents are seeing that the philosophical differences are growing greater and greater.

The influence of humanistic thought is readily evident in many school textbooks which subtly or blatantly attack Christian values. Controversy continues to rage over textbooks which espouse an agnostic, atheistic, humanistic, non-Christian position concerning life and reality. Many Christian parents and Christian leaders are deeply concerned over certain public-school textbooks containing non-Christian views.

The heart of Christian education is the centrality of Jesus Christ in every area of life. Every class is to be taught from that perspective. When you study history, for instance, you are going to study God's dealings with man through history. You are going to emphasize a great deal more the Christian beginnings of our nation, the reliance of our country's forefathers on biblical principles.

The Christian school is going to view everything through God's Word. The Bible becomes the standard for truth. You are not going to accept anything as truth unless it is consistent with God's Word.

This is the glory and the necessity of the Christian school.

Our First Baptist Academy summarizes its goals in its logo— "Education with a perspective beyond time," education of the total student—mind, soul, body. This is a vital task and our goal projects us to the cutting edge of life.

Christ-centered education is not an option; it is a divine imperative at First Baptist Academy. "In the beginning God" is the theme that dominates every subject whether it is math, English, art, or geology. Facts are bathed in divine truth. Each student is guided to think, to grow, and to achieve through biblical principle and command. Since its beginning in 1972, hundreds of students who have attended First Baptist Academy have developed strong and deep spiritual insights. Every effort is made by teachers to:

1. Bring each student into a right relationship with God through Jesus Christ.

2. Teach a sense of purpose in life.

3. Encourage high goals and standards for living.

4. Develop respect for others.

5. Emphasize responsibility to God, home, and country.

6. Prepare the student for advanced studies.

At the academy God is supreme; Christ is king; and the Holy Spirit is free. This is the power which is ingrained into every student from little children in kindergarten to young people graduating from high school.

The First Baptist Academy of Dallas holds to the historic Christian view of life as presented in the Bible. We consider the school as an extension of the home and a partner with the parents in the education of the child. As part of a family, we help guide a child's growth with God's Word and our own God-given talents by providing a well-rounded education which develops the whole person spiritually, socially, intellectually, and physically.

Our First Baptist Academy is a fully accredited school encompassing kindergarten through twelfth grade. It is staffed by excellent, experienced, certified, and dedicated teachers. Its board of trustees is a prayerful, wise, and progressive body of support for the administration and faculty.

Our students are as well or better equipped in basic college preparation as most students in the Dallas area. There are, admittedly, enrichment and exotic programs available elsewhere which we cannot offer at this time, but we will eventually.

Our athletic program has excelled above all other private schools in the area. Witness the football and baseball championships these past seasons and the championship playoffs so narrowly missed by our basketball team. These championships include our girls' volleyball, basketball, and baseball programs. It is our goal to provide stadium facilities for our athletic program in the future.

If students are not reached for Christ in the elementary and secondary level, it is highly unlikely that higher education will reach them. If we can accomplish this program in First Baptist Academy, we can be used of God to produce more Christian leaders for this generation than we have seen in the last one hundred years of secular indoctrination. We are a part of the greatest school system in the world, God's school system.

The Church in the Summertime

Is the summertime God's quitting time in the vineyard of the Lord? Never, never. A thousand times no. Summertime is one of the best of all seasons in the year to do God's work. Outdoor revivals are possible and are everywhere. Retreats and church camps are the order of the day. Choir tours enhance the magic of church music for hundreds who can share in it. Vacation Bible School brings together hundreds of youngsters, each of whom is a challenge to win to the Lord. In our part of the world many of our professional people go down to the Rio Grande Valley to minister to the thousands who live on the border.

Summertime is closing time? It is the grandest, greatest opening time for the message of God in all the year. Pastor, take advantage of it!

11

Administering the Ordinances

General Observations About the Church Ordinances

The Meaning of the Word *Ordinance*

The word *ordinance,* as we use the term in the church, refers to a religious rite ordained by the Lord Jesus Christ. Upon his authority and institution, and following the practice of the apostles, we receive the ordinances of the church from his and their gracious hands. The word *ordinance* in the Old Testament represents something prescribed, enacted, and usually refers to a matter of ritual. For example, according to Exodus 12:14, the Passover was "an ordinance forever"; that is, a permanent institution. The word *ordinance* in the New Testament is a translation of four different Greek words. Although not technically referring to just the two ordinances of baptism and the Lord's Supper, I like the translation of the Greek word *paradosis* in 1 Corinthians 11:2. "Now I praise you, brethren, that ye remember me in all things, and keep the ordinances, as I delivered them to you." That is what we are to do, faithfully and scripturally and perpetually.

The Number of New Testament Ordinances

By the institution of Christ Jesus and by the example and practice of the apostles, the number of the ordinances in the New Testament are only two. The marks of an ordinance are, (1) it must be an outward symbol divinely appointed to represent a great fact and truth of the gospel and the personal relationship of the believer to the fact and truth, and (2) there must be a divine mandate

199

making the observance of the ritual obligatory, universal, and perpetual. These two criteria are plainly and evidently present in baptism and the Lord's Supper, the only two ordinances accepted and practiced in the New Testament church.

The Authority to Administer the Two Ordinances

The ordinances are to be administered by the authority of the church. They do not belong to the legislature or to the courts or to the Congress or to the judiciary or to the city council. They belong to the church and are to be kept and administered only by the church. The validity of the ordinance, therefore, does not depend upon the personal character of the administrator (although we would pray that he would always be a holy and godly minister of the gospel). The ordinance does not belong to a man. That is why, if a man is baptized by a preacher who turns out to be an apostate, his baptism is not invalidated. Baptism does not belong to any preacher, nor is its authoritative administration lodged in him. That is also why the church must receive the candidate for baptism, not a man, even though he be the preacher. Even Simon Peter did not arrogate to himself that authority; namely, to personally receive candidates for baptism. In Acts 10:46-47 the great apostle first asked, "Can any man forbid water, that these should not be baptized, who have received the Holy [Spirit] as well as we?"

Only under the direct leadership of the Holy Spirit and as an ordained deacon-evangelist-emissary of the mother church in Jerusalem, did Philip baptize the Ethiopian treasurer in Acts chapter 8. The ordinance is a church ordinance, administered by those sent out by the Holy Spirit from the church to the ends of the earth.

Symbolic, Not Sacramental Channels of Grace

Because of the pagan, idolatrous world in which the gospel was initially preached, the two ordinances early came to be regarded with superstitious veneration in the first Christian centuries. They then became instruments of a perverted doctrine that ensued in a sacramental grace. This sacramentalism became a powerful weapon in the hands of the clergy to hold over the people the constant threat of excommunication and damnation, all of which characterized the church at its worst. Sacramentalism is ever a curse to the preaching as the believing of the true gospel.

The ordinances are not sacraments; they are not the means and the channels of saving grace. The ordinances are symbols and visible representatives of the vital, central truth of the gospel. The ordinance of baptism sets forth our death to sin and our resurrection to a new life in Christ. Baptism is burial and resurrection (Rom. 6:3-5). Christ died for our sins according to the Scripture. He was buried, and the third day he was raised according to the Scriptures (1 Cor. 15:1-4). Paul said that is the gospel. We have died with Christ, we are dead to the world. We have been buried with Christ. No longer do the blandishments of the world reach us. We are raised with Christ to a new, triumphant, resurrected life. All this is symbolical in our baptism. There is no sacramental efficacy in the rite at all. It is entirely symbolic, representative, a "setting forth."

The Lord's Supper represents the atonement of Christ as the only means of our justification (God's receiving us as righteous) and the only support for the new life we have in Christ. There is no magic in it. The Supper is memorial in nature (1 Cor. 11:23-26). It "shows forth," it depicts, it dramatizes, it pictures the suffering death of our Lord on the cross.

The superstition of the magical powers of a priest to turn common bread and common juice of pressed grapes into the actual body and blood of Jesus is an overwhelming development. When little children wave their hands over something that is miraculously to be changed to something else, they say, "hocus-pocus." Where did they get such a phrase? They got it from the priests in the church whom they heard saying in Latin, *Hoc est corpus meus,* as they moved their magic hands over the tray of bread and the chalice of wine. What amazing magical power! No wonder the children picked up its astonishment!

Just exactly, then, what did Christ mean when he said, "This is my body" and "This is my blood"? Certainly not his actual body and blood, for he was standing there before them in the flesh when he uttered the words. Plainly and most evidently we know what he meant. He meant, "This bread, so broken and crushed, represents my body,'' and ''This fruit of the vine, red from the crushed grapes, represents my blood.'' It is exactly like this:

A wealthy member of our dear church invited me into his palatial home. As we stood in the beautifully walnut paneled library, I saw an oval picture of an old-fashioned girl on the wall. He pointed to it and said, ''That is my mother.'' Then with tears he continued: ''I never saw her. She died in childbirth when I was born. Some day, when I get to heaven, after seeing my Savior, I want first of all to see the face of my angel mother. Heaven will be heaven because she is there.'' Then he spoke with many tears as he pointed to the old-fashioned girl in the picture.

I could have exclaimed, ''*That* is your *mother*? That is nothing but a piece of paper and cardboard covered with ink! Yet you ridiculously cry out, '*That* is my mother!' '' I did nothing of the kind. I knew what he meant. ''That picture represents my angel mother. I never saw her, but some day in heaven I shall see her face to face and love her aboundingly for giving her life for me.'' It is exactly so with our own Lord Jesus. This is his body, and this is his blood, and it pictures our lovely Lord until that preciously beautiful day in heaven when we see him face-to-face and thank him for giving his life for us.

There is no sacramental magic in the ordinances. When we observe them, we make a personal profession of faith in the spiritual truths they symbolize. When a man is baptized, it means that he has given himself to the Lord in faith for the forgiveness of his sins and the regeneration of his soul. When a man shares in the Lord's Supper, it means that he believes that Christ has made an all-sufficient atonement for his sins. The ordinances, therefore, are not magical forms, they are not secret, mysterious instruments and channels of grace for those who receive them. Rather, they are vivid representations of the vital, dynamic, central facts and truths of Christianity, and when the believer receives them, he is making a personal profession of faith in the great doctrines the ordinances depict. They are outward symbols of tremendously meaningful spiritual, inward experiences with Christ our Savior.

Administering the Ordinance of Baptism

Baptism the Pledge of Our Allegiance to Christ

Baptism is commanded in the Great Commission (Matt. 28:19-20). It is the first public act of a believer in his confession of faith in Christ. It is ordinarily the door into the visible, local church. It is the initial ordinance (Acts 2:41; Acts 8:12; 1 Cor. 12:12-14; 1 Pet. 3:21).

The act of baptism involves a personal obligation on the part of the believer to promote the cause of Christ represented by the work of the church. The true New Testament church is a soul-saving, baptizing, teaching, preaching, evangelistic institution and the baptized believer is now a part of that great, missionary, worldwide ministry. We are united by the Spirit in the worship of God in praise, in thanksgiving, in prayer, and in the diffusion of the saving message of Christ to every creature. We are joined together in the body of our Lord for instruction, for spiritual growth, and for mutual helpfulness. It is a great, glorious, mighty, significant day when we are baptized into the body of Christ, the bride and church of our Lord.

Receiving the Candidate for Baptism

When a believer comes forward before the people to accept Christ as his Savior, he is thereafter presented to the church as a candidate for baptism (Acts 11:47; Acts 2:41; Acts 8:36-39). He is then handed this letter:

DEAR FRIEND IN CHRIST,

We rejoice with you in the decision you have made to follow our Lord in believer's baptism. Your obedience to the command of Christ will be a blessing to you, and to us as we share again the picture of our Lord's death, burial, and resurrection.

The ordinance of baptism is observed each Sunday at 6:30. This is just prior to our evening worship which begins at 7:00 PM. Our baptismal committee will assist you in the preparations for this ordinance. You will meet with the committee and with the assistant pastor for a final word of instruction and prayer at 6:00 PM in Grace Parlor, on the ground floor of the Criswell Building. A member of the baptismal committee will go

204 CRISWELL'S GUIDEBOOK FOR PASTORS

with you to the robing rooms and will graciously care for any needs you have during this time.

You will need to bring only one change of undergarments. The church provides towels and a heavy baptismal robe. Hair dryers are also provided.

We count it a high honor and privilege to share this glad hour with you. We would also encourage you to invite your family and friends to share this special occasion. Our staff and church family will pray for you and encourage you in every way we can. We pray God's richest blessings upon you as you join your life with ours to serve him through the fellowship of this church.

Faithfully yours,

The Pastor

With his response in coming, everything is now ready for the administration of this holy ordinance.

How to Baptize Beautifully

The baptismal service ought to be a beautiful and deeply spiritual occasion whether held in a creek, a river, a pond, or in a church baptistry. I have baptized for years in all of such places. In a creek or a river I would stand in the middle of the stream with an open Bible, preach the gospel to the people watching from both banks, then make an appeal for Christ. In a baptistry I make the rite a part of the great soul-winning effort of the church. The ordinance is a gospel message in itself, and a powerful one at that.

Meticulous care should be taken that all necessary arrangements be made for the holy observance. If in a stream, that the depth and access to the water be just right. If in a baptistry, that the temperature of the water be exactly correct. The depth of the water in either place ought to be such as to make the immersion easy and effectively beautiful. Too shallow a depth of water makes a beautiful baptismal service impossible. Better too deep than too shallow.

In administering the ordinance itself, we ought to be solemnly deliberate in every movement. If the meaning of baptism is felt in the soul of the preacher, he will automatically baptize as he ought to baptize. Baptism is a death, a burial, and a resurrection. Remember to feel that, believe that, and the rite will come naturally to the administrator. We do not throw our beloved dead into the grave. We carefully and tenderly lower them into the grave. Since baptism is a burial, we also should baptize our candidates that way. We should not throw them into the water, dash them into the water, or splash the water all over everywhere as we lower the candidate into the watery grave. Contrariwise, we shall lovingly and tenderly lower them down into the water, then raise them up in triumphant exaltation.

In our baptistry we have a bar welded to the floor. The candidate places his feet under the bar. This helps him to stand upright and steady and to keep that straight posture as he is lowered into the water.

I have the believer cross his hands high on his chest while I pray, then with one hand on both his, I place my other hand on his back, slip my hand upward toward his neck as he goes down into the water, place my other hand over his face (actually closing his nose) for just a moment as he is buried under the surface, then raise him up as he pulls his right foot backward to help push his body upward. I do not use a handkerchief or a towel in the ceremony, covering the face. I could not imagine John the Baptist doing such a thing or James, Peter, Paul, or you.

The formula of the prayer that I pray before the believer is baptized is very simple. I vary it many times, but the central substance is always the same. It is this: "In obedience to the Great Commission of our Lord Jesus Christ, and upon your open and unashamed confession of faith in him as your personal Savior, I baptize you, my brother—or sister (then I call their name)/in the name of the Father and of the Son and of the Holy Spirit." Sometimes I will say at the beginning, "Following the footsteps of our Lord Jesus, even through the waters of the Jordan, and upon your profession of faith." Sometimes I will say, "And setting forth before our very eyes the burial and resurrection of the Lord Jesus." Sometimes I will say, "We are buried with our Lord in the likeness of his death and we are raised with our Lord in the likeness of his resurrection." But always the rite is (1) in obedience, (2) upon confession of faith, (3) and in the name of the Triune God.

Teaching and Training After Baptism

What we do with the candidate after he is baptized is another matter, and one in which most preachers and most churches are tragically weak. So many times we "dip them and drop them" and let them go. We need to remember that baptism is an *initial* rite. It is the first and very beginning. The rest of the pilgrim way is no less the responsibility of the church to teach, to train, to instruct, to help, to encourage, to be all that the Lord intended for the pastor and the church to be to "one of these little ones." The church teaching and training is almost as vital as the church evangelizing and witnessing.

Administering the Ordinance of the Lord's Supper

The Difference Between "Worthy" and "Worthily" in Paul's Discussion

Reading Paul's discussion of the observance of the Lord's Supper in the church at Corinth (1 Cor. 11:17-34), we are increasingly conscious of an all-important facet of that observance: it must be done in a worthy, spiritually effective manner. Because the church at Corinth did not thus "discern the Lord's body," many among their members were "weak and sickly" (v. 30) and many had actually died. How important it is that we do it right! To observe the ordinance in a wrong and unworthy way is to eat damnation to oneself and to drink condemnation to one's soul.

Do you notice the use of the adverb "unworthily" in 1 Corinthians 11:27 and 29? An adverb modifies a verb and refers to the manner of doing a thing. Paul does not use the adjective "worthy" which would refer to a noun, a person. The discussion of the apostle does not revolve around our worth in approaching the Lord's table. If it did, not one of us could ever partake; we are not worthy the least of God's mercies. We are lost, undone sinners; we are to be pitied in our weakness and frailty. But that is the reason for the Supper which portrays the atoning sacrifice of our Savior. "God commended his love toward us, in that, while we were yet sinners, Christ died for us" (Rom. 5:8). It is because we are *not* worthy, because we are *not* lovely, because we are lost and dying, that Christ came to seek and to save us. And it is because, being sinners, we have found hope and refuge in him that we share in this holy ordinance of the breaking of bread.

A deacon and Sunday School teacher in one of my churches never shared in the Lord's Supper. When I asked him why, he replied, "I am not worthy, and the Bible says that if we eat and drink not being worthy we eat and drink damnation to our souls." He had missed the meaning of the message in 1 Corinthians 11 altogether. The admonition does not concern our personal worth at all. Who among us is worthy of the love and suffering of our dear Lord? The discussion concerns *the manner* (adverb, "worthily") in which we observe the ordinance. With every means and wisdom at our disposal, we ought to make arrangements for the service of memorial to be beautifully and spiritually kept.

Arrangements for the Lord's Supper

All the physical matters that pertain to the actual observance of the Lord's Supper ought to be in the hands of the deacons. In a way, this is in keeping with the purpose of the ordination of the seven in the mother church at Jerusalem recorded in Acts 6:1-6. The apostles gave themselves to prayer and to the ministry of the Word while the seven gave themselves to the serving of tables. This would mean the purchase and careful keeping of the trays of the broken, unleavened bread, and the trays that hold the several cups. (It has been a long, long time since I was in a church where all the congregation drank out of one large cup.) The preparation of all the elements, the arrangements for the holding trays in the Lord's Supper table, and their care after the memorial service is over, is the responsibility of the deacons.

A Spiritual Means of Observing the Lord's Supper

Humbly, and not by any means as a perfect model for anyone else to follow but only as one way of doing it, let me describe in detail how we observe this holy ordinance.

The elements are placed in front of the pulpit, on the Lord's Supper table. In the middle of the table and directly in front of the pastor is a bowl of water with a towel alongside. In the middle and a little to either side are two stacked trays of broken, unleavened bread, with the top tray on either side holding a large piece of unbroken bread covered with a white napkin. Beyond that is a silver pitcher in a silver tray with a large silver chalice, the pitcher filled with the crushed fruit of the vine. On both ends of the table are stacked the trays that hold the cups filled with the red juice of grapes. I take my place behind the table with a deacon seated on either side and the serving deacons seated on the front pews before us.

At the beginning of the service, I usually read the passage in 1 Corinthians 11:23-26, Paul's description of the initiation of the ordinance by our Lord Jesus Christ. One of our fellow preachers is then called upon to lead the thanksgiving, the eucharistic prayer. I then wash my hands in the bowl of water and dry them with the towel.

Uncovering the left tray of bread, I take the large piece of unleavened bread, break it, and place the stacked trays on the table close to the deacon on my left side. I do the same thing with the right stack of bread trays, placing them, after the breaking of the top piece of bread, close to the deacon on my right side.

When I am seated, those two deacons stand up together, and the serving deacons seated in the pews in front come forward according to a prearranged schedule, two by two. Simultaneously the two deacons to my left and to my right give the bread trays to the deacons who have come forward. Two by two, one on either side of the building, these deacons take their assigned places in the sanctuary, waiting until all the deacons have taken their places.

They then pass the trays down the rows of pews through the congregation, and each participant takes a piece of the broken bread, holding it in his hand. The serving deacons then return two by two to the front of the church, returning their trays to the deacons who stand on either side of me. The trays are then restacked in the same order as they were given out.

The deacons on either side of me then serve the deacons seated in the pews at the front of the church. They then serve the men seated on the platform. Returning to their respective places, one of them places the tray in my hand and I serve the two deacons seated on either side of me. Thus all the people are seated holding the broken bread in their hands.

The pastor then asks all the people to kneel in the presence of the Lord. We then sing together:

> Let us break bread together on our knees,
> Let us break bread together on our knees;
> When I fall on my knees
> With my face toward the throne of grace,
> O Lord, have mercy on me.

On our knees I then read 1 Corinthians 11:24 like this: "This is my body which is broken for you; take, eat . . . in remembrance of me." After our eating, I then ask the people to be seated again.

With the cup I read the introductory words in 1 Corinthians 11:25, "After the same manner also he took the cup." I call upon a fellow preacher to lead the second thanksgiving (eucharistic) prayer. The serving deacons then come forward two by two and take the trays of cups to the congregation, returning them to the front as they did the trays of bread. After all are served, I then pour in the large silver chalice the red fruit of the vine out of the silver pitcher, then ask all our people again to kneel. We sing a second time:

> Let us drink the cup together on our knees,
> Let us drink the cup together on our knees;
> When I fall on my knees
> With my face toward the throne of grace,
> O Lord, have mercy on me.

Then I read 1 Corinthians 11:25, "This cup is the new testament in my blood: this do ye, as oft as ye drink it, in remembrance of me." After drinking the cup, we then are seated again.

We close the service, singing a hymn as Jesus and the apostles did in Matthew 26:30. We join hands across every aisle from side to side in the sanctuary, and sing "Blest Be the Tie." It is a sweet, sweet service, It is done in the most worthy and Christ-honoring manner we know how.

Personal Persuasions About the Lord's Table

Allow me to write here some personal persuasions I hold in my heart about the observance of this holy and beautiful ordinance.

1. In my humble opinion, it is best to observe the Lord's Supper

with as little speaking as possible. To talk throughout the time of the observance is to take away the message that God would speak to us through the symbols. One time I attended one of the largest, downtown, famous churches of America whose pastor was almost a household word in the Christian community. In their observance of the Lord's Supper, he had a microphone by the side of his chair and he spoke and talked and preached and commented and read all the way through the Supper. It greatly bothered me. God is speaking to us in the symbols of Christ's body and blood. We ought to be silent before the Lord, listening to his voice.

2. How often should the Lord's Supper be observed? The Lord left this to us. He merely directed, "As oft as ye eat this bread, and drink this cup, ye do show the Lord's death till he come" (1 Cor. 11:26). If the phrase, "breaking of bread," refers to the Lord's Supper (and I suppose it does), then in Acts 2:42,46 the first Christian disciples observed it every day. We know the Christians at Troas observed it with Paul on a Sunday (Acts 20:7). Apparently, according to the word of the Lord Jesus, we can observe the ordinance as often as we like, once a week, once a month, once a quarter, however we are led by the Spirit to do.

In our dear church we observe the Supper once a month. We seek to observe it at night. The Greek word *deipnon* in 1 Corinthians 11:20, refers to a meal eaten at night. I would think that the word *Supper* in any language in the earth would refer to an evening meal. It is not a breakfast. It is not a brunch. It is not a midday dinner. It is not a tea. It is a supper, and a supper is eaten at night. Thus Paul writes in 1 Corinthians 11:23, "That the Lord Jesus *the same night* in which he was betrayed, took bread." I like to observe the Supper at night. But out of deference to older people, and others who cannot be present at night, once a quarter we observe the ordinance at the morning worship hour.

3. Should the Lord's Supper be a concluding part of a preaching service or should the Supper alone be observed at the stated worship hour? I think it depends upon the pastor and upon the occasion. We do both. Sometimes (most of the time) we observe the ordinance at the conclusion of our preaching and evangelistic appeal. Sometimes, such as at the early service on Sunday when the time for the quarterly observance comes, we observe the ordi-

nance alone. But whenever and whatever, I always make an appeal for souls before we share in the symbols, and God always honors the appeal with a gracious harvest.

4. Should we use fermented wine or grape juice in the cup? It is a most unusual thing that in the four accounts in the New Testament recording the institution of the Lord's Supper, not one of them ever uses the word *wine* (Matt. 26:26-30; Mark 14:22-26; Luke 22:19-20; 1 Cor. 11:23-26). That is most remarkable. The symbol lies in the red, crushed fruit of the vine. That is enough. There is no point in its being soured (fermented).

5. What about separating the audience between those who ought to partake and those who ought to be excluded?

As a boy in the little village church where I grew up the separation was done in one of two ways. The pastor would say, "Now all of you who are baptized believers in good standing with the church rise while all the rest of you will remain seated." Then the elements would be served to those standing. The rest were not to receive them. Or the pastor would say, "Now all of you who are baptized believers in good standing with the church move to this side of the church auditorium and the rest of you move to the other side." The pastor and deacons would then serve the elements to those on the designated side of the auditorium.

But even as a little boy, such a procedure seemed wrong to me. I looked at those standing or at those seated on the correct side of the church house, then I looked at those on the wrong side of the division, and sometimes it appeared to me that those on the wrong end of the division were better people than those at the correct end. Not knowing, and not understanding, and not being acquainted with the nuances of theological thought, I was deeply disturbed by what our little church did. And now that I am older I have not changed my mind nor am I convinced that such a dividing procedure is right. It is God alone who is able to divide the sheep from the goats. Let him do it, not us. Then let us pray that we all can be on the right side of God's flock.

What we ought to do, I think, is to preach the truth as it is revealed to us in the Holy Scriptures, and then allow the Spirit of God to do his convicting work. Plainly and emphatically the Bible teaches us (Matt. 28:19-20) this sacred order: one, we are to be saved; two, we are then to be baptized upon that profession of faith; three, we are thereafter to observe the things Jesus has given us to keep. The order is as inspired as the content. No unbeliever is to take the Lord's Supper. No unbaptized person is to take the Lord's Supper. Paul would add in 1 Corinthians 11:17-20 that no church in division and in turmoil can really share in the Lord's table. But having preached the truth faithfully and prayerfully, then if the service of memorial is to be publicly held, let the people in their own consciences decide what to do. Otherwise, observe the ordinance privately, inviting only church members in good standing to attend.

A Closing Meditation of Love for Jesus

My heart moves me to close this chapter on the holy ordinances with a prayerful meditation. O Lord, how we need thee! And how merciful thou art to us poor, unworthy sinners!

If we had been present that night Jesus was tried before the Sanhedrin, would we have spoken out for him? If we had been in the judgment hall of the Roman procurator when Pontius Pilate condemned him to death, would we have defended him? If we had been one of the disciples that awesome and terrifying day of the cross, would we have stayed by his side amid the taunts of the crucifying mob? Or would we have been like Peter, cursing and swearing that we never knew him, and like all the other disciples, forsaking him and running away to save our own lives?

Lord, Lord, forgive us. What would we have done?

The nails that crucified our Lord were made of iron. The spear that pierced his side was forged on an anvil—cold, sharp, terrible. But those sharp nails and that terrible spear were also made of bitter hatred, sinful greed, open hostility. Do I also so crucify my Lord, driving those nails through hands and feet and piercing through his side with that cold spear? How much of me is found in the shadow of that mob that reaches down through history? What part of me hammers out nails and forges sharp spears that break and tear the body of our Lord and of his people?

O God, forgive me and make me anew, a regenerated soul in thy Son, Christ Jesus. How much we love him! How much we owe him!

A long, long time ago (in the 1100s) an unknown Christian pilgrim wrote a hymn to the Lord Jesus in Latin. It was translated into German by Paul Gerhardt and set to music by the incomparable J. S. Bach. In an English translation it reads like this:

> O sacred Head, now wounded,
>> With grief and shame weighed down,
> Now scornfully surrounded
>> With thorns, thine only crown;
> How pale thou art with anguish,
>> With sore abuse and scorn!
> How does that visage languish
>> Which once was bright as morn!
>
> What thou, my Lord, hast suffered
>> Was all for sinners' gain:
> Mine, mine was the transgression,
>> But Thine the deadly pain;
> Lo, here I fall, my Savior!
>> 'Tis I deserve Thy place;
> Look on me with thy favor,
>> Vouchsafe to me thy grace.
>
> What language shall I borrow
>> To thank thee, dearest Friend,
> For this thy dying sorrow,
>> Thy pity without end?
> O make me thine forever,
>> And should I fainting be,
> Lord, let me never, never
>> Outlive my love to thee!

God grant it, Lord, as we break bread together, praise thee together, and love thee forever and ever. Amen.

12

The Ordination of the
Pastor and the Deacon

The Two Ordained Officers of the Church

In the New Testament there are two officers of the church that are set aside in ordination, in "the laying on of hands." They are the pastor and the deacon (Acts 6:5-6; Phil. 1:1; 1 Tim. 3:1-13; 4:13; 2:7). They are the preacher and the layman, the pulpit and the pew, the vocational and the avocational, the salaried and the unsalaried, the prophet and the people. Separated they are like two hemispheres that bleed themselves white. Together they are the strength and the power of the Lord. When they are one in Christ they make an unbeatable team. Like a pair of scissors—one blade will not work. Two are needed. They sharpen each other.

Happy is the church that has a wonderful pastor. Blessed is the pastor who has a group of concentrated deacons whose hearts the Lord has touched. Marvelous is the life of the congregation when they can behold love and harmony in the two.

Meaning of the Descriptive Words

There are three words in the New Testament that refer to the office of the pastor. The three words are used interchangeably (Acts 20:17,28; Titus 1:5-7; 1 Pet. 5:1-4). One is the word *episkopos,* translated in the English language "bishop." The original word is made up of two Greek words: a preposition *epi,* meaning "over"; and a noun *skopos* meaning "a watcher" (from the verb *skeptomai,* meaning "to look around," "to survey"). Literally, therefore the word *episkopos* ("bishop") means an

215

overseer. He is the officer in the church that oversees all the work of the Lord. The title refers to his assignment. He is responsible for the life and well-being of the congregation. The entire work heads up in him. He is *the* leader of the church.

The second New Testament word that refers to that same office is *presbuteros,* translated in the English Bibles as *elder.* The word for an old man, an ambassador, in Greek is *presbus.* The word *presbuteros* is the comparative form of *presbus.* The noun form literally refers to one more advanced in years, a senior, an elder. It thus became an apellation of dignity, referring in Jewish life to a member of the Sanhedrin and in the Christian church to the office of the ruling ministers (Heb. 13:7,17,24). The word *elder* primarily and essentially describes the dignity of the office of pastor (1 Tim. 5:17-19). It is a cheap, sorry church that looks upon its pastor as a hireling, as a paid errand-runner of the deacons, as an object of charity. It is a great, strong, mighty church (however small the numerical membership) that looks upon the pastor as an ambassador from the courts of heaven, as God's man for their people. Our dear First Baptist Church here in Dallas loved and revered the far-famed pastor, Dr. George W. Truett, their under shepherd for forty-seven years. They always called him "The Pastor." When I came to be pastor of the congregation upon the death of Dr. Truett, I inherited the same reverential respect accorded him, even though I was forty-three years younger than the mighty man of God. It is a great church; there is a reason why God has blessed it so. God will bless any church that loves and respects its pastor.

The third word in the New Testament that refers to the office of the pastor is *poimen,* translated "shepherd," "pastor." The word literally describes a herdsman, one who tends the flock. This word refers to the shepherdly love and care of the pastor for his people. Jesus is called the chief Shepherd (the Great Pastor), in 1 Peter 5:4. He laid his life down for the sheep. The same devoted love ought to characterize the pastor of the church. He ought literally to give his life in ministering to the flock of God, the people of the church.

The word in the New Testament for "deacon" is *diakonos.* The word in classic Greek referred to the servant (slave) of a king, especially one who acted in the capacity of a waiter, serving food and drink. Thus in the New Testament the word was used to describe the office of those who cared for the poor in the church and who distributed to them the money collected in their behalf. The deacons of the church were the servants of the church. They were chosen for that assignment, to help, to save, to care for the temporal necessities of the people.

The idea of a "board" of deacons is as strange and unknown to the New Testament church as would be a band of Hitlers and Stalins composing the chosen twelve apostles of the Lord. A ruling board is an idea imported from the corporate life of American business. It has no place in a true, New Testament church. A deacon-led church will always be a weak, pitiful congregation, floundering before every wind of secular change. God ordained the pastor, the elder, the bishop to be the spiritual leader and ruler of the congregation. Where he is that and truly that and capably that, the church grows in strength and will forever. Where he is not that and where he becomes a hireling of the deacons, the church withers and dies. God in his infinite wisdom set the order and the constitution of his true church. Blessed and happy is the congregation that follows that order in the mind and purpose of heaven.

It is far better to refer to "the fellowship of deacons" than to refer to "the board of deacons." The word *fellowship* (Greek *koinonia*) is a beautiful, wonderful New Testament word, translated "communion"; "fellowship." Let us use it. It is God's word for his people.

It has been my experience through the years that without fail the deacons need and desire a real leader, a real pastor. They want the preacher to stand before them and tell them what ought to be done, to present a challenging program to them. They are ready to follow, to work, to build, to go if they have a man of God and a man of vision to lead the way.

Upon a day the chairman of the deacons of one of the largest churches in our denomination came to see me here in Dallas. He wanted me to talk to his pastor. He said: "We love our pastor but he doesn't lead us. At our deacons' meeting he just sits there and if a decision has to be made, he answers, 'Whatever you deacons decide will be fine with me.' We want him to speak up, stand up, tell us what we ought to do, and where we ought to go. Please talk to him and see if you can't change him." Of course, I couldn't do such a thing, but his plaintive, pathetic appeal moved my heart. A worthy deacon wants to move, to achieve, to do things for his Savior, and he depends on the pastor to help him do it.

Ordination of the Pastor-Preacher

1. Article IV of the By-Laws of our church concerns "Ordination and Licensing," and it reads like this:

A. *ORDINATION.* The church shall consider a man as a candidate for ordination if he shall have fulfilled the following qualifications:

1. He must have received a specific calling to a definite preaching ministry in the kingdom of our Lord such as (1) to be a pastor of a church, (2) to be a chaplain in the armed forces of our country or in one of our institutions, (3) to the office of an evangelist as a distinct calling from God, or (4) to fill a specific assignment in the work of our Lord that requires ordination.

2. He must demonstrate a deep conviction and personal knowledge of the doctrines of the church and a proficiency in expressing them as a preacher and teacher of the faith.

3. He must be a member of the church unless the candidate has been a member of the church previously and the ordination committee determines that an exception to this requirement is warranted.

B. *LICENSING.* The church shall have the privilege and authority to license a man to exercise his gifts in the preaching of the Gospel when the licensing committee is convinced of his Christian character and of his evident call to the ministry. As in ordination, he should be a member of the church unless there is a most evident and applicable exception. It is understood that an ordination is the setting aside of a minister for a specific calling in which ordination is required, whereas a license to preach is the approval and recommendation of the church that the man might be received as a minister of the Gospel.

It can be seen from this paragraph that licensing a man to preach is the public commendation of the church of a brother to the Christian world that he exercise his gifts for the Lord in a sympathetic, prayerful atmosphere. It is a word of approval and recommendation of a man as a preacher-minister of the Gospel.

Ordination, on the other hand, is the setting aside of a God-called preacher for a particular office, it may be that of a pastor, or of a chaplain, or of a staff assignment, or of an evangelist, or of some other specified assignment in the church or in the denomination. Ordination, or the public investiture of church officers with official authority, is strictly scriptural. It is not, however, the ultimate source of ministerial authority. This is found in the call of the Holy Spirit and the election by the church, of which ordination is the public recognition and the completing act.

The word *ordain* in the King James Version of the New Testament never denotes the ecclesiastical ceremony of ordination. The word is used six times in connection with the sacred office and is, in each instance, the translation of a different Greek word. Mark 3:14; Acts 1:22; 17:31; and 1 Timothy 2:7 refer not to a formal ceremony of ordination but to the choice or appointment to a sacred office. The same is true in Acts 14:23, and in Titus 1:5, although here the word may possibly include the whole procedure, both the choice and the ordaining ceremony.

Although the word *ordain* is not used, there are three instances of ordination or the public setting apart to church office found in the New Testament: that of the seven in Acts 6:6; that of Barnabas and Saul in Acts 13:1-3; and that of Timothy in 1 Timothy 4:14. Then we could add also the admonition in 1 Timothy 5:22 to "lay hands suddenly on no man." Evidently, the ultimate responsibility of admitting to the ministerial office is here devolved first, on the ministry itself, then on the church. They only, therefore, may act in setting apart to the sacred office. But ordination confers no new grace or power. That is a gift of the Holy Spirit.

2. The procedures we follow in the ordination of a preacher-pastor are these:

(1) There is a conference between the candidate and the pastor of the ordaining church at which time the reasons for the ordination are discussed.

(2) A time is set for the candidate to appear before the committee on ordination appointed by the church. The committee is presented a letter in writing requesting his ordination (often written by a sister church), and the candidate is introduced to the committee.

(3) The committee thoroughly and at length interrogates the candidate concerning his conversion, baptism, church membership, call to the ministry, doctrinal understanding, personal integrity, and sometimes a thousand other things beside. There is no limit to the probing of the committee to ascertain the calling and usefulness and dedication of the candidate. He is to be systematically and searchingly examined.

(4) The committee reports to the pastor of the ordaining church, and if the report is favorable, a time is announced for the public administration of the candidate and the church votes for a council to be called and to proceed with the ordination.

(5) At the time of the ordination, an ordaining council (a presbytery) is organized with the ordained preachers present (in many churches ordained deacons are included). A moderator is elected (usually the pastor of the ordaining church) and a clerk.

(6) The ordination committee then makes its report to the church and to the ordaining council and presents the candidate. The candidate then publicly tells of his experience of grace and his call to the ministry. At this time, in many instances, the council and anybody in the church can ask the candidate any questions he or she would like. (This has to be watched; it can get out of hand both in length of time and in content.)

(7) The candidate then kneels, facing the audience. The members of the council kneel around him. A previously chosen elder leads the ordaining prayer, after which each member of the council lays his hands on the head of the candidate. This actually is the ordination, the consecration, the "setting aside" (1 Tim. 4:14).

(8) After the council is seated and the candidate is seated, any service can follow that is wisely chosen: a charge to the candidate, a charge to the church, the presentation of a Bible, a testimony of prayerful remembrance on the part of the church, hands of fellowship and encouragement on the part of everybody present, just anything edifying.

(9) The benediction.

3. Should the candidate who is ordained belong to the church that ordains him? We follow that practice. If necessary he can letter in and letter out the same week. The basic situation in the Bible is this: a church sets aside one of its members for the work of the ministry, for the work whereunto God has called him. This custom of ordaining a brother in the church to which he belongs has been followed for the most part through all the years.

The Assignments of Pastors

1. The number of pastors (elders, bishops) in each church is not fixed by Scripture. It is possible that practically all the churches of the New Testament had a plurality of elders. We have that in our church. There are as many as twenty-five fellow pastors, fellow elders in the First Baptist Church in Dallas. We have our separate assignments in many different categories of ministries among the people.

The duties of pastors are the preaching of the gospel (such as we read in Acts 20) and the administration of the ordinances, the government and spiritual oversight of the church. Paul exhorts in 1 Thessalonians 5:12, "We beseech you, brethren, to know them that labour among you, and are over you in the Lord, and admonish you." In the book of Hebrews, we read, "Obey them that have the rule over you, and submit yourselves" (13:17). In 1 Peter 5:1-4 is a similar beautiful passage, outlining the shepherdly care of the pastor for his flock.

The pastor is to direct and supervise the public, religious instruction of the congregation, to administer the ordinances, to preside in all meetings of the church, and to watch over the personal experience and life of the members—exhorting, admonishing, reproving, rebuking those trusted to his care. Pastors do not constitute a priesthood with sacrificial mediating and absolving powers. Such priestly powers are the offspring of clerical ambition. Ministers in the New Testament are never designated as priests. They are always shepherds, pastors, elders, overseers. God said that is enough.

The Calling of a Pastor to a Field

When a church is without a pastor, it becomes a matter of deepest prayer and concern that the Spirit of God lead them to the one, exact man the Lord has chosen and called to be their under shepherd. A mistake here is tragic. It is like a marriage; nothing but sadness and sorrow come of a mismatched couple. There is a right man for a right woman in the elective purpose of God. Likewise, there is a right man for a right church in the will of heaven.

The church pulpit committee (appointed by the church) and the church itself must find that man. The Holy Spirit will lead them.

On the pulpit committee that recommended me to Dallas were seven representative people chosen by the congregation: The chairman of the deacons, chairman of the committee; the associate pastor who was also the minister of music; the president of the WMU; a denominational executive; a representative of the young people; a banker; and a president of a business firm.

Sometimes the pulpit committee can number scores of people who are broken down into smaller committees. Any way a church decides to do it is acceptable, only let the committee be representatives of *all* the worshiping congregation.

2. Never under any condition should a minister encourage a church to call him unless he fully intends and prepares to accept the call. This understanding is also a part of the work of the pulpit committee. The pulpit committee should never take to the church the name of a man nor should the church ever call a man, who, first, does not believe that God wills that he accept the call. Not to follow this admonition discourages the church, plays with the deep things of God, and makes the man who finally comes to be pastor feel that he is a second- or third-rate choice.

3. When a pulpit committee talks to a prospective pastor, what should he do? He has one thing to do: Is this the will of God for him? If there is a divine call, there is also a divinely appointed field of work. Every man in the ministry should, first of all, consider whether or not God calls him to a mission field. If he feels that God has called him to minister here at the homeland, then he must find God's assignment for him in his homeland. That means that he must earnestly pray that God will direct him to the right place.

Is this it? God will speak yes or no, possibly by several providences. He can invite trusted friends to pray with him about the decision. The nature of his work in his present field can be a sign whether or not he ought to leave. One sure way to know whether the right decision is being made is this: Having made the choice, is your heart at rest? If not, you had better reconsider and start all over again, especially with the family.

4. The pulpit committee, acting for the church, should make every financial arrangement necessary for the coming and continuing ministry of the pastor. The pastor should be worthily paid (Luke 10:7). It is interesting to note that the word *honor* in 1 Timothy 5:17 also means "pay." "Let the elders that rule well be counted worthy of double honour, especially they who labour in the word and doctrine." The arrangements with the new pastor should be done with business definitives: salary, vacations, parsonage (or allowance for a home), moving expenses, funds for travel to conventions, etc. Better have a full understanding *now* than misunderstanding and unhappiness later on.

When I came to the church in Dallas, I asked for two things, both of which were agreed to and granted: One, that I have an unfettered pulpit. I preach what God lays on my heart. Two, that the staff is completely and absolutely mine. This has proved a most wise request on my part. It adds immeasurable strength to the work of the pastor.

5. If the pastor accepts the call and settles down in the field, there are deep and everlasting obligations he assumes in coming as pastor.

The pastor accepts the scriptural doctrine in practice of that church and places himself under obligation to defend and to teach the doctrines that are believed by that church. It is not right that he accept a church if he does not believe in the doctrines that are held by the congregation. When he gives himself to the church, he is to invest all the faculties of his being that he might be the minister of Christ to edify and to protect the congregation. He is to give his very life for the sheep (John 10:11-12).

The Selection and Election of Deacons

1. Many churches appoint a new deacon nominating committee to search out and to nominate to the church men qualified to hold the office of deacon. Many churches select deacons by a secret ballot in a business meeting publicized for that purpose. However

the method, the church is the authoritative body to elect the men who are to serve in the fellowship of deacons.

2. Any service meaningful to the pastor and to the congregation can be followed in the ordination of deacons. But whatever order is followed, these things ought to be included. Each nominated or elected deacon ought to tell the congregation his experience of grace: his conversion, baptism, church membership, and his purpose of heart to serve the Lord and the church. An ordaining council ought to be called for the purpose of ordination; that is, the laying on of hands, the setting aside of the newly elected men for their sacred work. In fact, the ordination of a deacon can follow the same course as the ordination of a pastor with this exception: the pastor is a teacher according to the Word of God (1 Tim. 3:2), and the ordaining council must be sure that the candidate knows the doctrines of the faith. The deacon, on the other hand, is not called upon as such in the performance of his duties, and therefore does not need to be questioned so thoroughly concerning his intimate knowledge of the doctrines.

3. It has never been my privilege to be the pastor of a church that rotated the membership of its fellowship of deacons. But I can tell you positively and certainly that you will have a better and a stronger leadership for the church if you will rotate the men. When a man is elected for life, he may take things for granted— his attendance upon the meetings, his service in behalf of the people, his leadership in the congregation. A man may be one thing at thirty years of age and an altogether different thing at sixty years of age. If his life, work, and service are never reviewed, he can fall into any kind of disinterest, and nothing can ever be done about it. No political or business institution in the world would do a thing like that, never review the people who run the organization. You will find that only in the church.

It is infinitely better to ask the elected man if he will devote, say, three years of his best time and talent to the church, after which he rotates off and is not eligible for reelection until the passing of a year. In this way one third of the men rotate off each year and a group numbering one third are added each year. Deadweight and listless indifference can thus be eliminated and replaced with vibrant, dedicated men who are eager to go forward for Christ.

4. It is good church organization and it is according to the Scriptures (Acts 6:1-6) that the deacons be charged with the temporal, physical, financial responsibilities of the church. They can work closely with the pastor in all these things, but it is first and foremost their assignment to see that the house of the Lord and the redeemed congregation of God's people are beautifully cared for. The business office in every detail can report to them. The maintenance of all the facilities can be in their hands. Men love to do this kind of work. They take pride in doing it. Let them do it.

More and more, also, I see deacons beginning to lead the church in a tremendously meaningful witnessing program. They are more and more soul-winners, lay renewal leaders, flock ministers, greeters, ushers; in fact, just all-around, splendid, associate pastors. That is wonderful. God be praised for them all.

13

The Pastor Doing the Work of an Evangelist

The Command of God

The pastor is under the command of God to do the work of an evangelist (2 Tim. 4:5). The evangelist, according to the word of Paul in Ephesians 4:11, is one of the gifts of the ascended Christ to the church. Among the apostles, prophets, and pastor-teachers, he stands as a God-anointed, God-called minister in the household of faith. But the work that the evangelist does in his itinerant ministry the pastor is to do in his pastoral ministry. If he fails in this he fails God. If he is faithful in this he is faithful to God. There is no alternative. The pastor is to win souls to Jesus.

If we could speak in the language of Paul in 1 Corinthians 13 and in his soul-winning spirit the words would go like this:

Though I speak with the tongues of scholarship, and though I use approved methods of preaching, and fail to win my people to Christ, or to build them up in Christian character, I am become as the moan of the wind in a Syrian desert.

And though I have the best of preaching skills and understand all mysteries of religious psychology, and though I have all biblical knowledge, and lose not myself in the task of winning others to Christ, I become as a cloud of mist in an open sea.

And though I read all the homiletical books and attend denominational conventions, and institutes and summer schools, and yet am satisfied with less than winning to Christ and establishing my people in Christian character and service, it profiteth nothing.

The soul-winning preacher, the character-building pastor suffereth long and is kind; he envieth not others who are free from the task; he

227

vaunteth not himself; is not puffed up with intellectual pride.

Such a pastor doth not behave himself unseemly between Sundays, seeketh not his own comfort, is not easily provoked.

Beareth all things, believeth all things, hopeth all things.

And now abideth knowledge, methods, evangelism, these three; but the greatest of these is evangelism.

What Is Evangelism?

What is evangelism? It is taking seriously the first command of the Great Commission—going, making disciples. It is taking seriously the last appeal of the apostle Paul, "Preach the word, do the work of an evangelist" (2 Tim. 4:2,5).

What is evangelism? It is recreating in the world of today the method and the manner of the New Testament Christians. Words can hardly describe the desperate urgency and the immediate hopefulness with which they preached the message of the cross, the resurrection and the glorious appearing of our Lord. Evangelism, winning the lost, the confession of our faith, is New Testament Christianity. We must never forget that economic reform, political enlightenment, culture, and learning are by-products of the Christian faith. The main thing has always been and will always be the restoration of the soul, without which the rest is vain.

What is evangelism? It is the acceptance of the underlying and predominant thesis of the New Testament that men are lost without Christ. It was our Savior himself who spoke most, and most solemnly, on the tragic denial of heaven to the soul that willfully turns away from the overtures of God's grace and mercy. It was Simon Peter who said, "There is none other name under heaven given among men, whereby we must be saved" (Acts 4:12). It was John who wrote, "And whosoever was not found written in the book of life was cast into the lake of fire" (Rev. 20:15). Whether we believe in literal, physical flames or not, the New Testament teaches, and history confirms, that men are woefully lost without Christ. Every ruined city on the continents, every white cross in military cemeteries, in some tragic way brings to our hearts anew the conviction that men more than anything else need God and the Christian way of life.

What is evangelism? It is intercession for the lost. It is the anguished cry of Jesus as he weeps over a doomed city.

It is the cry of Paul, "I could wish that myself were accursed from Christ for my brethren, my kinsmen according to the flesh" (Rom. 9:3).

Evangelism is the heartrending plea of Moses, "Oh, this people have sinned . . . . Yet now, if thou wilt forgive their sin—; and if not, blot me, I pray thee, out of thy book which thou hast written" (Ex. 32:31-32).

It is the cry of John Knox, "Give me Scotland or I die."

It is the declaration of John Wesley, "The world is my parish."

It is William Carey with his Bible in his hand and the burden of the world on his heart.

It is the prayer of Billy Sunday, "Make me a giant for God."

It is the sob of the parent in the night, weeping over a prodigal child.

Evangelism is the loving spirit of the shepherd who seeks the lost sheep, of the father who prays and waits for the prodigal son.

It is the secret of a great church.

It is the secret of a great preacher and of a great Christian.

A burden for the souls of lost men would bring to our churches a revival such as we have not known since the Spirit in fullness came on Christ's church at Pentecost.

To the end that our people might be saved, that our churches might live and grow, that Christ might be glorified and honored, let us give ourselves to the main task for which every minister is called and every church exists—evangelism, the hope of the world.

Evangelism—the Reason for the Growth of Churches

There is a reason for the growth of great churches. That reason is evangelism; evangelism in the pulpit, in the Sunday School, in the city, in the country. Evangelism, the soul and spirit of every organization and endeavor of the church.

Where churches have been evangelistic, they have grown. Where they have failed to win souls, they have inevitably died and are dying. Upon the occasion of the visit of the late Dr. Rushbrooke to America, I asked him why his denomination in one of the great nations of the world was gradually dying. He replied, "It is because they have lost the spirit of evangelism." What breath is to the body, what soul is to the man, evangelism is to the church. What color and fragrance are to the flower, what water is to the sea, what power is to the engine, evangelism is to the church.

Other churches may live by their political alliances and be the strength of their state-supported institutions, but free churches, repudiating both, must ever remember that evangelism made us and evangelism alone can preserve us. There is a judgment of God upon us if we fail in this vital matter. "Remember therefore from whence thou art fallen, and repent, and do the first works, or else I will come unto thee quickly, and will remove thy candlestick out of his place . . . . He that hath an ear, let him hear what the Spirit saith unto the churches" (Rev. 2:5,7).

The Pastor Evangelical and Evangelistic

The pastor who believes the gospel of the New Testament, preaches it fervently and faithfully, and wins souls for Jesus will fall into all kinds of criticism from those of the new enlightenment. He is "an anachronism." He "does not keep up with the times." He is not "sensitive to the sweeping social changes in the world." He is not "preaching to the present generation," And he is "answering questions no longer asked." No matter. Remember that Paul had those who hounded him wherever he went as he preached the gospel of the grace of the Son of God. But he never stopped. He preached all the more fervently (Gal. 1:6-24; 6:11-17). Let us do the same.

The true pastor must ever strive to keep his heart warm by the fires of God's love and grace. Let no root of bitterness grow in his soul. Pray, be sweet and tender, and witness to the lost that they might be saved. Just keep on doing the soul-winning work to which Jesus called you.

We are found to find others.

We are told to tell others.

We are won to win others.

We are saved to save others.

Let us follow the holy example of that unknown Christian who wrote:

Lord, give to me Thy love for souls,
  For lost and wandering sheep,
That I may see the multitudes
  And weep as Thou didst weep.

From off the altar of Thy heart
  Take Thou some flaming coals,
Then touch my lips and give me, Lord,
  A heart consumed for souls.

O fire of love, O flame divine,
  Make Thy abode in me.
Burn in my heart, burn evermore
  Till I burn out for Thee.

One of the liberal denominations of America through its news media attacked one of its ministers for objecting to some of its Christ-denying literature. He was an Evangelical in a hotbed of semi-Unitarians. Because of the pastor's objection he was labeled a Bible worshiper, a liar, and it was suggested that he had a naive and illogical mind.

In the same issue of the denominational magazine attacking the minister was an article attacking all evangelism and evangelistically minded Christians. The entire group of Evangelicals was called togetherness boys, hate mongers, right-wingers, desecrationists, Neanderthal-types, perverted brethren, apostles of discord, human dinosaurs, Pied Pipers, literalists, authoritarians, opinionated, immature, fanatics, Separatists, Lilliputian creatures, plus a score of other implications which are worse than those named! The magazine referred to fundamental preaching as poisonous vapor, hate, twisted doctrine, and paranoiac barbarism.

If these people won the lost to Christ, built up the churches, sent out missionaries, ministered to the needs of the people, then we could abandon our Bible, forget about our Lord's Great Commission, keep our money to ourselves and rest at ease in Zion and watch the kingdom of God advance from our ivory towers. The trouble is, these self-styled superior religionists who scoff at evangelism as being crude and backward and barbaric do nothing but preside over a dying church and a dying witness and a dying denomination. One of them says: "See that ecclesiastical moron preaching every Sunday to thousands and thousands of people? If he were sophisticated like me, he would be preaching to a congregation of one hundred and fifty!"

Another says: "See that Bible-believing, stupid ignoramus baptizing over five hundred every year? If he were an intellectual Athenian philosopher as I am he would be baptizing three a year as I do!"

Another one says: "See that narrow-minded gospel-preaching pastor over there, delivering the same message his forefathers did, with a Sunday School attendance averaging over eight thousand every Sunday. If he were enlightened as I am, he would average seventy-five as I do!"

No liberal ever built a great church, held a mighty revival, or won a city to the Lord. They live off the labor and sacrifices of those who paid the price of devoted service before them. Their message, which they think is new and modern, is as old as the first lie, "Yet, hath God said" (Gen. 3:1). They live in another world from us and they preach another gospel that is not a gospel but a tragic perversion of the truth (Gal. 1:6-9). C. T. Studd wrote of the difference in a poem entitled, "I'm Not Going Your Way," a conversation between a young, modern entrepreneur and an old-time gospel preacher.

I'm Not Going Your Way

"You're just out of date," said young Pastor Bate
To one of our faithful old preachers
Who had carried for years, in travail and tears,
The Gospel to poor, sinful creatures.
"You still preach on Hades, and shock cultured ladies
With your barbarous doctrine of blood;
You're so far behind, you'll never catch up.
You're a flat tire stuck in the mud."

For some little while a wee bit of a smile
Enlightened the old preacher's face,
Being made the butt of a ridiculous cut
Did not ruffle his sweetness and grace.
Then he turned to young Bate, so suave and sedate,

"Catch up, did my ears hear you say?
Why I couldn't succeed if I doubled your speed;
My friend, I'm not going your way."

Let the true pastor never turn aside from his great calling to preach the whole counsel of God, warn men of their sins and the judgment of the Lord upon them, call the lost to repentance and faith, baptize converts in the name of the Triune God, and build up his congregation in the love and wisdom of the Lord. If he does this, he will have completed the work for which the Holy Spirit did choose him. What a blessed reward to hear the voice of the Father saying, "Well done, thou good and faithful servant: . . . enter thou into the joy of thy lord" (Matt. 25:21). Do not be deterred or discouraged by what others say about you. Just keep on winning souls to Jesus.

The Organization of the Church Like the Organization of an Evangelist

In the work of an evangelist, great effort is poured into organization devised for winning the lost. In the tremendous Philadelphia campaign of Billy Sunday, the organization reached down to the last city block. The entire city was touched by it and moved by it. As a result of the revival, more than six thousand souls were baptized into the churches of the metroplex. If the pastor is under authority to do the work of an evangelist, then he must do the same thing; namely, he must use his church organization to win the lost. To what better use could they be dedicated? And what a powerful instrument for witnessing the pastor has in the marching members of his many-faceted ministry through the church. The way the church is put together is inherently, intrinsically made for soul winning, for reaching people. It is the thing that comes naturally.

The Sermon as an Instrument of Evangelism

The sermon and the pulpit are instruments in the hands of the evangelistic pastor to win souls for Jesus (1 Cor. 1:18-20). Sorrowfully, there is a modern tendency to turn aside from evangelistic preaching, as though the people outside the church could be reached by lowering our standards and changing our eternal message. The spirit of compromise, secularism, and ecumenism are seen everywhere. It is more dialogue without decision communication without conversion, universalism without personal salvation. This is not the method of the New Testament (Acts 2:40). The apostles preached for a verdict. Jonathan Edwards profoundly believed that the sermon was an agency and a vehicle for conversion. He restored the sermon to its primacy as the center of worship. He made the sermon the focal point of worship, not the sacraments. He expected something to take place when he preached. The one principal aim of preaching was to win others to Christ. Edwards had no desire to be clever, only to be clear.

Charles G. Finney believed exactly as Edwards. He believed in the centrality of the sermon as an agency of conversion. Of his own preaching he wrote, "Conviction occurred under every sermon that I preached." The aim of the preacher is primarily the conversion of his hearers. The seeking note ought to be heard and felt in very sermon.

Jonathan Edwards in his pulpit sought a verdict. Charles G. Finney expected results and he had them. C. H. Spurgeon ended his sermons with an appeal to the lost. Even the sermon preached primarily for edification ought to have in it saving features.

There ought to be tremendous purpose in preaching, and one of those primary purposes is reaching for the lost. Could you imagine an insurance salesman presenting all the good, fine points of his company and contract then never asking his prospect to sign on the dotted line? It is no less unthinkable that the pastor delivers the saving message of Christ and then expecting no results, extending no invitation, dismisses the people with an empty benediction. The pastor ought to expect a harvest.

A young man was complaining to Spurgeon about the fact that he had no conversions on a regular basis. Spurgeon replied, "You do not expect to have conversions at every service, do you?" The young man answered, "No." Spurgeon thereupon observed, "Then you will never have them." A man ought to preach with expectancy and he ought to work with the persuasion that God will bless his ministry of appeal.

The Construction of the Evangelistic Sermon and Service

The evangelistic service in the church (and that ought to include every worship service) ought to have these common characteristics:

1. The people in attendance must have a mind-set for evangelism. The appeal for the lost is not strange or new to them.

2. The atmosphere of the church must be one of warm welcome. No babies are ever born in a snowbank or an iceberg. They are born in the warm matrix bathed by a mother's blood.

3. There must be the contribution made by the Christ-devoted, soul-loving greeters and ushers.

4. The church must be filled with the love of a precious fellowship. Who wants to seek Christ in a congregation torn by dissension?

5. The faithful attendance of God's people. If we are not interested enough to come, why should we expect the lost to come?

6. Good, soul-warming music. Music can literally kill an evangelistic service, and too often does.

7. A vast preparation before the meeting. This includes visitation, prayer meetings, personal intercession, confession, commitment, all the virtues that Christ can use in reaching the spiritually indifferent.

8. A warm-hearted pastor preaching an evangelistic, gospel sermon. If he will dedicate himself to turning all he says into an appeal expressed in the climactic invitation, God will use him mightily.

Phillips Brooks said, "It does not take great men to do great things; it only takes consecrated men."

9. In summary, if there is prayer, preparation, the presence of the people, the preaching of the Word, and the presence in power of the Holy Spirit, there will be a hallelujah service of salvation and soul saving. It never fails. But if these ingredients are not present, the service is sterile and barren.

Once a church in our city asked for the loan for a year of our leader of visitation and evangelism. We acquiesed and he went there to lead the work for a year. After about six months he quit and came back home to us. I asked why. He replied that he taught and led the congregation in a visitation, soul-winning ministry. They went from door-to-door, they talked and prayed with the lost, they won them to Christ, and the new converts promised to attend the services of the church, publicly confess their newfound faith in Christ, and become baptized members of the church. But Sunday would come, they would be present in the audience, and nothing happened. It was heartbreaking. The leader went back to the homes of his new converts with the question: "Why did you not come forward? You were there. I saw you. Why did you not respond?" The converts could not answer; they could not verbalize the inward reason. But our leader of evangelism answered the question for them and for me. He said the lack of response was due to the coldness of the pastor and to the frigid atmosphere in the church. The pastor and the church must change if the people who ought to be won to Christ are changed.

The construction of the evangelistic sermon must have three vital remembrances:

1. The preacher must believe that men are lost in their sins apart from personal faith in Christ.

2. He must believe in his deepest soul that Christ and Christ alone is the power of God unto salvation. He cannot be a Universalist and be a soul-winner.

3. He must so pray in faith that he believes the Holy Spirit will bless the message he delivers to the saving of the lost. God, having called him, will use him for this divine purpose.

An effective evangelistic sermon must possess these ten ingredients:

1. Be biblical in content
2. Simple in construction
3. Personal in its concern
4. Winsome in its appeal
5. Uncompromising against sin
6. Present pardon in Christ
7. Preached with energy and zeal
8. Delivered in marvelous expectancy
9. Utter reliance upon the Holy Spirit

If the pastor will follow these admonitions, he will have souls as his crown of rejoicing at most services.

Prayer and outreach ministries and evangelistic preaching will not fail. And how wonderful the results! Somebody who knew wrote these lines:

> When I enter that beautiful city,
> Far removed from earth's sorrow and fear;
> I want to hear somebody saying:
> It was YOU who invited me here.
>
> When to welcome me over the River,
> The loved ones of earth should draw near,
> I want to hear somebody whisper,
> It was YOU who invited me here.
>
> When the glad harps of heaven are ringing,
> With music so tender and clear,
> I want to have somebody singing;
> It was YOU who invited me here.
>
> To this happy home I might not have come
> Had YOU not invited me here.

The Pastor Extending the Invitation

As a famous London pastor lay dying, his friends gathered around and asked, "Do you have one last word for the world?" The loving pastor replied: "Yes, I do. Tell the pastors of the world this, 'O preacher, make it plain how a man can be saved!' "

When the pastor has shown the sinner that he is lost, when he has presented Christ's redemptive plan of salvation, then he is to draw the penitent into an open confession of his faith in Jesus (Matt. 10:32-33; Rom. 10:9-10). How does he do that effectively? How can the pastor extend an invitation that pulls at the heart-strings of a lost man? Here are some suggested things to consider.

1. It must be in the heart of the preacher to make appeal to his people. He must pray to this end that God will help him do it effectively. More than life the good pastor desires the salvation of the lost and the complete consecration of his congregation. The invitation must start in *him,* in his deepest soul. If the pastor has it in his heart to win his people, he will somehow know how to do it (John 7:17). The Holy Spirit will help him.

2. The sermon must lead up to this climactic consummation. Whatever the subject, the message must be turned to the need of the soul for the grace and mercy of God. This is not difficult, for the purpose of preaching is to lead men to give their hearts and lives to the way and will of God. Before the sermon begins, the ultimate end of appeal must be kept in view. The preacher is not just talking. He is preaching with a purpose. He is reaching for a verdict. He is a pleader for the souls of men. One of the corollaries of the invitation is to add substance and meaning to the pastor's message.

3. Many pastors close their sermons with a prayer while the heads of the people are bowed in prayer with him. In this prayer the preacher prays for the lost and for others who are to be included in the invitation. During the time while the people wait with bowed heads, the preacher can ask for those who are moved toward God to raise their hands, asking for remembrance in the intercession. The preacher can then appeal for a commitment after he leads the prayer.

4. At the end of the prayer the congregation can be asked to stand as the choir begins to sing the invitation hymn. Some preachers leave the congregation seated while the invitation hymn is sung, but that practice makes it difficult for some to reach the aisles. I have begun having the congregation stand with bowed heads at the conclusion of my sermon. While they are thus standing and praying, I pray with them and for them, then make the appeal for souls, whereupon the choir begins to sing the invitation song.

5. The invitation can be for anything the Spirit lays upon the heart of the pastor. Beside the appeal for the lost to confess their faith in the Lord, the invitation can be for baptism and church membership, for the transfer of church letters, for those who cannot get church letters to come forward by statement. The invitation can be for Christians to reconsecrate their lives to the Savior, for young people (and older people, too) to answer God's will for special service. The invitation can be for healing and for prayer. The pastor must be led by the Holy Spirit in the invitation he extends.

6. Music plays an all-important part in this appeal. How the

choir looks and acts at this time of response is destiny-determining. The choir must pray as earnestly as the pastor. They must feel the need and the desire for Christ to come into the hearts and lives of the people. At invitation time they are almost as important as the pastor in winning the lost.

7. Sometimes when I have made appeal for the lost in asking them to raise their hands for prayer, I first ask those who raised their hands to come forward. Then I ask those who did not raise their hands, but who want to be saved, to come forward. Often I ask a friend or relative to make a personal invitation to the lost to respond, quietly and prayerfully doing it as we sing with bowed heads. Sometimes I have made appeals for Christians to reconsecrate their lives to the Lord, reminding them that a lost man may (and usually will) follow you down to the front.

8. If our people in the church have prayed, invited, telephoned, taught in Sunday School, witnessed face to face with the lost and the unchurched, God never fails to bestow the harvest. After all, Jesus is in the business of saving souls. That is what he said (Luke 19:10).

9. The length of the invitation is in the will of God. As long as people are responding, the congregation will stay there in deepest interest forever. When the Spirit's work is done, the pastor ought to sense the time has come for the close of the appeal. To continue beyond that time is hurtful, but to close before that time could mean the eternal destruction of a lost soul. The pastor must be led by the Spirit.

The Genius of the Invitation

Because of the deep, everlasting consequences involved in the invitation at the end of the sermon, let me write of this all-important appeal at further length. Most pastors and preachers do not know how to extend an effective invitation. They are timid about it, fearful before it, and hesitant to press the appeal for Christ. Because of this lack of tremendous conviction and confidence, many pastors in many churches do not present an opportunity for the lost and the unchurched to come to the Savior. This is a tragedy, because any pastor can learn how to invite men to Christ and any evangelical congregation can be brought to a loving, praying care for souls. The answer lies in the hands of the pastor. What a responsibility he has to learn how!

Timidity and hesitancy in the pastor himself can defeat an invitation. Do not say, "Is there one here who will raise his hand for prayer?" Say rather, "How many will raise their hands for prayer?" If the meeting is in the church of the pastor, let him come down from the pulpit expecting to greet those who come; or, if he remains in the pulpit to press the appeal, let him arrange for others to come to the front in great expectancy.

Appeal to that lost man. His eternal soul is at stake. "What shall it profit a man, if he shall gain the whole world, and lose his own soul?" (Mark 8:36).

Joseph Addison Alexander wrote of the doomed man:

> There is a time, we know not when,
>   A point we know not where,
> That marks the destiny of men
>   For glory or despair.
>
> There is a line by us unseen,
>   That crosses every path,
> The hidden boundary between
>   God's patience and His wrath.

James Russell Lowell spoke of the present crisis, and God gives to each one of us a choice.

> Once to every man and nation
>   Comes the moment to decide,
> In the strife of truth with falsehood,
>   For the good or evil side.
>
> But to every man there openeth
>   A high way and a low
> And every man decideth
>   Which way his soul shall go.

How awesome our decision!

Give the invitation positively, affectionately. Tell the ones who listen what they should do, not what they should not do. In your appeal answer, "Yes, Lord, I will." "Yes, Lord, I am coming, now." "You mean to be saved sometime: be saved now. Jesus stands outside the door of your heart. Open that door. Say to him, 'Come in, Lord Jesus, come into my heart, come in today, come in to stay, come into my heart, Lord Jesus!' "

Make the sermon shorter and the invitation longer. Give emphasis to your teaching and preaching instruction to the congregation that they witness to and win souls for the Lord. The big event is conversion, salvation, regeneration, redemptive reconciliation, homecoming, accepting, receiving, believing! Make the emphasis come alive in the way you conduct the whole service.

In the invitation quote Scripture freely. Tell them what God says in love, in warning, in promises. Keep everything in an atmosphere of prayer; one can be saved sitting quietly, listening, praying.

Appeal to the lost man to find relief, release, rest. Earthly satisfactions are never deep and lasting. Restlessness, dissatisfaction, burden, are the costs of rejecting Christ. Jesus said:

Come unto me, all ye that labour and are heavy laden, and I will give you rest.

Take my yoke upon you, and learn of me; for I am meek and lowly in heart: and ye shall find rest unto your souls.

For my yoke is easy, and my burden is light (Matt. 11:28-30).

Appeal for victory in Christ. Many live defeated and broken lives, crushed by sinful habits, vicious lusts, a desire to be free, to experience mastery over self. The delivering, victorious Christ is able to set men free and to keep them by his power.

If the Son therefore shall make you free, ye shall be free indeed" (John 8:36).

I can do all things through Christ which strengtheneth me (Phil. 4:13).

Appeal on the basis of the sacrifice and love of Christ for us. He died for us, took our sins away on the cross. Have you ever thanked him for it?

Appeal on the basis of example for children. If one parent is a Christian and the other is not, it is difficult for children.

Appeal to honest investigation (John 7:17). If the Bible is right, then the unbeliever is wrong. He has everything to lose in this life and in the life to come. If the skeptic, atheist, and infidel are right (and they absolutely are not), then the Christian is still ahead—he has more joy and satisfaction in life.

Appeal to friendship and fellowship with Christ. The world is full of lonely people. Christ is the true friend. He leads to himself and to the fellowship in the church.

Remember, the gospel deserves a response, and Christ's call to men expects an answer.

Dr. Lee R. Scarborough, an evangelist in his own right, president of the Southwestern Baptist Theological Seminary, and professor of "The Chair of Fire" (the chair of evangelism), always did one thing in an evangelistic service: he got the people to move, to respond. I have watched him many times; he would make appeal after appeal until he gained an answer. If the service is stiff, hardened, and cold, it has to be broken up by the spirit of the preacher and the people of God. No sinner will respond in an iron, strait-jacketed service. God must move through his people.

Let the preacher extend the dry service, or continue the one blessed with souls, by saying, "If five will come for prayer, for reconsecration, for some one who is lost, we shall continue the appeal." Then if five come forward, the invitation can continue in power. He can say, "If ten shall come, we shall continue the appeal." In this way all have a deepening part in the length of the invitation.

The preacher can ask for all who are praying for someone in the congregation to be saved at the service, to come forward and pray for them. If there happened to be no one to respond (and what an indictment on the people of the church!) then he asks all the leaders of a department in the Sunday School, such as the Junior Division, to come forward and pray for the lost.

Each night at invitation time the pastor can invite a group to come forward for prayer. The first night it can be all the preachers present. The second night all the deacons. The third night all the staff and elected church leadership. And on it can continue throughout the period of services (or Sunday by Sunday). Their coming breaks a barrier sometimes felt in a hesitancy on the part of the lost to come down to the front in a confession of faith. It is also a revival in a revival.

With heads bowed for prayer, the preacher can ask all who will truly consecrate their lives to the Lord raise their hands. Then he can ask all who are willing to accept Christ as their Savior to raise their hands. Then he can ask both groups to come forward, the saved becoming an "escort," a "convoy," for the unsaved.

With heads bowed, ask four questions. First, all those who are members of *this* church raise your hands. Second, all those who are members of other churches in the city raise your hands. Third, all those who have their church membership out of town, raise your hands. Fourth, all those who belong to no church raise your hands. Talk, pray, and plead with the last two to respond to the appeal of Christ to come forward, be saved, or to join the church.

Many church members are tormented and afflicted with doubts about their salvation. Ask them to raise their hands if they want to be saved and know it. This is an appeal so needed for assurance of salvation.

The Many-faceted Invitation

The many-faceted invitation can follow numerous courses. Praying in hope that the pastor will consider these further suggestions, they are written here in the belief that they can be used in the services to bring men to Christ. No one pastor would seek to employ all of them, but any preacher can be encouraged in his soul-winning appeal by carefully studying them. So here are further ways to press the appeal for our Savior.

1. Invite Christians to remain for a prayer meeting (come forward for a prayer meeting). Invite them to bring their unsaved friends into the service, in a room, or at the front of the auditorium. Read a Scripture, sing a hymn, kneel in prayer. Have testimonies of those who have been blessed during their prayer meeting—ask if any have accepted Christ as Savior.

2. Appeal to the congregation while the invitation hymn is sung.

Those desiring to seek the Lord, come to the pastor who remains at the front before the pulpit, or to an announced room for an after-service.

3. With heads bowed, a solo is sung or the organ is played. All who have burdens to bear, need Christ's strength, need his cleansing power, raise their hands (or stand for prayer). Then ask them to come forward, with those accepting Christ as Savior. At the conclusion of the invitation, ask those who should have accepted Christ but did not to raise their hands for prayer. Say: "If some here who should have come forward but did not, we would like to pray for you before the service closes. You desire to keep the door of salvation open until you have entered. You do not mean to reject salvation finally, but intend to be saved, even though you do not tonight. If you would like to be remembered in prayer, raise your hands. We shall not ask more."

4. Ask Christians to raise their hands, then ask the unsaved to raise their hands.

Or ask Christians who wish prayer for unsaved loved ones or friends to raise their hands, then ask for those unsaved loved ones or friends to raise their hands. Invite these unsaved after the prayer to come to the front.

5. All bow their heads, ask Christians to raise their hands and quote John 3:16. This gives workers time to see whose hands are not raised.

Then ask for hands raised of Christians who are sorry they became Christians. This is a glorious testimony. No one is sorry; every Christian is glad. Then ask the unsaved to join this company of glad Christians.

6. With bowed heads and closed eyes, ask all who will accept Christ to stand for prayer. Then ask a Christian to stand with each one; then *all* come to the front.

7. Ask the praying Christians to stand who are asking God to save friends or loved ones so we may pray with them. Then before the prayer, ask the unsaved to stand as an indication of gratitude that people are praying for them.

8. In a sermon on Matthew 22:42, "What think ye of Christ?" weigh evidence for and against the claims of Christ as found in the New Testament. First, bring witnesses against Christ, the atheists,

infidels, skeptics, modernists, and quote their statements. Then call out the witnesses, one by one, to testify for Christ, the prophets, apostles, angels, Father's voice from heaven, martyrs, Christian leaders, scientists. The audience is the jury. Ask all who believe that Jesus Christ is an imposter, deceiver, not what he claimed to be, to stand. (If one should stand, thank him for his courage, tell him you have several books you would like for him to read.) Then ask all who believe Jesus Christ is all he claimed to be—Son of God, Savior of the world, very God of very God with all authority in heaven and in earth—to stand.

Invite those who have never before personally received and acknowledged Christ before men to come to the front during the hymn. If the Spirit leads, have all the Christians be seated after pleading for the unsaved to continue standing. Plead that they obey the words of Matthew 10:32-33 and Romans 10:9-10.

9. Ask various ages to stand. Emphasize the value of making a decision as early in life as possible. It becomes harder and harder as we grow older.

Demonstrate: those converted after 50 stand. Count.
those converted between 40-50 stand. Count.
those converted between 20-40 stand. Count.
those converted under 15, 10 stand. Count.

Now take the groups in reverse order. Those who became Christians under age fifteen stand again. Invite others in that age bracket who will now become Christians to stand. Go through all the age groups that way. Those standing for the first time, come forward.

10. Close the service with everyone praying. Saved, unsaved, those who had accepted the Savior, rise, give thanks to God. Come forward. With heads bowed, carefully, fully explain the plan of salvation. Having accepted Christ, come.

11. All bow heads, a duet is sung, or a solo such as "Precious Lord, Take My Hand." Ask the people to make whatever decision God indicates, rededicate themselves to Christ, forgive others, accept Christ as Savior, answer God's call. Then after the song, ask all who made some decision to raise their hands. Ask those who raised hands to come to the front.

12. Preach on Romans 10:9-10. Ask everyone in the house who

can honestly do so to stand and confess Christ in these words: "I am trusting Jesus Christ as my Savior and Lord," or "I believe God raised Jesus Christ from the dead and I am trusting him as my Savior and Lord." Ask all, one by one, in the house to make this confession. Encourage the unsaved to rise and make this confession along with others in token of their initial commitment to Christ. Scores of Christians can make their confession in a few minutes. (This should be done individually, not in groups or while seated.) Now bow heads in prayer and thank God for all who made their confession. Before concluding the prayer, ask for raised hands of all who made the confession the first time. These came forward.

13. If a child is the first to come, ask him publicly: "Do you believe Jesus died for you? Are you ready to receive Jesus as your Savior and Lord? Do you believe that he will receive you now? Are you willing to trust Jesus and serve him as long as you live? Are there other people here whom you would like to receive Jesus?" Then press the appeal for others to come.

14. At a big, special evangelistic convocation, invite deacons (or other leaders) to lead the way and come to the front, face the audience in a line on either side of the pastor. Invite Sunday School teachers to come to the front, face the audience, then all who will receive Christ to come stand by their teachers. Ask the teachers to say a word of encouragement (or go into the audience to speak with their pupils).

15. Invite recent converts to lead the way. They are new in the Christian life, glad, happy in Christ, and recommend Jesus to others. You might ask a new convert to give a word of testimony.

Invite aged Christians to come. Ask them if they are disappointed in Christ. Would they like to renounce the Christian faith? Abandon the Christian hope? What better evidence? Did you ever hear of a Christian giving up his Christian hope on a deathbed? Skeptics, blasphemers, die in terror but the Christian dies in sweet assurance.

16. Invite all Christians to come forward to pray. As Christians gather to the front, invite the unsaved to come with them, give you their hand, kneel for prayer and invitation. This can be used

toward the end of a revival and when the congregation is not too large.

17. Invite intercessors to come forward, those who are definitely praying for the salvation of loved ones or friends. Announce the invitation hymn, then invite those for whom prayer is being made to come to the front for prayer and instruction. Whether any lost come or not, have the prayer meeting.

Invite all the burdened to come to the front, those who need prayer for themselves or for loved ones and friends. Speak of the necessity for asking in order to receive. Invite those to come who are confused regarding salvation, who need assurance and victory. Dismiss the audience, then pray with these.

18. After the message, have a moment or two of silent prayer. Then any anxious souls can raise their hands to be remembered in prayer. Then have the hymn of invitation, inviting those to come forward.

Prolonged seeking is unnecessary, unscriptural. God is ready to save any soul instantly if that soul is ready to accept the free gift of salvation. We do not have to persuade God—God has been reconciled to the sinner. The perfect, finished work of Christ on the cross is for our complete salvation (2 Cor. 5:21; John 1:12; 5:24; 6:37).

19. Extend an invitation to young people. Ask those who have already publicly given their lives to full-time service to come to the front. Then invite those who also feel called and who are seriously considering a call. Then ask those who have never definitely felt the call to full-time Christian service but are willing to enter it if God should call them to come forward. Then appeal to unsaved young people to receive the Lord Jesus as Savior and come to stand by these.

20. On an appropriate occasion, extend an invitation, after a sermon on 1 Corinthians 9:24-27; 2 Timothy 2:1-5; Hebrews 12:1-2. Appeal for a team of nine or eleven Christians to come to the front who can recommend Christ and stand as witnesses. If more than eleven come, welcome them all. Cheerleaders are usually girls—can they recommend Christ? Let a dozen or more come to the front. Then invite the unsaved to come forward.

214 CRISWELL'S GUIDEBOOK FOR PASTORS

21. Preach on the cross. Arrange for a lighted cross. All lights are turned out except those lighting the cross. The organist plays "The Old Rugged Cross" or "Near the Cross." Extend the invitation, having the people come to the cross. Some may find it easier to come forward in the semidarkness.

22. After a sermon on assurance of salvation, ask all who have the assurance to come and shake the hand of the pastor. As they come, invite others who lack assurance to come, remaining at the front. Then invite the unsaved to come. Those who do not want to die unsaved, come. Maybe they are not ready to receive Christ now, but plan to do so some day, come.

23. Use the story of Samuel's call. Have worthy Christians testify how God saved them in youth. Ask those who gave testimonies to remain in the front. Bow heads in prayer. As God calls, speak to each heart, ask those who hear God's call in their hearts to come forward. Then sing an invitation hymn, asking all others to come who will trust Jesus.

Lead in a prayer that all repent: "Lord Jesus, I am a sinner lost and perishing, but I come to thee. I now receive thee as my personal Savior. Save me from my sin; make me thy child; give me eternal life; write my name in the book of life; receive me into thy kingdom. Help me to confess thee before men and to love thee as long as I live. Thank thee, Lord, for hearing and answering my prayer, for Jesus' sake, Amen."

24. On a decision day in a Sunday School department, the pastor brings a short message to the whole assembly. Then dismiss the group to their several classes where the teachers offer prayer and explanation, seeking to win their pupils to Christ. At a signal the classes reassemble. All those who took Christ as Savior stand, and come forward as an indication they received Christ. Sing a song, then invite others who will accept Christ to come. If no one responds, ask the Sunday School teachers or other Christian leaders who wish to be better teachers to come, and give the pastor their hand.

The Pastor Receiving New Converts

1. Every one who comes forward at the preacher's invitation ought to be prayed with or talked with individually. This can be

the work of the godly deacons, of the pastor's fellow ministers, and of others chosen for their spiritual understanding. It is a serious moment when souls turn to seek Christ. The pastor and his people must realize this and ask the Spirit's leadership in dealing with them. Whether in a counseling room, or at the mourner's bench, or in some kind of an after service, or seated together in a pew, the souls who come forward must be under the care, love, and concern of the pastor. He must receive them as trophies of grace and care for them as the doctor and the nurse would do for a newborn babe. Their needs are as different as there are people. They are not to be looked upon as bucketsful, oceansful, nameless aggregate, but rather as individual souls for whom Christ died. Their counseling after they have responded to the invitation is too important not to be earnestly provided for by the pastor.

2. The presentation of new members to the church ought to be done with rejoicing. If the pastor has prayed and worked and visited with his people, he cannot help but be overwhelmed with gladness at the harvest.

When I came to the church here in Dallas, the congregation greatly noticed how I received new members. They were not accustomed to such rejoicing and welcoming. Some of them said to me, "How much better to say, 'God bless you,' shake their hand, and conclude by saying, 'You may now be seated.' " If I did that now, the church would think I had lost my joy in the Lord. Each convert, each new member, is presented one by one with words of infinite welcome.

The recruit has now enlisted in the army of the Lord. He is ready to be trained in spiritual warfare and become a full-fledged fighting soldier for Jesus. That teaching and training is the assignment of the church. It is a lifelong task that must be done faithfully and carefully.

Some Things That Help the Pastor's Soul-winning Ministry

Open for the pastor to use are some marvelous procedures that not only help the church in its soul-winning ministries, but also build faith and Christian character in the people who share in them. Here are some of the activities.

1. Any pastor will succeed gloriously in his work or any evangelist if he is able to build a personal soul-winning program with his people. There can be no substitute for the personal, individual witnessing of the people of God.

No logical argument ever offered is so powerful as the warm-hearted love of a mother for her children, or the tears in devoted eyes pleading for the Savior.

No sermon ever preached could take the place of a pastor. Paul went from house to house, with many tears, testifying to all who opened the door of repentance toward God and faith toward our Lord Jesus Christ (Acts 20:20-21,31).

No tract in the world was ever so effective as the track of a man's footsteps on the threshold of a neighbor's home.

No attack against sin and Satan was ever so deadly as the knock of a soul-winner at a door of his friend. Earth's portals are shaken and hell's foundations quiver at the sound of the soul-winner's voice.

With all our organization, plans, drives, campaigns, sermons, choir's songs, and everything else attendant to worship services, this is first and foremost, that the people themselves offer to God the personal testimony of their souls. What says Revelation 12:11? "And they overcame him [the dragon] by the blood of the Lamb, and by the word of their testimony." Nothing however perfected can substitute for personality. It is the tone of the voice, the flash of the eye, the clasp of the hand, the bended knee, the knock at the door that moves the heart Godward. A man may easily battle against logic, refuse argument, spurn organization, but personal love expressed in tears and tenderness has in it the power of God.

If the pastor is to have a soul-winning church, it must be one where personal testimony is preached as a life-style, the order of every day. It must spring from the heartbreak of a mother for her child, a father for his family, the pastor for his flock, the teacher for her class, the lawyer for his partner, the man next door for his neighbor.

Jesus came from earth to heaven, God in the flesh, visiting and witnessing from city to city, from house to house (Luke 19:10).

The eternal picture of our Lord is in Revelation 3:20, knocking at the door of the human heart.

He taught us as sowers to go forth into the field to plant the word of life, not wait for the field to come to us to be sowed.

He taught us as fishers of men to launch out into the deep and let down our nets, not wait for the fish to jump up into a boat.

He taught us as shepherds to seek the lost sheep until we find it, not build a fine sheepfold on the edge of the wilderness, and if some stray sheep happens to come along, wander in, and be saved.

Our Lord's great word was to "Go."

2. Another program to help the pastor in his soul-winning ministry is the neighborhood prayer meeting. Every revival meeting ought to be preceded by these periods and places of intercession. Anytime and any place where two or more are gathered together is a good time and a good place to pray. Have a leader sing a Christian hymn, read from the Bible, ask for special requests, then all (if possible) take part in the intercession.

3. The home group Bible study is a powerful instrument in the hands of the pastor for soul-winning. The number of these is only limited by the number of qualified, dedicated leaders willing to lead them. Choose a home (or homes), invite all in the geographical area to come, have each one to bring a dessert (or the host provides a little something for refreshments), then let the chosen teacher open God's blessed Word for the group, all participating in the study. These home Bible classes can reach friends and neighbors otherwise uninterested in attending church. Under the direction of the pastor, these home meetings can be marvelously useful (but always under the surveillance of the pastor).

4. The most spectacular of all the adjuncts in soul-winning is the revival crusade. They command the utmost of our genius, talent, publicity, prayer, organization, music, preaching, and everything else that pertains to the kingdom of God. The purpose is to proclaim the gospel through every means possible to every person possible, especially to persons not ordinarily contacted by the church.

We are concerned about the social and ethical transformation of society. We believe, however, that the only ultimate transformation of society can occur as a result of individual regeneration with appropriate teachings of the principles of Jesus Christ over and over again to those who have been renewed by faith in him as Savior and Lord. As one great leader has written, "To talk of changing society may sound visionary and unrealistic, however, to think of changing society without changing individuals is utterly absurd." Therefore, through evangelistic campaigns, in addition to many other facets of church evangelism and development, we seek to lead individuals to a personal confrontation with Christ that will result in conversion and in their commitment to Christ as Lord.

5. One other great adjunct in helping the pastor do the work of an evangelist is the prospect file. These prospects can be gained from newcomer files kept by the utility companies, from a city census, from an inside census (asking every Sunday School member to give the name and address of a prospect), from church visitor cards signed by visitors at the worship services, and from families and friends who are burdened for the welfare of the lost and unchurched.

It has been suggested to me that the pastor ought to define what we call a "prospect" for our church. A prospect is not someone who is active in another church and who says that sometime he would like to visit our congregation because he has heard so much about us. Rather, a prospect is someone who is not attending any church or someone who has moved to the city and who does not have a church home. There are many people who say that they belong to certain denominations; but when you ask further, you, learn that they were christened into the denomination as an infant and have never been converted or actively identified with the work of the Lord. These people are also prospects. They need to be won to Christ; they need to be taught the way of the Lord. If God will help us to mediate the saving grace of the gospel of Jesus, we ought to offer ourselves as instruments in his hands to lead them to our Savior.

We immediately follow up all church visitors who indicate on the card an interest in us.

We use our teenagers to survey neighborhoods in a door-to-door census.

We constantly use our Sunday School in age-group visitation.

The discerning, caring pastor has many people to help him in many ways if he will let the Holy Spirit guide him in these soul-winning approaches.

14

The Pastor's Concern for Children

Children As a Heritage from the Lord

It would be impossible to emphasize too much the importance of children in the life and destiny of the church. They are the only material out of which God makes his preachers, missionaries, church members, and kingdom workers. They are the race itself, the church itself, and the redeemed of God itself, tomorrow. He is a wise pastor who takes time for their care and upbringing.

Is not this according to the word of the Lord? The psalmist said:

Lo, children are an heritage of the Lord: and the fruit of the womb is his reward.

As arrows are in the hand of a mighty man; so are children of the youth.

Happy is the man that hath his quiver full of them: they shall not be ashamed, but they shall speak with the enemies in the gate (Ps. 127:3-5).

Of the Lord Jesus it is written:

And Jesus called a little child unto him, and set him in the midst of them,

And said, Verily I say unto you, Except ye be converted; and become as little children, ye shall not enter into the kingdom of heaven.

Whosoever therefore shall humble himself as this little child, the same is greatest in the kingdom of heaven,

And whoso shall receive one such little child in my name receiveth me.

But whoso shall offend one of these little ones which believe in me, it were better for him that a millstone were hanged about his neck, and that he were drowned in the depth of the sea.

255

Take heed that ye despise not one of these little ones; for I say unto you, That in heaven their angels do always behold the face of my Father which is in heaven.

For the Son of man is come to save that which was lost.

Even so it is not the will of your Father which is in heaven, that one of these little ones should perish (Matt. 18:2-6,10-11,14).

The Pastor Who Notices Children

1. He is a smart as well as a wise pastor who notices the children in the family. Pastor, speak to the children by name if possible. Take time to make them feel welcome to come to speak to you. There is no compliment that is ever afforded the pastor that is more precious than that a child feels drawn to him. Such a friendship establishes later the rapport that is needed for the child to share his decision for Christ with the pastor and with the church.

2. When a family moves to town, call the child by telephone. Better still, if you know the family is coming, call the child by long-distance telephone. Such a kindness will overwhelm every member of the family, that you thought to do such a thing. There is a tremendously gifted executive who has belonged to our dear church for years. When I learned he was moving to our city, I called his boy. I told him all about our church with its camp, retreats, recreational areas, everything. When the family arrived in town and Sunday came, that boy proudly and emphatically announced: "I don't know about you, but *I* am going to the First Baptist Church. Dr. Criswell is a personal friend of mine!" He was only nine years old! Having the boy, we had them all.

3. When the pastor visits in a home for any reason (a death in the family, to win a prospect), let him be sure to draw the children into the circle of discussion and witness. Pray for the child as you pray for the rest of the family. When the family joins the church, make much of the children in the group. They are *really* important and make everybody feel that way.

4. The pastor ought to be a part of all the activities that are planned for the children. The whole world ought to know of his deep interest. By announcement from the pulpit of their activities, by public prayer for their happy training and teaching, with words of commendation and appreciation for their adult leadership, let

the pastor be forever identified with the children's work in the church.

The pastor ought to visit the children's classes and departments whenever possible—Sunday School, Church Training, RA's, GA's, Mission Friends, all of them. In Vacation Bible School, for example, speak to all the groups from the youngest to the oldest. Such a pastoral concern will not only build a beautiful relationship with the children, but will also express appreciation for the adult leadership.

With the children do not be afraid to be a part of a fun situation if it will enable you to communicate with them later one. If acting clownish at a retreat or a camp or a party will establish a good rapport with the children, do it. Do not be afraid to laugh—at yourself or at something that happens. A child (like an adult) moves very quickly from hilarity to serious attention. Their loud cheering and laughter and applause only sets the stage for your saving message. Children will listen to you when you stand up to preach on Sunday if they have had a good time with you on Saturday.

When a function is planned for children, let the pastor give them his attention and time. Do not let the adults preempt his time away from the kids. This is *their* time.

A child, like an adult, responds to personal attention. Write a personal message in the child's Bible, for example, if you have opportunity.

Have your picture made with the youngster whenever occasions arise. Especially is this an effective thing to do when the child comes in for his baptismal conference with the pastor, when he is baptized, and even at childrens' parties.

The pastor will never make a mistake by emphasizing by every way possible the activities planned for children. Children's music programs, children's Christmas hours, Easter and Christmas baptismal services, special evangelistic appeals, these and a thousand other interesting things can make the child literally delight in the church.

Folks said the downtown church in Dallas could never be a children's church. Who would bring a child so far? It was an adult church and was forever destined to remain that way (that is, if it lived at all). But God blessed the children's program that was begun years ago. Our church is now a children's church with hundreds and hundreds of babies and Beginners and Primaries and Juniors. It can be done anywhere.

5. In the pulpit it is always good for the pastor to use illustrations from his own childhood. Youngsters notice that immediately and identify with the truth the preacher is proclaiming. On the way home after church many families discuss the message delivered at the worship hour. A story that involves children gives the parents a splendid opportunity to talk to their youngsters about the services and about the meaning of the message.

And it is not beside the point to remember that children love color. The pastor ought to think about wearing eye-appealing clothing. The pastor should not look like a gravedigger and an undertaker all the time. Brighten things up with a pretty tie and a handkerchief to match!

The Children's Programs

All the programs for children in the church ought to have an outreaching, evangelistic appeal. Everything done ought to mean something for Christ.

The first and most important program for children in the church is the Sunday School. This work must be prayerfully and carefully furthered. Reaching a child for the teaching ministry on Sunday will enable the pastor to reach a whole family. I have never seen a baby come to church by itself. Beyond the baby are father, mother, brothers, sisters, grandparents, aunts, uncles, cousins, and a whole array of everybodies.

In our children's divisions we have multiple departments for each grade group. Although women superintend most of the Nursery and Beginner departments (with several exceptions where men lead), beginning with the Primary Division the departments are directed by men. Each department has classes with a man teaching boys and a woman teaching girls.

There are many gifted women who could ably lead these departments but we have used men in order to:

1. Give these children a fine example of a man who will lovingly serve the Lord. Many times these children have no such father in

the home. Remember, it is easy for a child to get the idea that church is only for women and children.

2. Using men in places of leadership has helped us to develop the young men who join our church.

3. A man who is in a place of leadership will lead his family to stay in the church.

We use this same philosophy in staffing our training hour departments.

Possibly a typical review of the many other children's programs in the church can be seen in some of the things the Junior Division does.

1. Our fall program provides a Western roundup where the boys and girls bring their friends and family for a fun time and the pastor closes the evening with a special word around the campfire, encouraging the boys and girls and their friends and parents to get back into the work of our church after their long summer holidays.

2. At Christmastime, the month of December begins with our boys and girls having an old-fashioned Christmas Day at our encampment. They hunt mistletoe, cut down a few straggly trees, have a world of fun, eat an old-fashioned Christmas dinner, and then are a part of an evangelistic emphasis where a gifted missionary will make an appeal for Jesus. The pastor will help in the invitation time. He will be a part of the day. Or, they may go out overnight to our camp for a winter minicamp. A number of missionaries will be gathered to teach them. Then they will have an evangelistic service, giving the boys and girls and their special guests an opportunity to trust in the Lord as Savior or to give their lives for some special place of service.

3. In February the division will have a day when they bring the boys and girls together to give extra time to memorizing a prescribed course in the Scriptures. They will then have a time for the youngsters to skate after their time of study and memorizing.

4. Retreats in the springtime have been invaluable in gathering children together for a day of playing ball, flying kites, hiking, and a dozen other kinds of play. This will be during the morning. In the afternoon the leaders plan a special way to present the pastor to these children so that they relate to him in a happy, fun

way. The pastor may be "Bat Man" or "Big Bird" or a gorilla or a rabbit or something that the kids are caught up in at the time. Whatever, it is employed in such a way that the kids feel that their pastor is interested in what they are interested in. Then, after a fun time like this, the pastor or an invited speaker will talk to them about the Lord Jesus and make an appeal. Many of them will respond.

A youngster was being counseled by one of our missionaries during the summer camp. When the missionary inquired about the time the child had been saved, the child replied, "Oh, yes, I know that I have been saved. Jesus saved me at Junior Retreat the year Dr. Criswell was the rabbit."

5. Our summer camp program involves hundreds of our boys and girls. The camp has been instrumental in more young men and women going into the ministry, in mission service, or in other Christian service than any other program of our church. I believe in the camp program and diligently promote it. I spend time with the campers each year.

Every boy and girl from our church has the privilege of bringing someone who does not belong to our church to our camp. We have gained a large number of families through the influence the camp had on these boys and girls who became acquainted with us through this activity.

6. Our Vacation Bible School departments are set up so that boys go to one department for their age group and the girls go to another. This has been instrumental in our reaching kids who like being with his or her "own kind." And I find that the teachers in these Vacation Bible School departments like working just with boys or just with girls. One superintendent who has directed sixth grade boys has been a superintendent of boys for twenty-two years. He likes it and the kids like it.

The Dedication of a Baby

Nothing is more meaningful or more beautiful than the dedication of a baby at the stated worship services of the church. The father and mother come forward with the child and the group is presented to the waiting congregation, along with all the other members of the family who are present. They all kneel, with the father holding the child in his arms. The pastor then prays a dedicatory prayer, giving the child to God, and pleading in behalf of the Christian family that the child will be reared in the love and admonition of the Lord. A little white Bible, or another small remembrance can then be presented to the parents.

The Child's Public Response at Church Services

1. A good rule to go by in a child's expressed desire to go forward in response to an invitation to accept Christ is this: be grateful that the heart of the child is thus moved Godward and Christward and heavenward. Never interdict the response with such answers as, "You are too young," or "You do not understand," or "Wait awhile," or "Some later time." Anytime is a good time and an acceptable time when a child wants to move toward God. Encourage him with the loving and enthusiastic words, "Wonderful! let us go."

But what if the child is very young? When he says, "I want to tell the pastor that I love Jesus; I feel in my heart that Jesus loves me," he may be only a few years old. Let the youngster come forward with rejoicing on the part of everyone. We call that "A Step Toward God." We have a place on the decision card for that to be marked. In the days and years that follow, the child can be led into a consciousness and confession of sin, of being lost, and of accepting Jesus as his personal Savior. But for the moment, the child "loves Jesus" and desires the whole world to know the precious fact that he does.

2. When the day comes that the child has a conversion experience, then at the invitation in the church service he comes forward, openly confessing his faith in the Lord Jesus as his personal Savior. This public confession of Christ is in accordance with the mandate written in the Holy Scriptures. Jesus says in Matthew:

Whosoever therefore shall confess me before men, him will I confess also before my Father which is in heaven.
But whosoever shall deny me before men, him will I also deny before my Father which is in heaven (Matt. 10:32-33).

Paul wrote of salvation in Romans:

That if thou shalt confess with thy mouth the Lord Jesus, and shalt believe in thine heart that God hath raised him from the dead, thou shalt be saved.

For with the heart man believeth unto righteousness; and with the mouth confession is made unto salvation (Rom. 10:9-10).

Having repented of our sins and accepted Jesus in our hearts, we are publicly to confess him with our mouths.

It is a good and a beautiful thing for the family to come forward with the child and, kneeling down with him, join in the prayer of the pastor as he thanks God for the heavenly decision. After the prayer, the child is presented to the church as a new convert. He is then publicly given a little book I have written entitled, *Joining the Church*. The child is then placed in a new members class for children. There he studies the book for six weeks under the direction of a godly teacher. After the six weeks course is finished, an appointment is made with the pastor to visit with him about the doctrines learned in the book. The appointment includes the parents who are to bring the child with them. At the meeting in the pastor's office, when then the pastor sees that the child is well prepared for baptism and for church membership, a time is set for the family to come forward to present the child for baptism and church membership and a time is set for the administration of the holy ordinance.

3. The child's visit to the study of the pastor is hopefully a great event in the life of the child, but most certainly in the ministry of the pastor. It gives him a beautiful opportunity to visit with the family, talking about the things of God and especially about the rearing of the child. The bold truth about the whole arrangement is this: the parents may need to know about conversion, baptism, and church membership as much as the child.

During this session with the child and with the parents present, the pastor is by no means to let the conference be taken up with "adult talk." Sometimes the parents want to "just talk." The conference is mostly for the child, and he needs to feel and to know that he and he alone is the center of the love, concern, prayer, and attention that brings the group together. Let the pastor give the child the time that he needs.

If the child is plainly not ready for baptism, if he does not know the book, and if he does not realize what he is doing, then the pastor can arrange for another conference with the family. The teacher of the new members' class or the responsible staff member can be made aware of the situation and can follow up on all the things necessary for the full instruction of the child. No child should ever be baptized who does not realize what he is doing.

4. Why should a child be encouraged to come forward at the church service two different times? One time to accept Jesus publicly as Savior and the second time to be received for baptism and church membership? The answer arises out of the long years of my pastoral work with children. Youngsters often have the unstated idea that they are saved by becoming church members. Most of us sadly realize that the average church usually has far too many members who have had no regenerating experience with Christ. Though members of the church they are still unsaved. For the child to be baptized and to become a member of the church and not be saved is tragic.

In seeking to be certain that the child knows that to be saved is one thing (Jesus only can wash our sins away and save our souls from hell), and to be a church member is another thing (the preacher can do that, make a church member by baptizing the candidate upon the authority of the congregation), I used to try to teach this truth to the youngster by saying: "See, I have *two* hands, not one hand. This hand represents what it is to be saved. This other hand represents what it is to be baptized and to be a church member. They are two different hands; thus conversion and church membership are two different things." But try as I might, I still could not teach the doctrinal truth effectively. It was then that I decided to have the child *do* two different things. One time he comes forward confessing Jesus as Savior, repenting of his sins, and asking the Lord to forgive him and to save him, to come into his heart forever. This is conversion, salvation, regeneration. The other time the child comes forward, after his conference with the pastor, is to join the church by baptism. This procedure accomplished the purpose in the best and most meaningful way I have ever known.

5. Let me add an emphatic word about the conference the child has with the pastor before baptism. I cannot underscore too heavily or too much the marvelous spiritual blessings that accrue

from that meeting. It helps the pastor become more familiar with the people of his congregation. He gets to know the children. The meeting strengthens the ties of the family to the church. It gives the pastor an opportunity to clarify any misunderstanding on the part of the child or of the family concerning salvation and church membersip. And it also provides the pastor with a unique opportunity to encourage parents who need to make decisions for Christ to do so.

The Important Teaching Instrument, *Joining the Church*

Because of the importance of the little booklet *Joining the Church* in the development of the Christian experience of the child, it is published here word for word.

First is a brief introduction from my own life's experience:

When I was a little boy and gave my heart to the Lord, I was immediately baptized; but no one said anything to me about the meaning of the holy ordiance. It was only in after years that I learned it's true and beautiful significance. I made a resolution when I began my pastoral ministry that every child who came forward to be baptized would be faithfully taught the scriptural meaning of the ordinance. This little book is the fruit of that resolution. May it prove a blessing to every child and to everyone who studies it.

Then follows the four chapters of the book, "What It Means to Be Saved," "What It Means to Be Baptized," "What It means to Take the Lord's Supper," and "What It Means to Be a Good Church Member." Each chapter is followed by questions and answers that the child (and an adult for that matter) ought to learn.

CHAPTER I

WHAT IT MEANS TO BE SAVED

Without Christ as my Savior I am a condemned sinner (John 3:18). I am utterly lost (John 3:36). As a condemned sinner I am spiritually dead (Ephesians 2:1). I have no hope and I am without God in the world (Ephesians 2:12).

But when Christ comes into my heart, He forgives my sin

(Acts 10:43), He writes my name in the Book of Life (Revelation 21:27), He saves my soul (Luke 19:10). Believing in Christ as my Savior, I am a new creation (II Corinthians 5:17). I am a child of God (John 1:12).

For Christ to be a Savior to me I must realize that I am a lost sinner and that He came into the world to save me (Isaiah 53:6; I Timothy 1:15; Matthew 1:21). I am saved forever by repenting of my sins (Luke 13:3) and believing in Jesus as my Savior (John 3:14-16; John 5:24; Acts 20:21; II Timothy 1:12).

When I repent of my sins and ask Jesus to save me, I am immediately and publicly to confess Him as my Savior and Lord (Matthew 10:32-33; Romans 10:9-10).

QUESTIONS AND ANSWERS

Question: From what does Jesus save us?

Answer: From our sins. (Mark 2:1-11; Matthew 26:28; I John 1:7).

Question: What is sin?

Answer: Sin is disobedience to God, or breaking of the law of God. (I John 3:4).

Question: Who has sinned?

Answer: All of us have sinned. I have sinned. We all have sinned. (Romans 3:10,23).

Question: What is the penalty for my sins?

Answer: Death. (Ezekiel 18:4; Romans 6:23). I die two ways; one, my body dies (if I did not sin, I would never die); two, my soul dies. I am separated from God forever. The Bible calls that the second death, hell.

Question: How can I be saved from this death?

Answer: I can be saved from eternal death by trusting Jesus as my Savior. I am sorry for my sin and turn from it (this is repentance) and look to Jesus to forgive me (this is saving faith). (Acts 16:30-31).

Question: Do I work for this great salvation?

Answer: I do not work for my salvation. It is a free gift of

God. It is wholly of grace. I just receive it; I just take it; I just accept it. My salvation is something God gives me through faith in Jesus Christ. (Romans 4:2-5; Ephesians 2:8-9).

Question: Why should I seek to do good works?

Answer: Because Jesus has saved me and I seek to honor Him in my life. (Ephesians 2:10; James 2:26; John 15:14). If I am truly saved, I will obey my Lord. Good works are the result of my salvation, not the means by which I obtain it. Only after the tree is made good, can it bring forth good fruit. (Matthew 12:33).

Question: What are the steps of salvation as we turn in saving faith to Jesus?

Answer: The steps of salvation are
(1) Repentance: Being sorry for my sin and turning from my sin to Jesus.
(2) Faith: Accepting Jesus as my Savior.
(3) Confession: Publicly declaring my faith in Jesus.

CHAPTER II

WHAT IT MEANS TO BE BAPTIZED

The "doctrines" of a church are its beliefs and teachings. The "ordinances" of a church are its observances, called "ordinances" because Christ commanded or "ordered" them. In a New Testament church there are two "ordinances." These two ordinances are baptism and the Lord's Supper.

Baptism is a burial and a resurrection. We are buried with Christ in the likeness of His death and we are raised with Christ in the likeness of His resurrection. (Romans 6:23; Colossians 2:12; Galatians 3:27). It shows forth three things:

1. It portrays or pictures the death, burial, and resurrection of Jesus.

2. It portrays or pictures our death to sin and our resurrection to a new life in Christ.
3. It proclaims our faith. Our faith is that if we die and are buried, we shall be raised from the dead by the power of the Lord.

Baptism is the first of the two church ordinances. It is the doorway into the church. We are all baptized by the Holy Spirit into the body of Christ. The body of Christ is His church. Water baptism portrays that work of the Spirit that adds us to the body of Christ (1 Corinthians 12:13).

QUESTIONS AND ANSWERS

Question: Who baptized Jesus?
Answer: John the Baptist. (Matthew 3:1)
Question: Where was Jesus baptized?
Answer: In the Jordan River. (Matthew 3:13)
Question: Why was Jesus baptized?
Answer: To fulfill all righteousness. (Matthew 3:15)
Question: What is baptism?
Answer: It is a burial and a resurrection. (Colossians 2:12)
Question: What is the meaning of baptism?
Answer: It pictures three things: (Romans 6:23; Galatians 3:27)
           1. It pictures the death, burial, and resurrection of Jesus.
           2. It pictures our death to sin and our resurrection to a new life in Christ.
           3. It pictures our faith that if we die and are buried we shall also be raised from the dead.
Question: Does Jesus command us to be baptized?
Answer: Yes. According to His Great Commission in Matthew 28:18-20, all are to be baptized who accept Jesus as their Savior.
Question: In what name are we commanded to be baptized?
Answer: In the name of the Father and of the Son and of the Holy Spirit (Matthew 28:19)

Question: In Acts 8:26-39, what was the first thing the eunuch wanted to do after he heard the gospel of Jesus?

Answer: He wanted to be baptized. (Acts 8:36)

Question: What was the one requirement he had to meet before he could be baptized?

Answer: To believe in Jesus with all his heart. (Acts 8:37)

Question: How was the eunuch baptized?

Answer: He was lowered beneath the baptismal waters (buried with Christ) and he was raised out of the baptismal waters (resurrected with Christ). (Acts 8:38-39)

Question: According to Acts 2:41; 10:44-48, who should be baptized?

Answer: Those who have repented of their sins and have accepted Jesus as their Savior.

Question: Are we lost if we are not baptized?

Answer: The Bible says we are lost if we do not repent (Luke 13:3). The Bible says we are lost if we fail to believe on Jesus (John 3:18). Nowhere does the Bible say we are lost if we are not baptized.

Question: Why, then, should we be baptized?

Answer: Because of our love for the Savior, Jesus Himself set the example and Jesus Himself commanded us to be baptized. Baptism is an act of obedience on the part of one who believes in Jesus.

Question: How is baptism rightly administered?

Answer: The believer is immersed in water, in the name of the Father and of the Son and of the Holy Spirit. This is according to the institution of Christ and the practice of the Lord's apostles.

CHAPTER III

WHAT IT MEANS TO TAKE THE LORD'S SUPPER

The second (and recurring) church ordinance is the Lord's Supper. It was instituted by our Savior the night in which He was betrayed and delivered to die for our sins on the cross (Matthew 26:20-30). We are not saved by partaking of the Supper. It is a memorial of the death of Christ, that we may ever remember his sacrifice for us (I Corinthians 10:16).

Who may take the Lord's Supper? Those who have trusted Jesus as their Savior and who have been baptized in obedience to His command. In the Great Commission recorded in Matthew 28:19-20, three things are very plain: first, we are to make disciples (the literal translation) of all nations; second, we are to baptize these converts in the name of the Father and of the Son and of the Holy Spirit; third, we are to teach these converts to observe the things Jesus has commanded us, one of those things commanded being the observance of the Lord's Supper. The order Jesus gave is very plain. It is one, two, three. One, we must trust in Jesus, become a disciple of Jesus. Two, we are to be baptized, "buried with the Lord, raised with the Lord." Three, we are to observe the things Christ has given us to keep, one of which is the Lord's Supper.

This order of one, two, three is as much inspired as the content of the Great Commission. Before I have the privilege of taking the Lord's Supper I must (first) be converted, I must (second) be baptized, then I am ready (third) to sit at the Lord's table.

QUESTIONS AND ANSWERS

Read 1 Corinthians 11:23-29

Question: What are the two elements of the Lord's Supper?

Answer: Bread and "the fruit of the vine" (Matthew 26:29) the red juice of crushed grapes held in a cup.

Question: What do these two elements symbolize?

Answer: The bread represents the body of Christ and the cup represents the blood of Christ.

Question: Why are these two elements *not* the actual body and blood of Jesus?

Answer: Because when Jesus instituted the Lord's Supper and said these words, His body was standing before the disciples and His blood was still coursing through His veins. The bread and the cup ''show forth the Lord's death.'' The very words ''in remembrance of me'' suggest their symbolic nature. Jesus said He was ''the door'' (John 10:9), ''the vine'' (John 15:1), ''the Good Shepherd'' (John 10:11), and we understand perfectly what He meant. We understand also the symbolic meaning of His words regarding the bread and the cup.

Question: How often should we observe the memorial of the Lord's Supper?

Answer: Jesus left that to us. He said, ''as often as ye eat this bread and drink this cup . . .'' We could observe the Lord's Supper every day, every week, every month, every quarter.

Question: How should we take the Lord's Supper?

Answer: We should take the Lord's Supper in deepest humility and reverence. The adverb ''unworthily'' (notice it is not an adjective) in I Corinthians 11:27-29 refers to our manner of observing the ordinance, not our own worth. Because we are sinners and the sacrifice of Christ has made atonement for our sins, we observe the Lord's Supper in overflowing love and gratitude.

Question: What is meant by the words in I Corinthians 11:26, ''till he come''?

Answer: The words ''till he come'' plainly teach us that our Lord Jesus will come a second time, which is the joy and hope of all those who truly believe in Jesus (Acts 1:11; I Thessalonians 4:16).

CHAPTER IV

WHAT IT MEANS TO BE A GOOD CHURCH MEMBER

A church is not the building in which the people meet. A church is a congregation of baptized believers voluntarily associated together for the purpose of proclaiming the Gospel, observing the ordinances, and fellowshipping the love and grace of the Lord Jesus. Jesus founded the church (Matthew 16:18) and so loved it that He gave Himself for it (Acts 20:28; Ephesians 5:25).

QUESTIONS AND ANSWERS

Question: As a church member should I attend the services of the church?

Answer: According to Hebrews 10:25, "Not forsaking the assembling of ourselves together" I must faithfully attend the services of the church.

Question: As a church member should I witness for Jesus?

Answer: According to Luke 24:45-48, Acts 1:8, we are to witness to the saving grace of Jesus to everyone everywhere.

Question: As a church member should I read my Bible and pray every day?

Answer: According to John 5:39, Acts 17:11, I Timothy 4:13-16, Revelation 1:3, I am faithfully to read my Bible and, according to Luke 18:1, I Thessalonians 5:17, I am to pray always.

Question: Does God have a plan for me to support the church?

Answer: According to I Corinthians 16:1-2, I am every first day of the week (Sunday) to give to God a proportionate part of my income. The people of God under the law gave at least a tenth (Leviticus 27:30-33). Those who love Jesus will give even more. It is a holy privilege to give (II Corinthians 8:9; II Corinthians 9:6-7).

The Prayer That Closes the Conference
of Pastor with Child

After my conference with the child and with the family regarding the book the youngster has studied, *Joining the Church*, I then ask him to kneel down by my side and repeat a prayer after me, word for word, phrase by phrase. Usually the family will kneel also with us. Then the child, kneeling, repeats after me this prayer:

Our Father in heaven   (the child repeats out loud)
We thank Thee for Jesus   ,,
That he died on the cross   ,,
To save us from our sins.   ,,
We thank thee for our church   ,,
Bless me as I join the church   ,,
Bless me as I am baptized   ,,
And after I am baptized   ,,
Help me to be a good church member   ,,
May I grow in grace   ,,
And in the knowledge of the Lord   ,,
Bless my dear father   ,,
And my sweet mother   ,,
And the circle of our home   ,,
May I be a joy to them   ,,
As long as I live   ,,
And an honor to thee   ,,
Forgive our sins   ,,
Keep us close to thee   ,,
In Jesus' dear name, Amen.   ,,

This is a precious and meaningfully moving way to close the conference with the child and with the family.

15

The Pastor as Counselor
and Shepherd of the Flock

The Pastor's Opportunity to Do Good

The pastor has many opportunities to serve God and man.

He has an opportunity to know Christ as his personal Savior and to walk with him as a friend.

He has an opportunity to depend upon God for the answers to every human need.

He has an opportunity to preach the wonderful and heavenly tidings of the gospel.

He has an opportunity to win people to Jesus.

And he has an opportunity to minister as a shepherd-counselor to the needs of the people.

Oh, what a beautiful life the pastor can live! Every opportunity is a golden invitation from the courts of heaven to be a messenger of encouragement and salvation. The very angels must envy our place of service.

The people need us. They need our love, our prayer, our friendship, our encouragement, our understanding, our sympathy, our counsel. I wish I had a life to live that could be dedicated to the ministry of personally helping people in a time of need. Some day, sometimes, somewhere, every one of us will desperately need the presence and prayers of the preacher. He is God's man to show the right way or to give us strength to follow what we ought to do.

The shepherd tending his flock, the pastor living in love and encouragement among his people, is the picture the New Testament presents of this God-called servant (1 and 2 Timothy). As

273

the Lord visited the couple he made in the Garden of Eden, as the Lord Jesus visited in the days of his flesh, so the pastor is the very representation of heaven in his holy assignment of visiting with his people.

Prayer, even fervent prayer, is not enough, nor is prayer plus incessant Bible study enough. We must also live with our people, minister to our people, encourage, and guide our people. In Luke 14:23 the Lord sent his servants out into the highways and hedges. In Acts 20:20 Paul visited the lost from house to house among the people at Ephesus.

The pastor who sows the seeds of God's love in the community where he lives will some day reap a precious harvest (Ps. 126:6). Mingling with the people will not only sharpen our swords but put the iron of God in our souls as their champions (Jer. 1:5-8; Ezek. 3:15-21).

The Pastor's Visitation

If the pastor would really succeed in his work, let him minister to the needs of his people. To begin with, he will have a soul-saving response from them. A survey was made by a national retail organization concerning the success of salesmen. Forty-eight percent of the salesmen made one call; 25 percent of the salesmen made two calls and quit; 88 percent of the salesmen quit after one, two, or three calls. Twelve percent of the salesmen kept on calling. The 12 percent who kept on calling did 80 percent of the business. The 88 percent who quit by the third call did only 20 percent of the business. It pays to keep on visiting!

But more than that, the pastor who knows, loves, visits, and ministers to his flock has a place in their hearts sacred forever. I once heard of a church conference called to fire the pastor. The congregation was present to the last man, all having agreed to get rid of him. But before the vote was cast, one of the men, looking at the pastor, was smitten in his heart and stood to say: "Brethren, when my wife died our pastor stood with me through all those days of sorrow, prayed for me, helped me, encouraged me. I cannot vote against him." Thereupon another stood up to say: "Brethren, when my child was sick unto death the pastor prayed with her throughout the night. We believe it was his prayer that saved our child. We cannot vote against him." Another stood up to say: "Brethren, the pastor buried my mother who loved him dearly. In her old age he visited her, read the Bible to her, prayed with her. I cannot vote against him." When the session was over, no vote was taken except to affirm unanimously that they loved their pastor and praised God for his ministry in their midst. This is what a shepherdly love will do.

The example of the great pastors of the world is always one of personal contact with the people. The pulpit is the throne of the preacher, but the throne is not stable unless it rests on the affections of the people. To win the affections of the people, you must visit with them and know them and talk to them and let them talk to you. The man with whom you have wisely and tenderly conversed on vital, personal religion cannot turn a cold, critical ear toward you on the Lord's Day, nor does he. The man who visits has the love of the people.

When the pastor has established personal religious relations with his hearers, to them, even the simplest sermons are clothed with sacred power. There are many instances where the pastor cannot visit all of his people. In that event he ought to have a church staff that helps him in the work. But whether it is he or the representative who goes for him, the pastor who is loved is the one who remembers his people and cares for them in their distress.

Some of the characteristics of a good pastoral visit are these:

1. The visit ought to be religious. That is the reason we are there, not to talk about the weather or the political or economic situation, but to talk about the Lord.

2. The visit should not be stuffy and stiff and formal. A sour visage and a formal style are not necessary for religious conversation.

3. The visit ought to overlook no one. It ought to include everyone in the home, children, domestics, everybody. The visitation among the people ought to be impartial. It ought to be to the poor as well as to the rich. There ought to be no favortism in our ministry to the people.

4. Ordinarily, visits should be short. That is especially true in hospital visitation.

5. The visit ought to be confidential; whatever the people dis-

close to the preacher privately ought to be something kept in his heart. He ought not be a busybody, carrying around what he has learned about other people.

6. In every case, the great purpose of his heart ought to be to win people to Christ.

7. The visit always ought to close with a prayer.

There are many, many advantages in the pastor visiting among his people and being close to his congregation. It keeps his life from degenerating into mere professionalism. He brings religion into the life of the people. Religion is not a theory; it is a living, personal reality. He can bring consolation and encouragement to dejected, afflicted spirits, with new hope springing up in his own heart and in their hearts. There is many a man that may be faultless in rhetoric and logic and learning and orthodoxy, but he fails to move the people because he does not come within the range of their experience. The preacher has three books to study, the Bible, himself, and his people.

The Shepherd's Heart

When Dr. George W. Truett was invited to be president of Baylor University, he declined with one of the most beautiful sentences I ever heard. He said, "No, I cannot come, for I have sought and found the shepherd heart." When we consider such passages as Jeremiah 10:21 and Jeremiah 12:10-11, how pleased must the Lord in heaven have been with his earthly servant.

1. The pastor possesses the ministry of comfort. We are admonished to "weep with them who weep." For the lonely, the sorrowful, the sick in heart, the defeated, and when death tears asunder the circle of the home, no one can take his place as he brings eternal hope to those who grieve in the distress of earthly separation.

2. The pastor possesses the ministry of encouragement, especially in the day of severe illness. Sickness can suddenly cut down any man or woman in the very prime of life. Our hope and help is in Jesus, the Great Physician. The saintly John Greenleaf Whittier wrote:

The healing of his seamless dress
Is by our beds of pain;
We touch him in life's throng and press,
And we are whole again.

The congregation can help the pastor with his ministry among the sick. They ought to notify the pastor immediately.

There are some things to remember in hospital visitation:

(1) Make the visit brief.

(2) It is prudent to visit in the hospital in a rested, healthful condition. If you yourself are "puny," you had better stay at home awhile. It is easy to pick up a virus.

(3) We ought to go in the spirit of prayer and loving solicitude.

(4) The visit with the sick ought to be cheerful and encouraging. We ought to let them tell us what is on their hearts and be sympathetic in listening.

(5) If the person is a Christian, we can encourage him in the remembrance that God is leading us closer to him through our illnesses. If the person is not a Christian, we ought to say a good word for Jesus, pointing to our salvation in him.

(6) We ought always to pray. Anytime we make a visit, especially to the sick, we ought to pray.

3. The pastor possesses the ministry of joy. Romans 12:15 admonishes us to "rejoice with them who do rejoice." The friendly contacts made by the pastor in social engagements are invaluable. It is great when the people love to have the pastor present upon glad, gala occasions. Not all the life of the pastor is filled with tears and sorrow. Some of his ministries are ineffably happy.

4. The pastor possesses the ministry of feeding, nurturing, and maturing the members of his flock. Growing greater Christians is his supreme task after he has won their souls in saving faith to Christ (John 21:15-18). We are admonished by the Lord to take care of his little ones (Matt. 18:2-6,11). These "little ones" can refer not only to small children but also to the new converts in Christ. Their cultivation and training are the especial and particular responsibility of the pastor.

The pastor ought always to have a new members class. It should be revolving and ongoing throughout the year. All new converts are babes in Christ and need spiritual help. Review the plan of salvation, assurance of salvation, and what happens when a person is saved. Explain the importance of baptism, church membership, the Lord's Supper, tithing, and the stewardship of life and talents. Describe the two natures, the certainty of temptation and the assurance of forgiveness. Discuss what our joy depends upon. Explain the importance of reading, studying, meditating upon the Word of God. Emphasize the importance of prayer and a quiet time with the Lord. Deal with the Christian attitude and the privileges and duties of a Christian. Teach the person the work of the Holy Spirit and the fruit of the Spirit. Urge witnessing of one's faith to others and the winning of others to Christ. Show the reasons of Christian separation from the world and unto Christ. Start them on Bible study.

5. The pastor possesses the ministry of loving commendation and appreciation for his people (Rom. 16:1-16; 2 Tim. 1:16-18). Could anything the pastor does be sweeter or dearer than that? He can commend without flattery. He can write letters and say words of appreciation world without end. One of Dr. Truett's most meaningful ministries was that of writing personal letters in his own hand. The pastor can arrange for fellowship dinners for new members, maybe presided over by the deacons.

He can just love the people all the time.

> Blest be the tie that binds
> Our hearts in Christian love;
> The fellowship of kindred minds
> Is like to that above.
>
> —JOHN FAWCETT

The Pastor as Counselor

Let me suggest seven rules to be observed and remembered by the pastor-counselor.

1. The first rule of counseling concerns the matter of confidence. The pastor ought to keep confidential conversations confidential. He ought not to use them for sermon illustrations or to share them with others. Keep faith with the people. He must never betray the confidence placed in him.

When a counselee shares his innermost self, the experience becomes a sacred trust to the counselor. This trust must never be broken. Problem-solving with a professional is not breaking the trust when the motivation is to find answers; however, conversation which involves the life of a counselee for any other purpose is a violation of that trust. So, pastor, if you can't keep your mouth closed, don't counsel. Lives can be ruined and souls lost forever because an untrustworthy counselor betrays a trust.

2. The second rule of counseling is to be a good listener. Many times healing and help come from allowing a parishioner to pour out of his heart all his troubles. He does not expect you to do anything about it. Maybe you cannot. But he wants you to listen and by listening to his sorrows or problems, he finds strength to face them. Possibly the reason the confessional booth in the Roman Catholic church has endured through the years is because people need to find help through a listening ear.

3. A third rule for the pastor-counselor is to bring to the conference the spirit of prayer to know and to do the will of Christ. Aside from some kind of affliction entailed in a mental illness (we can be sick in our heads just as we can be sick in our livers), most if not all our problems can be solved in the love of Jesus. There is a saying, "Christ is the answer to every human need." That includes all our problems, too. There is nothing our Lord cannot do. Nothing is impossible with God. Let go and let God have his wonderful way in our lives. If the pastor can persuade people having trouble to seek to do the will of God, most things will turn from darkness to light, from sadness to joy, from hatred to love, from death to life. We all need Jesus.

4. A fourth rule of counseling is not to be afraid to say you do not know what to do. Do not hesitate to make a necessary referral when more is required than the pastor is capable of performing. There is no shame or loss of prestige in referral. No one of us is infallible or illimitable or inexhaustable in our abilities. The greatest doctors in the world refer all the time. For the pastor to do the same is no admission of weakness. Rather it is a loving strength shown to the soul in need.

5. A fifth rule of counseling concerns the human limitations of the pastor to enter fully in the troubling problem, usually in cases

of marital conflict. You do not know what goes on when a married couple go the their bedroom and shut the door. The couple themselves will not tell you, or if they do they will color or distort the truth.

We desperately need to do everything humanly and divinely possible to save the crumbling American family. Divorce is an evil. The orphaning of children is a tragedy. The repercussion lives forever. The scars are there eternally. The pastor needs to help the home in every way possible. That is one reason why he needs to pray.

6. A sixth rule of counseling for the pastor concerns his sessions with the women in the church. Do not allow them to recount to you the intimacies of their lives, no matter what the problem may be. Some pastors revel in this, encouraging the women to tell more and more. He gets the same feeling ("kick") out of the lurid details as he does out of a pornographic movie. Do not do it.

A distinguished family joined our church from another fine congregation in the city. When I saw the pastor of the church from which the family came, he said to me that he had made a great mistake and that is why he lost the group. He said that he allowed the wife and mother in the home to tell him the intimacies of her life in a counseling session. Thereafter, he told me, she was self-conscious and embarrassed every time she met him. Finally, she took her deacon-husband and children out of the church altogether. Truly, he had made a mistake. You can make it, too.

There is another danger in a conference, that if allowed, even can prove disastrous. When a woman begins telling the pastor about problems in her married life that involve marital intimacies, she can sense your interest, and it is easy for the sympathetic pastor to become emotionally involved. One time I was a part of a three-month preaching mission in Japan. Everywhere I went the pastor and the people were down, blue, discouraged. I asked the reason why. It was this. The president of their national convention and the pastor of their largest church had resigned his pulpit, resigned his preaching, and left the ministry. Why? He had gone off with one of the women in his congregation. How did it come about? She came to him for advice. She liked what she heard. She came back to him for counsel. He liked what he saw. The conferences continued even more intimately and finally it took him out of his ministry. What a tragedy for the people of God!

Let the pastor help in every way he can, but there is no need that he be told all the details of a marriage breakup.

7. The last rule for the pastor-counselor is to make sure that the session ends Godward, Christward, and heavenward. Let it never end in hopelessness. Maybe what is needed above all else is a closer walk with God (Luke 12:13-21). There are few things that personal repentance, humility, repudiation of the cheap values of the world, a complete commitment to Christ, and a resolution to place our Lord first in all things, will not solve.

May God bless the pastor to bring his counseling to that beautiful and happy end.

16

The Wedding Ceremony

An Opportunity for a Pastor

There are few events in the life of a family that have more meaning and greater potential for good than a wedding. The arrangement for the beautiful occasion opens the door for the pastor into the very heart of all the people involved. He is a wise pastor who takes advantage of the providence to counsel the couple in Christian homemaking and to encouraging the parties to make Christ and his church the center of their lives.

The Counseling Session Before the Wedding

Every couple the pastor marries should have a personal, heart-to-heart visit with him before the day of the wedding. At this session the pastor should do three things:

1. Talk to the couple about the Lord. If they are not Christian, seek to win them to Christ. If they are not church members, seek to win them to the church. By all means they ought to attend and to belong to the same church. A divided church life is not ideal.

2. The pastor should tell the couple how to build a Christian home that God will bless forever. I tell them:

"See, I have five fingers on this hand. Each stands for something you should do in building a Christian home.

One, say grace before you eat. Hogs and dogs do not do it, but you do it. Be thankful for God's blessings upon you.

Two, sometime during each day, read the Bible together (such as at the breakfast table) and pray.

Three, before you go to bed at night, kneel down together and pray out loud where the other partner can hear you talk to God. Nobody is perfect; we are all human. That means we make mistakes, misjudgments, and fall into misunderstandings. If we have been short-tempered, hasty, unsympathetic, brutal, or any other unhappy way during the day, it all will dissove away in the open prayer. God's Word says we are not to let the sun go down on our anger (Eph. 4:26). No couple should ever go to sleep at night estranged from each other, hurt at each other. Make it right before God and with one another before you go to sleep.

Four, dress up and go to church every Sunday. Appear before God in the presence of all his people in the best clothes you possess.

Five, take a part in the life of the church. Do something for God.

If a couple will heed that advice, they will enjoy an unbreakable homelife as long as the years shall last.

3. The pastor should tell the couple to see a doctor before their marriage. I do not think it is the place or the calling of the pastor to talk to them about the intimacies of conjugal relationship. The doctor can do it better.

No couple should have a child immediately after their marriage. It takes a little time to get acquainted. Take that time, then father and mother all the children you pray for and that God gives you.

The Christian Emphasis in a Wedding

The many attendant things that normally accompany a wedding can be chosen and followed according to the tastes and choices of the families, such things as wedding invitations, rehearsals and rehearsal dinners, printed programs to be followed at the wedding itself, the decorations of the church or chapel, the music to be played and sung. All of these arrangements and choices are entirely in the will of the families.

Just one observation ought to be made about it all: everything connected with the wedding ought to be distinctly and explicitly Christian. And that includes the music that is played and sung.

Format of the Wedding Service

The format of the wedding itself ought to go something like this:

1. After the lighting of candles, the seating of mothers, and

whatever music is offered, let the pastor go in first at the beginning of the wedding march, taking his place in the center of the chapel or sanctuary.

2. Following the pastor, the groom and the best man ought to enter, standing in front of and to the left of the pastor.

3. During the continuing wedding march, the bridesmaids, ringbearers, and all others taking part in the wedding should come forward, taking their assigned places.

4. Last of all, the bride should enter with the one who is to give her away to the groom.

Words Spoken by the Pastor Before Wedding Vows

After the minister comes in, the introductory remarks of the pastor before the wedding ceremony begins can take any form the preacher would like to make, and the prayer he prays can follow any supplication to which the Holy Spirit leads him. Here is an example of introductory remarks:

Because the image of God indwells us, we are able to know and personally experience love. It has been said, "He that abideth in love, abideth in God." This is a realization which is celebrated in worship. Where there is the presence of love, there should be worship, for God is the author of love and he is the Holy One whom we worship. Therefore, it is the heartfelt desire of _____ and _____ to welcome you—to welcome you to share and to celebrate their covenant and commitment of love during this time of worship.

In the past (time period), _____ and _____ have learned to know and to love each other. Now they have decided to live their lives together as husband and wife.

We have been invited to hear _____ and _____ as they promise to face the future together, accepting whatever may lie ahead. These surroundings were not chosen by chance, just as _____ and _____ believe that they did not meet by chance. They believe that God directed them to be in the same place at the same time and that it was God's will that helped them find each other. For the beauty around us, for the strength it offers, and for the peace it brings, we are grateful.

(_____) and (_____), nothing is easier than saying words, and nothing harder than living them day after day. What you promise now must be renewed and redecided tomorrow. At the end of this ceremony, legally you will be man and wife, but you still decide, each day that stretches out before you, you want to be married.

Real love is something beyond the warmth and glow, the excitement and romance of being deeply in love. It is caring as much about the welfare and happiness of your marriage partner as about your own. But real love is not total absorption in each other; it is looking outward in the same direction—together. Love makes burdens lighter, because you divide them. It makes joys more intense, because you share them. It makes you stronger, so you can reach out and become involved with life in ways you dared not risk alone.

The pastor then says, "Dear family and friends, having gathered in this beautiful place for the purpose of solemnizing the sacred rites of matrimony, who gives this woman to this man in wedlock?"

The father of the bride then answers, "We do, her mother and I" (or any appropriate answer).

The father then takes the right hand of the bride and places it in the right hand of the groom, and then he returns to be seated by the side of his wife.

The pastor then takes his place in the pulpit behind a kneeling rail if possible, nods for the couple to come up before him, nods for the best man and maid of honor to take their places on either side, then the wedding ceremony begins.

The wedding ceremony can follow any one of many patterns. These ceremonies are written out in Episcopal, Presbyterian, Methodist, Baptist, and other denominational manuals. Here is the ceremony I have used for years, all or in part according to the type of wedding (whether in the big auditorium, in one of the chapels, in my study, or in my home).

The Ceremony Itself

The wedding ceremony itself can go like this:

Holy and happy is the sacred hour in which two devoted hearts are joined in the bonds of matrimony. Here in our swelling breasts we are reminded of the myriad, magic charms of home, of the quiet fireside, where Christ and his peace that passeth all understanding is the respected, the cherished, and the permanent guest. Here we are reminded of the lengthening days when the eventide shadows are fringed with the silver of devoted companionship's purest sympathy.

Originating in divine wisdom and goodness, designed to promote human happiness and holiness, this rite is the foundation of home life and social order, and must remain so until the end of time. It was sanctioned and honored by the presence in power of our Savior at the marriage in Cana of Galilee, and marked the beginning of his wondrous works.

Marriage is of God. It is ordained of heaven. It is the first and the holiest institution among men. God himself gave the first bride away. God himself performed the first wedding ceremony. In the Garden of Eden our heavenly Father himself hallowed and sanctified the first home. In the wisdom of the Almighty, the first establishment is not the church, it is not of the state, it is not of the schools; it is of the home of the Lord God first speaks:

Genesis 2:15,18-24, 'And the Lord God took the man [whom he had made], and put him into the Garden of Eden. . . . And the Lord God said, It is not good that the man should be alone; I will make him an help meet for him. . . . And the Lord caused a deep sleep to fall upon Adam, and he slept; and he took one of his ribs, and closed up the flesh instead thereof; And the rib, which the Lord God had taken from man, made he a woman, and brought her unto the man. And Adam said, This is now bone of my bones, and flesh of my flesh: she shall be called Woman, because she was taken out of Man. Therefore shall a man leave his father and his mother, and shall cleave unto his wife: and they shall be one flesh.'

From that beautiful, Edenic day of purity and innocence until this present moment, in the strong love of a man for his wife, and in the love and reverence of a wife for her husband, we have found our highest hope and our sweetest promise for a fairer day.

Marriage and home are built upon the foundation of the

sublimest dedication known to the human heart—that of unselfish love and heavenly affection. With many tears and deep searching of heart, giving up her native home and country and people, Ruth spake of that dedication in these immortal words: "Entreat me not to leave thee, or to return from following after thee: for whither thou goest, I will go; and where thou lodgest I will lodge; thy people shall by my people, and thy God my God. Where thou diest, will I die, and there will I be buried: the Lord do so to me, and more also, if ought but death part thee and me."

The apostle Paul spake of that devotion like this: "Though I speak with the tongues of men and of angles, and have not [love], I am become as sounding brass or a [clanging] cymbal. And thought I have the gift of prophecy, and understand all mysteries and all knowledge, and though I have all faith, so that I could remove mountains, and have not [love], I am nothing. And though I bestow all my goods to feed the poor, and though I give my body to be burned, and have not [love], it profiteth me nothing. [Love] suffereth long and is kind; [love] envieth not; seeketh not her own, is not easily provoked; Beareth all things . . . [Love] never faileth: but whether there be prophecies, they shall fail; whether there be tongues, they shall cease; whether there be knowledge, it shall vanish away . . . Now abideth faith, hope, [love], these three, but the greatest of these is [love]."

The same inspired apostle Paul wrote on the sacred page: Ephesians 5:22-32: "Wives, submit yourselves unto your own husbands, as unto the Lord. For the husband is the head of the wife, even as Christ is the head of the church! . . . Therefore, as the church is subject unto Christ, so let the wives be to their own husbands in everything. Husbands, love your wives, even as Christ also loved the church and gave himself for it . . . So ought men to love their wives as their own bodies. . . . For we are members of his body, of his flesh, and of his bones. For this cause shall a man leave his father and mother, and shall be joined unto his wife, and they two shall be one flesh. This is a great mystery. . . ."

And it *is* a great "mystery"—how God can take two hearts and two lives and make them one is "a great mystery"—a mystery of heaven, but one that will be a strength and a blessing to you both as long as time shall last.

Realizing, therefore, the sacredness and the sanctity of the holy covenant you now make with one another, if you know of no barrier to such a union between yourselves, you will signify such by joining your right hands.

Do you, _____, in the presence of God and these assembled witnesses, promise to love and to cherish, in sickness and in health, in prosperity and in adversity, this woman whose right hand you now hold? Do you promise to be to her in all things a true and faithful husband, to cleave unto her, and to her only, as long as life shall last? Do you? (The man answers, ''I do.'')

Do you take her to be your lawful, wedded wife, as long as you both shall live? Do you? (The man answers, ''I do.'')

Do you, _____, in the presence of God and these assembled witnesses, promise to love and to cherish, in sickness and in health, in prosperity and in adversity, this young man whose right hand you now hold? Do you promise to be to him in all things a true and faithful wife, to cleave unto him, and to him only, as long as life shall last? Do you? (The woman answers, ''I do.'')

Do you take him to be your lawfully, wedded husband, as long as you both shall live? Do you? (The woman answers, ''I do.'')

(To the man) _____, do you possess a token of your love and affection to give to your bride, a seal of this holy covenant? (He answers, ''I do.'')

What is it? (He answers, ''A ring.'')

In all ages and among all peoples, the ring has been a symbol of that which is measureless; and thus, in this holy hour, a symbol of your measureless, boundless devotion. It is a circle; it has neither beginning nor ending; so down to old age and to death and forever you are to keep this vow inviolate, and the sign and the seal thereof will be this ring. As a ceaseless reminder of this sacred committal, place this ring on the wedding finger of your bride and repeat after me.

I, _____, take thee, _____, to my wedded wife, to have and to hold from this day forward, for richer for poorer, for better for worse, to cleave unto thee, and to thee only, as long as we both shall live. With this ring I thee wed, with loyal love I thee endow, all my wordly goods with thee I share, in the name of the Father, and of the Son, and of the Holy Spirit, blessed forever more, Amen.''

(To the bride) _____, do you possess a token of your love and affection, to give your husband, a seal of this holy covenant? (She answers, ''I do.'')

What is it? (She answers, ''A ring.'')

Invested with the same significance as the ring you have just received, a circle of precious gold indicating the longevity of your love and the pricelessness of your devotion, place this ring on the wedding finger of your husband and repeat after me:

''I, _____, take thee, _____, to my wedded husband, to have and to hold, from this day forward, for richer for poorer, for better for worse, to cleave unto thee, and to thee only, as long as we both shall live. With this ring I thee wed, with all the loyal love of my heart I thee endow, in the name of the blessed Trinity, the Father, the Son, and the Holy Spirit. Amen.''

And now by virtue of the authority invested in me as a minister of the gospel of Christ Jesus our Lord, and as the pastor of this beloved church, in the presence of God and these assembled witnesses, I pronounce you husband and wife, no longer two but one, one in interest, in destiny, in love, and in life.

And upon you, _____, and upon you, _____, his helpmate in all his work, may heaven's richest benedictions ever abide, making you a blessing to all who shall ever know and love you. To that end let us pray: [Here the pastor prays the prayer that God lays upon his heart.]

A final benediction can be added that goes like this:

May almighty God, with his word of blessing, unite your hearts in the never-ending bond of pure love.

May your children bring you happiness, and may your generous love for them be returned to you many times over.

May the peace of Christ live always in your hearts and in your home. May you have true friends to stand by you, both in joy and in sorrow. May you be ready and willing to help and comfort all who come to you in need. And may the blessings promised to the compassionate be yours in abundance.

May you find happiness and satisfaction in your work. May daily problems never cause you undue anxiety, nor the desire for earthly possessions dominate your lives. But may your heart's first desire be always for the good things waiting for you in the life of heaven.

May the Lord bless you with many happy years together, so that you may enjoy the rewards of a good life. And after you have served him loyally in his kingdom on earth, may he welcome you to his eternal kingdom in heaven.

And may almighty God bless you all, in the name of the Father, and the Son, and the Holy Spirit. Amen.

Suggested Alternatives in the Ceremony

There is no end to the variety that can be achieved in a wedding ceremony. For example, during the first part of the ceremony the beautiful sonnet of Elizabeth Barrett Browning written to her husband Robert Browning can be added:

> How do I love thee? Let me count the ways.
> I love thee to the depth and breadth and height
> My soul can reach, when feeling out of sight
> For the ends of Being and ideal Grace;
> I love thee to the level of everyday's
> Most quiet need, by sun and candle-light.
> I love thee freely, as men strive for Right;
> I love thee purely, as they turn from Praise;
> I love thee with the passion put to use
> In my old griefs, and with my childhood's faith.
> I love thee with a love I seemed to lose
> With my lost saints,—I love thee with the breath,
> Smiles, tears, of all my life!—and, if God choose,
> I shall but love thee better after death.

The ring vow can be changed in many ways. Here is one way that it can be repeated:

"With this ring—we pledge our love together—to Christ and to his church—even as he loved the church and gave himself for it.

"We ask his blessings upon the home we build in his name and the sign and the seal of that Christian commitment is this golden wedding band that binds us to one another and to our Savior forever.

"In the name of the Father and of the Son and of the Holy Spirit, Amen."

The Unity Candle

With increasing frequency I have watched couples share in a unity candle. It is a beautifully symbolic act.

One way to use a unity candle is to place a three-branched candlestick by the side of the pastor with the center candle unlighted. After the pastor pronounces the couple husband and wife, they then each take a lighted candle, set aflame the one in the middle, blow out each his and her candle, leaving the one in the center lighted. The pastor then asks the husband to kiss his wife, and they leave together while the recessional is being played.

Another way to use a unity candle is to place three candles on one stand at the front of the sanctuary. Before the groom's mother is seated, she with her accompanying husband light one of the candles. Before the bride's mother is seated, she with her accompanying husband light the candle on the other side, leaving the one in the center unlighted. After the ceremony, the bride and groom step down from the pulpit and before proceeding out of the church each takes one of the candles (the groom the one his parents lighted, the bride the one her parents lighted), light the candle in the middle, then blowing out the light each one holds, replaces them in their holders, leaving the one large candle burning in the center.

Another way of using the unity candle is for the pastor to call the two sets of parents to stand before him and the unity candle as he says:

> Life without love is like a tree without blossom and fruit. So it is now, that we turn for a moment to the parents of these two who have given so much love through the years. It must be a particular pleasure and a great satisfaction for these parents, _____ and _____,

_____ and _____, as they stand here with _____ and _____. You have watched them mature physically and helped them to mature spiritually. You have watched with love and affection as they have entered into this relationship with one another. You have cried, laughed, consoled, and been consoled, desired for, and realized many wishes come true from within your parental relationship. You have prayed many prayers and provided the guidance that has helped them to become the responsible Christian adults they are today. You have expressed your love in so many ways through the years as once again you do so now by standing beside them as they establish a home that will be so much stronger because of the Christian homes which they have known personally.

Who then, having played such an important role in helping these two become the persons they are, now promise their prayers and blessings to the formation of this new home?

Parents respond: "We do."

The parents then light their candle. Then the pastor goes to his place in the pulpit.

The Importance of the Christian Covenant

However and whatever the ceremony and order of the wedding, the service is to be deeply religious, Christian, and spiritual. People ought to feel that they have "been to church," especially the bride, the groom, and their families.

Remember, the building of the Christian home is one of the most important foundations in realizing the kingdom of God on earth. There is no such thing as a Christian church without a Christian home, and the home actually begins in the wedding covenant.

17

The Funeral Service

When Death Comes to the Home

The Need for the Pastor

The funeral service poignantly and pathetically, tenderly and sometimes tragically, cries out for the man of God. Where is he? Where can he be found? Does he have any word from the Lord? Is there any hope beyond the cruel grave? Is there life beyond the impenetrable darkness? Oh, for the man of God who can offer help and comfort in this sad, sad hour!

That man is the pastor. You will find him in the church. He has a message from heaven. His very presence and prayers are an immeasurable blessing. Without him we are lost like a blind man groping in the darkness of an unending midnight. But with him we are lifted up to the Light of life, we are consoled and comforted by his words from the risen Savior who said; "I am the resurrection and the life: he that believeth in me, though he were dead, yet shall he live: And whosoever liveth and believeth in me shall never die" (John 11:25-26).

The Message from Heaven for Waiting Hearts

There is no pastoral ministry that offers the open door of spiritual opportunity as does the presence of death in the home. Death is so universal. His visage is so stark and grim. His presence is so dark and dreaded. In his wake are oceans of heartaches and rivers of tears. This is the hour when the loving and caring pastor is needed most. Here let him be at his best, both spiritually and scripturally.

Present at the funeral service are so many who desperately need the Lord. There are the bereaved to be led to a sure and unfailing hope in Christ Jesus. There are the lost to be saved. There are the believers to be confirmed in the faith. There are families and friends who need to be challenged to lift up their eyes beyond the temporal, transitory moments of this brief life to the eternal verities, promises, and realities we know in Christ Jesus. The apostle Paul wrote of that assurance marvelously and triumphantly in these words:

For God, who commanded the light to shine out of darkness, hath shined in our hearts, to give the light of the knowledge of the glory of God in the face of Jesus Christ.

But we have this treasure in earthen vessels, that the excellency of the power may be of God, and not of us.

We are troubled on every side, yet not distressed; we are perplexed, but not in despair; persecuted, but not forsaken; cast down, but not destroyed.

Always bearing about in the body the dying of the Lord Jesus, that the life also of Jesus might be made manifest in our body.

For which cause we faint not; but though our outward man perish, yet the inward man is renewed day by day.

For our light affliction, which is but for a moment, worketh for us a far more exceeding and eternal weight of glory;

While we look not at the things which are seen, but at the things which are not seen: for things which are seen are temporal; but the things which are not seen are eternal.

For we know that if our earthly house of this tabernacle were dissolved, we have a building of God, an house not made with hands, eternal in the heavens.

For in this we groan, earnestly desiring to be clothed upon with our house which is from heaven:

If so be that being clothed we shall not be found naked.

For we that are in this tabernacle do groan, being burdened: not for that we would be unclothed, but clothed upon, that mortality might be swallowed up of life.

Now he that hath wrough us for the selfsame thing is God, who also hath given unto us the earnest of the Spirit.

Therefore we are always confident, knowing that, whilst we are at home in the body, we are absent from the Lord:

(For we walk by faith, not by sight:)

We are confident, I say, and willing rather to be absent from the body, and to be present with the Lord (2 Cor. 4:6-10, 16-18; 5:1-8).

Not Empty Eulogy—But Preaching the Gospel

The pastor should accept the funeral hour as God's open door for him to speak to the people about the fundamental, basic verities of life, death, earth, heaven, time, and eternity. To waste the hour in drivel with cheap eulogy and empty ostentation is to sin against the presence of the Holy Spirit. Speak the message of God. They will hear it as never before when they are seated in the service before you.

Never could I forget the first funeral service I was called upon to conduct in my first full-time pastorate out of the seminary. The town drunk, a no-account and worthless bum and sorry ne'er-do-well, had staggered onto the highway and had been killed by a passing car. What would the new pastor say about the life and death of a worthless blot on the human family like that? It seemed to me that half of the county seat town was there to hear what I would say.

I took the occasion of the funeral service to make an appeal for personal witnessing and prayerful intercession, one that lingered in the hearts of the people throughout the following years. "You knew this wretched man? How many of you prayed for him by name? How many of you sought to lift him up out of the gutter? How many of you sought to win him to Christ? How many of you offered to bring him to church? How many of you remembered him at Thanksgiving and Christmastime? How many of you reached out a loving hand to help him toward God? How many of you know whether he was lost or saved, is now with Jesus in heaven or is shut off eternally from God? Truly, it was a far different crowd who left the memorial service than the throng who came. Deep conviction moved the hearts of the people to a new day in personal soul-winning, all because of a memorial service for a drunken man!

The memorial hour ought not to be a ministry of misery but a marvelous message of Christian meaning. Preach the gospel. Open the Book of books and deliver the words of the Lord. You will never have a better opportunity to make an appeal for faith in the Christ who alone can save from death to eternal life.

The Sympathetic Pastor

When death comes to a home, a Christian believer should be the first one there to strengthen in the hour of need. If the visitor can be the pastor, so much the better. The pastor (or the assistant pastor) ought to call immediately at the home. Read the Bible, pray with the family, and offer whatever help is needed. The ministry of love will never be forgotten.

By far the most comforting and the most endearing thing that the pastor can do with a bereaved family is just to cry with them. A shepherd's heart will lead him to sympathize deeply and sincerely. This sympathy and love will mean more than all the words he could ever say. It is like the little girl who came home from school and told her mother that her little friend who sat at the desk next to hers was so sad. "Why?" asked the mother. "Because," replied the little girl, "because her mother had died." "And what did you do to help the little girl?" her mother asked. The child replied, "I just sat down by her side at the desk and cried, too." That was enough. God took care of the rest. "Weep with them that weep," reads Romans 12:15. That we are there in the hour of need—giving, caring, sharing Christ's love—helps most at a time of inexpressible sorrow.

The Order and Content of the Memorial Service

The order of the funeral service ought to be simple. It can go like this:

Song
Scripture reading
Prayer
Song
Message by the pastor
Benediction

The songs can be solos, duets, quartets, choirs, or congregational. If there are several ministers to share in the service, one can read the Scripture, one can lead the first prayer, and one can lead the benediction.

The service ought to be held at the church. When I die, I want to be buried from the church. This does not mean that a service in a funeral chapel is not acceptable. It is just that I think God's people ought to be buried from the church as a last witness and testimony to our commitment to the Lord Jesus Christ.

The message the pastor preaches ought not to be lengthy. The Holy Spirit will guide him in the words he ought to say, fitting the solemn and sacred occasion. An address of fifteen to twenty minutes is sufficient to deliver God's revelation and hope for us who remain in this earthly pilgrimage. The whole funeral service ought to be encompassed in a time period of about forty-five minutes.

Personal Observations About the Memorial Service

There are several things I feel ought to be observed in the funeral service.

1. The casket ought to be closed during the service. Why some families want it to stay open in front of the pulpit I will never know. An open casket placed before the preacher who is seeking to deliver his message is a horrible distraction.

2. The casket ought not to be opened after the service is over. Let the people go to the funeral home to see the dead, or let them come early to view "the remains," but after this time of viewing, let the casket be closed forever. It ought not to be opened again either at the church or chapel or at the cemetery.

3. The bereaved family should be seated at the front of the church or chapel before the pulpit and the preacher. To hide the family behind some screen where even the preacher cannot see them is an arrangement that must have come out of a false sense of shame in sorrow. The whole world expects the family to be filled with sorrow. Why should it be strange or something to be hidden that they would be grieved? There is nothing wrong about tears. After all, the service is public and not private and the purpose of the meeting is to afford the family and friends an opportunity publicly to thank God for the blessed hope we possess in Christ Jesus.

4. If the memorial service is for someone who believed in the Lord Jesus as personal Savior, the service ought to have a triumphant note throughout its length and breadth. Jesus died, but

he also rose again. If we die with him, we shall also be raised with him. Death is our entrance into glory. Paul expressed it victoriously in the great resurrection chapter of 1 Corinthians 15:

But now is Christ risen from the dead, and become the firstfruits of them that slept.

For since by man came death, by man came also the resurrection of the dead.

For as in Adam all die, even so in Christ shall all be made alive.

But every man in his own order: Christ the firstfruits; afterward they that are Christ's at his coming.

Then cometh the end, when he shall have delivered up the kingdom to God, even the Father; when he shall have put down all rule and all authority and power.

For he must reign, till he hath put all enemies under his feet . . .

Now this I say, brethren, that flesh and blood cannot inherit the kingdom of God; neither doth corruption inherit incorruption.

Behold, I shew you a mystery; We shall not all sleep, but we shall all be changed,

In a moment, in the twinkling of an eye, at the last trump: for the trumpet shall sound, and the dead shall be raised incorruptible, and we shall be changed.

For this corruptible must put on incorruption, and this mortal must put on immortality.

So when this corruptible shall have put on incorruption, and this mortal shall have put on immortality, then shall be brought to pass the saying that is written, Death is swallowed up in victory.

O death, where is thy sting? O grave, where is thy victory?

The sting of death is sin; and the strength of sin is the law.

But thanks be to God, which giveth us the victory through our Lord Jesus Christ.

Therefore, my beloved brethren, be ye stedfast, unmovable, always abounding in the work of the Lord, forasmuch as ye know that your labour is not in vain in the Lord (1 Cor. 15:20-25,50-58).

5. If the memorial service is for someone who was not a Christian, the pastor ought not to deny his pulpit message of judgment and accountability. He ought not to try to "preach a lost man into heaven." He should speak prayerfully and sincerely about the brevity of life, the certainty of death, the need of a Savior, the awesome eternity to come, then on the basis of these experienced realities, make an appeal for those who remain behind to give

their hearts and lives in faith to the Lord Jesus. There is no opportunity to make an entreaty for Christ like the memorial service for a lost man. We desperately need God's mercy and saving grace.

After the Memorial Service Is Over

After the memorial service is over, within the following few days, one more visit ought to be made to the home. This helps beyond compare. And sometimes it anchors a family in the church as nothing else will.

I also mail to the home a little booklet I have written entitled, "Our Home in Heaven." In these last several years I have followed the custom of mailing the little booklet to every home where a relative has died. This is a way of saying that we love and that we care.

Remembering the family *after* the funeral is over may mean the difference between victory and defeat.

A widow said, "If I had known ahead of time how desperately I would need help later, I would have replaced that guest book in the funeral home with a calendar, asking each visitor to designate a day in the future on which he would console by way of a visit, a card, or phone call." She likened the outpouring of sympathy at first to twenty ice cream cones handed to a starving child on a warm summer day. But later, when the youngster could have used a cone or two, she was left all but forgotten by her benefactors.

Sometimes this neglect causes mourners to become disillusioned about the local church. A widow may have pictured the church as the primary instrument of compassion and love. Yet, when she needed to share her burden, weeks after the funeral, her church was not there to help.

May God grant that such a forgetfulness could never be true of us. After, as well as before, we shall love, remember, and care for our bereaved people.

The Message at the Funeral Service

In delivering a message at a funeral service, I usually divide it into two parts. The first concerns the one who has died. I earnestly try to make every service deeply personal. I do not just go through a ritual that is impersonal and general. I speak of the loved one who is gone, his life, his work, his worth, his influence. The second part of the message concerns the word and promise of God. This is delivered from the Bible and is spoken with all the conviction of my soul.

Here are some of the texts, outlines, and suggested messages I have used at memorial services that have been blessed of God to the comfort and strengthened faith of the bereaved people.

To Die Is Gain

Philippians 1:21 "For to me to live is Christ, and to die is gain."

1. We gain a better body, a glorified, immortalized, resurrected body. In this present body of clay we are subject to all the sorrows and tears that life is heir to. Age, sickness, and finally death are the inevitable accompaniments of this house made of the dust of the ground. But in death and in the resurrection we gain a better body, one that can never grow old, know disease, suffer pain, and can never die. We gain a better body.

2. We gain a better home. However the beauty and the embellishments of any house we may possess in this world, it is nothing to be compared with our mansion in the beautiful city of God. According to the promise of Christ Jesus in John 14:1-3, our Lord through the years and centuries is preparing for us a mansion in heaven. We do not possess it in this life. Only in death do we move into our heavenly home. The longing of the Apostle Paul for his home in heaven expressed in Philippians 1:23 is the deep-seated hope every Christian feels when our life's journey is over. Our forefathers used to sing this old song:

> I am a stranger here,
> Heaven is my home.
> Earth is a desert drear,
> Heaven is my home.

> Sorrows and dangers stand
> Round me on every hand
> Heaven is my fatherland,
> Heaven is my home.

3. We gain a better inheritance. Our final inheritance is not here. It is in heaven. Our final reward is not here, it is in heaven. It is only beyond the gates of death that we ever hear the precious words of our Lord, "Well done, thou good and faithful servant; . . . enter thou into the joy of thy Lord" (Matt. 25:21).

4. We gain a better fellowship. All of us in this world live in a dissolving family circle. Mother is gone, or father is gone, or a child is gone, or our beloved grandparents are gone, or friends are gone. If we live long enough, we shall be strangers in this earth. Everyone we knew and loved will be gone. But the circle is unbroken in heaven forever and ever. There is no death there, no more sorrow and crying and pain, for these former things are all passed away.

But best of all, beyond our families and our friends who wait to greet us there, we shall see our Savior face to face. We shall sit down with Abraham and Isaac and Jacob in the kingdom of God and be with our Lord through all the eternities yet to come.

5. If "For me to live is Christ," then to die is gain." If for me to live is money, to die is a loss. If for me to live is pleasure, to die is a loss. If for me to live is self, to die is a loss. If for me to live is ambition, to die is a loss. If for me to live is sin, to die is a loss. If for me to live is this world, to die is a loss. But if for me to live is Christ, to die is a gain.

What God Has Provided for Us Who Love Him

Hebrews 11:40 "God having provided some better thing for us . . . ."

1. Death was not intended when God created the man and the woman and placed them in the Garden of Eden. God created them immortal, perfect, in the image of God to have fellowship with him. Sin and the judgment of death broke that holy and beautiful relationship. Death is an interloper, and intrusion, a horrible irruptive.

But the story is not done and the book is not finished with the judgment of death. God has provided some better thing for us. The grave is not our final resting place and corruption is not the ultimate consummation of our lives. There is another chapter to be written before the book is finally closed. That concluding chapter is one of victory and triumph in Christ Jesus.

2. Chapter 11 of the letter to the Hebrews recounts the heroes of faith. They are presented one after another. Their story is one of sorrow, tears, persecution, suffering, and death. Look at the verses that recount their suffering. From the shed blood of righteous Abel to the saints whose heavy and terrible trials described in Hebrews 11:33-38, the story is one of tragedy. But God provides some better thing for them. There is far more to life than the suffering we witness and personally endure here in this earth. God has provided heaven as an inheritance for his people.

3. Paul in 1 Corinthians 2:9 speaks of those wonderful and better things God has provided for them who love him. He avows that eye has never seen nor ear has ever heard nor heart has ever imagined the precious, heavenly things in store for the children of the Lord. But in verse 10 the apostle says that "God has revealed them unto us by his Spirit." What we cannot see or hear or feel by our natural senses we can know for truth, for fact, for reality, and for comfort through the Spirit of Jesus in our hearts. O heavenly truth! that the riches of all the promises we possess in Christ Jesus are ours now to behold, to be assured of, to be comforted by, and thus patiently to wait for their complete realization. This we achieve in our translation from this weary world to the heavenly world to come.

Precious is the hymn of Ellen H. Gates:

> I will sing you a song of that beautiful land,
>   The far away home of the soul,
> Where no storms ever beat on the glittering strand,
>   Where the years of eternity roll.
>
> Oh, how sweet it will be in that beautiful land,
>   So free from all sorrow and pain,
> With songs on our lips and with hope in our hands,
>   To meet one another again.

Memorial Service for a Mother

Proverbs 31:10,20,25-31

Who can find a virtuous woman? for her price is far above rubies.

She stretcheth out her hand to the poor; yea, she reacheth forth her hands to the needy.

Strength and honour are her clothing; and she shall rejoice in time to come.

She openeth her mouth with wisdom; and in her tongue is the law of kindness.

She looketh well to the ways of her household, and eateth not the bread of idleness.

Her children arise up, and call her blessed; her husband also, and he praiseth her.

Many daughters have done virtuously, but thou excellest them all.

Favour is deceitful, and beauty is vain: but a woman that feareth the Lord, she shall be praised.

Give her of the fruit of her hands; and let her own works praise her in the gates.

It is not without deepest meaning and significance that the wisest man in all the world closed his book of inspired proverbs with a tribute to a marvelous mother. We also would join him in his words of love and praise for her.

Our mothers' ministering love and self-giving sacrifice for us are beyond our power to reward. They cared for us when we were helpless. They watched over us like guardian angels. They prayed for us as we grew from childhood to adulthood. They loved us when at times we were unlovely. They are the best pictures of God that some of us will ever know.

There are many laurels to be won in this world and many crowns to be worn, but the greatest of victories ever achieved and the mightiest triumphs ever attained are those bestowed upon us by our dear mothers. Humble, sweet, precious, but also enduring as the Rock of Ages are their sweet ministries to us.

> The greatest battle that ever was fought—
>   Shall I tell you where and when?
> On the maps of the world you will find it not:
>   It was fought by the Mothers of Men.
>
> Nay not with cannon and battle shot
>   With sword or nobler pen;

Nay not with eloquent words or thought
From the wonderful minds of men,

But deep in a walled-up woman's heart
A woman who would not yield;
But bravely, bore her part;
Lo! there is the battlefield.

No marshalling troops, no bivouac song,
No banners to gleam and wave;
But, oh! these battles, they last so long—
From babyhood to the grave!

Yet faithful still as a bridge of stars
She fights in her walled-up town;
Fights on, and on, in her endless wars;
Then silent, unseen, goes down!

Ho! ye with banners and battle shot
With soldiers to shout and praise,
I tell you the kingliest victories fought
Are fought in these silent ways.

Oh, spotless woman, in a world of shame
With splendid and silent scorn,
Thou hast returned to God pure as you came,
The queenliest warrior born.

—Joaquin Miller

The Death of a Good Man

Acts 11:24 "For he was a good man, and full of the Holy Ghost and of faith: and much people was added unto the Lord." Barnabas, "the son of Consolation," was evidently dead when Luke wrote this verse, for the beloved physician used the past tense in referring to him. As the author tells the story of the first Christians in Antioch, he turns aside to write this note about the saintly and godly leader, who, coming to visit the work in the great Syrian city, rejoiced in the hand of the Lord upon them. Any good man rejoices in the power and extension of the gospel, and the people of the church no less rejoice in the power and presence of a godly man in their midst. A good man is God's demonstration of what he can do. Not a star or a planet or an ocean or a continent, but a good man. He is the pride and strength of the church and a blessing to the community and to the world.

There are things about the death of this good man for which we are sorry and sad.

We grieve because of the separation that takes him from us.

We grieve because of the loss of his dedicated hands from our common tasks.

We grieve because of the hurt and sorrow we see in the lives of his family and friends.

But there are things for which we are thankful beyond words to express them.

We are grateful for the family he leaves behind.

We are grateful for the church he loved and saved.

We are grateful for the Lord who so signally blessed him and in whose name he lived and prayed each day of his life.

And we are grateful for the heavenly home to which he has gone to wait for our coming when our task is also finished. He is not dead and thus ceases to be. He has just gone to another place, to another room. Robert Freeman wrote of that beautiful translation in these lines:

In My Father's House

No, not cold beneath the grasses,
  Not close-walled within the tomb;
Rather, in our Father's mansion,
  Living, in another room.

Living, like the man who loves me,
  Like my child with cheeks abloom,
Out of sight, at desk or schoolbook,
  Busy, in another room.

Nearer than my son whom fortune
  Beckons where the strange lands loom;
Just behind the hanging curtain,
  Serving, in another room.

Shall I doubt my Father's mercy?
  Shall I think of death as doom,

Or the stepping o'er the threshold
To a bigger, brighter room?

Shall I blame my Father's wisdom?
Shall I sit enswathed in gloom,
When I know my loves are happy,
Waiting in another room?

—ROBERT FREEMAN

Nor has he dropped out of our lives because he has moved away. He still lives in us in a thousand beautiful and precious ways. F. L. Hosmer expressed it for us in these meaningful stanzas:

Friends Beyond

I cannot think of them as dead,
Who walk with me no more;
Along the path of life I tread—
They have but gone before.

. . . .

And still their silent ministry
Within my heart hath place,
As when on earth they walked with me,
And met me face to face.

Their lives are made forever mine;
What they to me have been
Hath left henceforth its seal and sign
Engraven deep within.

Mine are they by an ownership
Nor time nor death can free;
For God hath given to love to keep
Its own eternally.

—F. L. HOSMER

The Death of a Little Child

2 Samuel 12:15-23

And Nathan departed unto his house. And the Lord struck the child that Uriah's wife bare unto David, and it was very sick.

David therefore besought God for the child; and David fasted, and went in, and lay all night upon the earth.

And the elders of his house arose, and went to him, to raise him up from the earth: but he would not, neither did he eat bread with them.

And it came to pass on the seventh day, that the child died. And the servants of David feared to tell him that the child was dead: for they said, Behold, while the child was yet alive, we spake unto him, and he would not hearken unto our voice: how will he then vex himself, if we tell him that the child is dead?

But when David saw that his servants whispered, David perceived that the child was dead: therefore David said unto his servants, Is the child dead? And they said, He is dead.

Then David arose from the earth, and washed, and anointed himself, and changed his apparel, and came into the house of the Lord, and worshipped: then he came to his own house; and when he required, they set bread before him, and he did eat.

Then said his servants unto him, What thing is this that thou hast done? thou didst fast and weep for the child, while it was alive; but when the child was dead, thou didst rise and eat bread.

And he said, While the child was yet alive, I fasted and wept: for I said, Who can tell whether God will be gracious to me, that the child may live?

But now he is dead, wherefore should I fast? can I bring him back again? I shall go to him, but he shall not return to me.

In complete trust that his little child was with God, David rose from the ashes of sorrow to live in the light and hope of the goodness of God. The child in God's elective purpose could not return to David, but David in God's time could go to the child. Thus in heaven God keeps for us these we have loved and lost for just awhile.

It was Jesus who took little babies and little children up in his arms who said, "Suffer little children, . . . to come unto me; for of such is the kingdom of heaven" (Matt. 19:14). In the arms of our dear Savior they are secure and safe and blessed. We can trust our loving Lord to take care of them even better than we ever could. What God has chosen is best.

It Is Best

Mothers, I see you with your nursery light,
Leading your babies all in white,

To their sweet rest;
Christ the Good Shepherd, carries mine tonight
    And that is best!

I cannot help tears when I see them twine
Their fingers in yours, and their bright curls shine
    On your warm breast;
But the Savior's is purer than yours or mine:
    He can love best!

You tremble each hour because your arms
Are weak; your heart is wrung with alarms,
    And sore oppressed;
My darlings are safe, out of reach of harm;
    And that is best.

You know that of yours the feeblest one
And dearest may live long years alone,
    Unloved, unblest;
Mine are cherished of saints around God's throne,
    And that is best.

You must dread for years the crime that sears,
Dark guilt unwashed by repentant tears,
    And unconfessed;
Mine entered spotless on eternal years,
    Oh, how much the best!

But grief is selfish, and I cannot see
Always why I should so stricken be,
    More than the rest;
But I know that, as well as for them, for me
    God did the best!

                                —HELEN HUNT

Beyond the cares, tears, and sorrows of this sin-cured world, our little ones are with our blessed Savior in heaven. The angels thus welcome the little child into their midst.

The golden gates were open
    And heavenly Angels smiled
And with their tuneful harpstring
    Welcomed the little child.

They shouted "high and holy,
A child hath entered in,
And safe from all temptation
    A soul is sealed from sin."

They led him through the golden streets
    On to the King of kings,
And a glory fell upon him
    From the rustlings of their wings.

The Savior smiled upon him
    As none on earth had smiled,
And Heaven's great glory shone around
    The little earth-born child.

On earth they missed the little one,
    They sighed and wept and sighed,
And wondered if another such
    As theirs had ever died.

Oh! had they seen through those high gates
    The welcome to him given,
They never would have wished their child
    Back from his home in Heaven.

            —AUTHOR UNKNOWN

Our services here are not in keeping with the joys experienced by our little children in heaven. The poem written by Mary Burroughs as she looked at Paul Thurman's painting, *The Pitcher of Tears*, expresses the truth so vividly and so poignantly.

Many days a stricken mother
    To her loss unreconciled
Wept hot, bitter tears, complaining
    "Cruel Death has stolen my child."

But one night as she was sleeping,
    To her soul there came a vision,
And she saw her little daughter
    In the blessed fields Elysian.

All alone the child was standing,
    And a heavy pitcher holding;

Swift the mother hastened to her
    Close around her arms unfolding.

"Why so sad and lonely, darling?"
    Asked she, stroking soft her hair,
"See the many merry children
    Playing in the garden fair.

Look, they're beckoning and calling,
    Go and help them pluck the flowers,
Put aside the heavy pitcher,
    Dance away the sunny hours."

From the tender lips a-quiver
    Fell the answer on her ears:
"On the earth my mother's weeping,
    And this pitcher holds the tears.

Tears that touch the heavenly blossoms.
    Spoil the flowers where'er they fall;
So as long as she is weeping
    I must stand and catch them all."

"Wait no longer," cried the mother;
    "Run and play, sweet child of mine;
Never more shall tears of sorrow
    Spoil your happiness sublime."

Like a bird released from bondage
    Sped the happy child away,
And the mother woke, her courage
    Strengthen for each lonely day.

                —MARY BURROUGHS

In heaven the little life God began down here will bloom in full beauty and glory up there. Thus an unnamed poet has expressed it:

I wonder, O, I wonder, where the little faces go.
That come and smile and stay awhile, and pass like flakes of snow.
The dear, wee baby faces that the world has never known.
But mothers hide, so tender-eyed, deep in their hearts alone.

I love to think that somewhere, in the country we call heaven,
The land most fair of everywhere will unto them be given:
A land of little faces—very little, very fair—
And every one shall know her own and cleave unto it there.

O grant it, loving Father, to the broken hearts that plead!
Thy way is best—yet oh to rest in perfect faith indeed!
To know that we shall find them—even them, the wee white dead—
At Thy right hand in Thy bright land, by living waters led!

—AUTHOR UNKNOWN

Ere sin could blight or sorrow fade,
Death came with friendly care;
The opening bud to heaven conveyed,
And bade it blossom there.

—SAMUEL TAYLOR COLERIDGE

Dear Little Hands

Dear little hands, I miss them so!
All through the day, wherever I go—
All through the night, how lonely it seems,
For no little hands wake me out of my dreams.
I miss them through all the weary hours,
I miss them as others miss sunshine and flowers
Daytime and nighttime, wherever I go,
Dear little hands, I miss them so.

—AUTHOR UNKNOWN

A child is loaned to us for just awhile. The little life belongs to God in heaven. Thus the poet Edgar A. Guest writes in his poem, "I Lend This Child to You."

I'll lend you for a little while
A child of mine He said,
For you to love the while he lives
And mourn for when he's dead.

It may be 10 or 11 years, or 22 or 3
But will you, till I call him back
Take care of him for me?

He'll bring his charms to gladden you
And should his stay be brief
You'll have his lovely memories
As solace for your grief.

I cannot promise he will stay
Since all from earth return
But there are lessons taught down there,
I want this child to learn.

I've searched this wide world over
In my look for teachers true,
And from the throngs that crowd life's lanes
I have selected you.

Now give him all your love
Nor think your labor vain
Nor hate me when I come to call
To take him back again.

I fancied that I heard them say,
"Dear Lord, Thy will be done.
For all the joys this one shall bring
The risk of grief we'll run.

We'll shelter him with tenderness
And love him while we may
And for all the happiness he brings
Grateful forever stay."

And should the angel come to call
Much sooner than we've planned,
We'll brave the bitter grief that comes
And try to understand.

—Edgar A. Guest

In Memory of a Soldier

John 15:13 "Greater love hath no man than this, that a man lay down his life for his friends."

No great gift is ever bought without sacrifice. No great work is ever wrought without toil and effort. The greatest gifts are bought at the greatest sacrifices. The greatest works are wrought at the greatest forfeitures of life.

It is thus with our country. It was born in blood and in the sacrifice of the lives of our forefathers.

Our nation lives today because of the wall of steel built around it by the armed forces of our country. But, beyond and above the wall of steel made by bayonets and cannon and dreadnoughts is the wall of human life protecting us from ravages of our enemies. For our homes this soldier boy laid down his life. For our country this lad paid the price in his own blood.

God has an eternal reward in heaven for this Christian youth. He has called him to a greater life in an upper and better world. An unknown author has penned our love and appreciation in these words:

> In memory of a soldier boy,
>   So strong and brave and true.
> O skies of God, shine tenderly
>   And wear your robes of blue.
>
> O breezes, softly, gently waft
>   The fragrance of these flowers
> Upon the air in memory
>   Of this honored boy of ours.
>
> How bravely marched the young lad forth
>   To battle and to strife.
> How nobly, for "our country's sake"
>   Was offered his brave life.
>
> His battle cry was "freedom"
>   His motto, "for the right."
> And God looked down upon him there
>   So loyal in His sight.
>
> And God saw that he was weary
>   And had done his duty well,
> And we know we crowned with laurels
>   His soldier boy who fell—
>
> Upon the field of duty and
>   He called him home to rest
> In sweeter peace eternal, on
>   Christian tender loving breast.
>
> —Author Unknown

On the Separation of a Couple by Death

Revelation 7:9-17

After this I beheld, and, lo, a great multitude, which no man could number, of all nations, and kindreds, and people, and tongues, stood before the throne, and before the Lamb, clothed with white robes, and palms in their hands;

And cried with a loud voice, saying, Salvation to our God which sitteth upon the throne, and unto the Lamb.

And all the angles stood round about the throne, and about the elders and the four beasts, and fell before the throne on their faces, and worshipped God,

Saying, Amen: Blessing, and glory, and wisdom, and thanksgiving, and honour, and power, and might, be unto our God for ever and ever. Amen.

And one of the elders answered, saying unto me, What are these which are arrayed in white robes? and whence came they?

And I said unto him, Sir, thou knowest. And he said to me, These are they which came out of great tribulation, and have washed their robes, and made them white in the blood of the Lamb.

Therefore are they before the throne of God, and serve him day and night in his temple: and he that sitteth on the throne shall dwell among them.

They shall hunger no more, neither thirst any more; neither shall the sun light on them, nor any heat.

For the Lamb which is in the midst of the throne shall feed them, and shall lead them unto living fountains of waters: and God shall wipe away all tears from their eyes.

Where are our loved ones when they are separated from us by death? Do they cease to be, forever gone? No. They have left us to live on another shore.

Beyond the Horizon

When I go down to the sea by ship,
And Death unfurls her sail,
Weep not for me, for there will be
A living host on another coast
To beckon and cry, "All Hail."

—ROBERT FREEMAN

The sweet memory of a loved partner will bless us forever.

Should You Go First

Should you go first and I remain
  To walk the road alone,
I'll live in memory's garden, dear,
  With happy days we've known.
In Spring I'll wait for roses red,
  When fades the lilac blue,
In early fall when brown leaves fall
  I'll catch a glimpse of you.
Should you go first and I remain
  For battles to be fought.
Each thing you've touched along
    the way
  Will be a hallowed spot.
I'll hear your voice, I'll see your
    smile.
  Though blindly I may grope,
The memory of your helping hand
  Will buoy me on with hope,
Should you go first and I remain
  To finish with the scroll,
No length'ning shadows shall
    creep in
  To make this life seem droll.
We've known so much of happiness,
  We've had our cup of joy,
And memory is one gift of God
  That death cannot destroy.

—ANONYMOUS

Will we know each other in heaven? Jesus says that we will.

And one of the malefactors which were hanged railed on him, saying, If thou be Christ, save thyself and us.

But the other answering rebuked him, saying, Dost not thou fear God, seeing thou art in the same condemnation?

And we indeed justly; for we receive the due reward of our deeds: but this man hath done nothing amiss.

And he said unto Jesus, Lord, remember me when thou comest into thy kingdom.

And Jesus said unto him, Verily I say unto thee, To-day shalt thou be with me in paradise (Luke 23:39-43).

He and the repentant thief knew each other.

Paul says that we will. "For now we see through a glass, darkly; but then face to face: now I know in part; but then shall I know even as also I am known" (1 Cor. 13:12).

We shall not really know each other until we get to heaven.

The writer of Hebrews says that we will.

And these all, having obtained a good report through faith, received not the promise:

God having provided some better thing for us, that they without us should not be made perfect.

Wherefore seeing we also are compassed about with so great a cloud of witnesses (Heb. 11:39 to 12:1).

The great cloud of witnesses look down upon us. We shall know them as they know us.

John says that we will.

And I turned to see the voice that spake with me. And being turned, I saw seven golden candlesticks;

And in the midst of the seven candlesticks one like unto the Son of man clothed with a garment down to the foot, and girt about the paps with a golden girdle.

His head and his hairs were white like wool, as white as snow; and his eyes were as a flame of fire;

And his feet like unto fine brass, as if they burned in a furnace; and his voice as the sound of many waters.

And he had in his right hand seven stars; and out of his mouth, went a sharp two-edged sword: and his countenance was as the sun shineth in his strength.

And when I saw him, I fell at his feet as dead. And he laid his right hand upon me, saying unto me, Fear not; I am the first and the last:

I am he that liveth, and was dead; and, behold, I am alive for evermore, Amen; and have the keys of hell and of death (Rev. 1:12-18).

The sainted apostle John recognized the living Lord Jesus immediately.

An unknown poet has written:

> Where do our loved ones go,
>   after life's last "good-bye"?

Is there a home beyond,
    where they shall never die?
Questions like these arise,
    challenging thoughtful men,
It is my firm belief,
    I shall see them again.
To that Fair Land unknown,
    far from this earthy shore,
God calls His loved ones Home,
    to live forevermore,
They shall be happy There,
    dwelling with Him,
    and when He calls me, I believe
I shall know them again.

A Message to Those Asking "Why?"

Romans 8:28-39

And we know that all things work together for good to them that love God, to them who are the called according to his purpose.

For whom he did foreknow, he also did predestinate to be conformed to the image of his Son, that he might be the firstborn among many brethren.

Moreover whom he did predestinate, them he also called: and whom he called them he also justified: and whom he justified, them he also glorified.

What shall we then say to these things? If God be for us, who can be against us?

He that spared not his own Son, but delivered him up for us all, how shall he not with him also freely give us all things?

Who shall lay any thing to the charge of God's elect? It is God that justifieth.

Who is he that condemneth? It is Christ that died, yea rather, that is risen again, who is even at the right hand of God, who also maketh intercession for us.

Who shall separate us from the love of Christ? shall tribulation, or distress, or persecution, or famine, or nakedness, or peril, or sword?
As it is written, For thy sake we are killed all the day long; we are accounted as sheep for the slaughter.

Nay, in all these things we are more than conquerors through him that loved us.

For I am persuaded, that neither death, nor life, nor angels, nor principalities, nor powers, nor things present, nor things to come,

Nor height, nor depth, nor any other creature, shall be able to separate us from the love of God, which is in Christ Jesus our Lord.

The will of God is always for the good and the blessing of his children. He makes no mistakes. The poet A. M. Overton has so beautifully written:

He Maketh No Mistake

My Father's way may twist and turn,
My heart may throb and ache,
But in my soul I'm glad I know,
He maketh no mistake.

My cherished plans may go astray,
My hopes may fade away,
But still I'll trust my Lord to lead
For He doth know the way.

Tho' night be dark and it may seem
That day will never break;
I'll pin my faith, my all in Him,
He maketh no mistake.

There's so much now I cannot see,
My eyesight's far too dim;
But come what may, I'll simply trust
And leave it all to Him.

For by and by the mist will lift
And plain it all He'll make.
Through all the way, tho' dark to me,
He made not one mistake.

—A. M. OVERTON

Some day, according to what Paul writes in 1 Corinthians 13:12, we shall understand the purposes and elective choices of God for us.

Sometime We'll Understand

Not now, but in the coming years,
It may be in a better land,

We'll read the meaning of our tears,
　　And there, sometime, we'll understand.

We'll catch the broken threads again,
　　And finish what we here began;
Heaven will the mysteries explain
　　And then, ah, then, we'll understand.

. . . .

God knows the way, He holds the key,
　　He guides us with unerring hand;
Sometime with tearless eyes we'll see;
　　Yes, there, up there, we'll understand.

　　　　　　—MAXWELL N. CORNELIUS

Until the day when God will make it plain why we suffer separation, bereavement, sorrow, and we find faith and hope in the Lord Jesus Christ who was so loved and adored by John Greenleaf Whittier:

Household Voices

I long for household voices fond,
　　For vanished smiles I long.
But God hath led my dear ones on,
　　And He can do no wrong.

I know not what the future hath
　　Of marvel or surprise,
Assured alone that life and death
　　His mercy underlies.

And if my heart and flesh are weak
　　To bear an untried pain,
The bruised reed thou wilt not break
　　But strengthen and sustain.

And so beside the silent sea
　　I wait the muffled oar;
No harm from him can come to me
　　On ocean and on shore.

I know not where his islands lift
　　Their fronded palms in air;

I only know I cannot drift
Beyond His love and care.

—JOHN GREENLEAF WHITTIER

A Message About Heaven

Revelation 21:1 to 22:5

And I saw a new heaven and a new earth: for the first heaven and the first earth were passed away; and there was no more sea.

And I John saw the holy city, new Jerusalem, coming down from God out of heaven, prepared as a bride adorned for her husband.

And I heard a great voice out of heaven saying, Behold, the tabernacle of God is with men, and he will dwell with them, and they shall be his people, and God himself shall be with them, and be their God.

And God shall wipe away all tears from their eyes; and there shall be no more death, neither sorrow, nor crying, neither shall there be any more pain: for the former things are passed away.

And he that sat upon the throne said, Behold, I make all things new. And he said unto me, Write: for these words are true and fiathful.

And he said unto me, It is done, I am Alpha and Omega, the beginning and the end. I will give unto him that is athirst of the fountain of the water of life freely.

He that overcometh shall inherit all things; and I will be his God, and he shall be my son.

But the fearful, and unbelieving, and the abominable, and murderers, and whoremongers, and sorcerers, and idolaters, and all liars, shall have their part in the lake which burneth with fire and brimstone: which is the second death.

And there came unto me one of the seven angels which had the seven vials full of the seven last plagues, and talked with me, saying, Come hither, I will shew thee the bride, the Lamb's wife.

And he carried me away in the spirit to a great and high mountain, and shewed me that great city, the holy Jerusalem, descending out of heaven from God,

Having the glory of God: and her light was like unto a stone most precious, even like a jasper stone, clear as crystal;

And had a wall great and high, and had twelve gates, and at the gates twelve angels, and names written thereon, which are the names of the twelve tribes of the children of Israel:

On the east three gates; on the north three gates; on the south three gates; and on the west three gates.

And the wall of the city had twelve foundations, and in them the names of the twelve apostles of the Lamb.

And he that talked with me had a golden reed to measure the city, and the gates thereof, and the wall thereof.

And the city lieth foursquare, and the length is as large as the breadth: and he measured the city with the reed, twelve thousand furlongs. The length and the breadth and the height of it are equal.

And he measured the wall thereof, an hundred and forty and four cubits, according to the measure of a man, that is, of the angel.

And the building of the wall of it was of jasper; and the city was pure gold, like unto clear glass.

And the foundations of the wall of the city were garnished with all manner of precious stones. The first foundation was jasper; the second, sapphire; the third, a chalcedony; the fourth, an emerald;

The fifth, sardonyx; the sixth, sardius; the seventh, chrysolyte; the eighth, beryl; the ninth, a topaz; the tenth, a chrysoprasus; the eleventh, a jacinth; the twelfth, an amethyst.

And the twelve gates were twelve pearls; every several gate was of one pearl: and the street of the city was pure gold, as it were transparent glass.

And I saw no temple therein: for the Lord God Almighty and the Lamb are the temple of it.

And the city had no need of the sun, neither of the moon, to shine in it: for the glory of God did lighten it, and the Lamb is the light thereof.

And the nations of them which are saved shall walk in the light of it: and the kings of the earth do bring their glory and honour into it.

And the gates of it shall not be shut at all by day; for there shall be no night there.

And they shall bring the glory and honour of the nations into it.

And there shall in no wise enter into it any thing that defileth, neither whatsoever worketh abomination, or maketh a lie: but they which are written in the Lamb's book of life.

And he shewed me a pure river of water of life, clear as crystal, proceeding out of the throne of God and of the Lamb.

In the midst of the street of it, and on either side of the river, was there the tree of life, which bare twelve manner of fruits, and yielded her fruit every month: and the leaves of the tree were for the healing of the nations.

And there shall be no more curse: but the throne of God and of the Lamb shall be in it; and his servants shall serve him:

And they shall see his face; and his name shall be in their foreheads.

And there shall be no night there; and they need no candle, neither light of the sun; for the Lord God giveth them light: and they shall reign for ever and ever.

This description is of our eternal home. This is our final resting place. This is where we shall live forever.

All that we have ever feared or dreaded is passed away. The song we sing is so true:

> There's no disappointment in heaven,
> No weariness, sorrow, or pain;
> No hearts that are bleeding and broken,
> No song with a minor refrain.
>
> There'll never be crepe on the door-knobs,
> No funeral train in the sky
> No graves on the hillsides of glory,
> For there the saints never die.
>
> I'm bound for that beautiful city
> My Lord has prepared for His own,
> Where all the redeemed of all ages,
> Sing "Glory" around the white throne.
>
> Sometimes I grow homesick for heaven
> And the glories I there shall behold
>> What a joy that will be
>> When my Saviour I see
> In that beautiful city of gold.
>
> —F. M. LEHMAN

When our task is finished, heaven is our welcome and an open door into everlasting bliss. Dr. Horatius Bonar wrote the following beautiful expression of heavenly faith. The song was sung at his funeral:

Heaven at Last

> Angel voices sweetly singing,
> Echoes through the blue doom ringing,
> News of wondrous gladness bringing;
>> Ah, 'tis heaven at last!
>
> On the jasper threshold standing,
> Like a pilgrim safely landing;

Jenter and Fort Gordon

don, Ga.

own that

324-62-1209

lly completed the

RATOR COURSE (201-31C10)
13 WEEKS/1 DAY
19 May 86)

varded this

oma *   *   *

y vested in us by the Department of the Army

our signatures and the seal of this institution,

Ga. this _19th_ day of _May_ 19_86_

PETER A. KIND
Brigadier General, USA
Deputy Commanding General

See, the strange bright scene expanding,
  Ah, 'tis heaven at last!

Sin forever left behind us,
Earthly visions cease to blind us,
Earthly fetters cease to bind us;
  Ah, 'tis heaven at last!

Not a teardrop ever falleth,
Not a pleasure ever palleth
Song to song forever calleth;
  Ah, 'tis heaven at last!

Christ himself the living splendor,
Christ the sunlight mild and tender;
Praises to the Lamb we render:
  Ah, 'tis heaven at last!

Broken death's dread bands that bound us;
Life and victory around us;
Christ the King himself hath crowned us;
  Ah, 'tis heaven at last!

—HORATIUS BONAR

The Committal Service

Brevity Called For

Above all else, the committal service at the graveside should be brief and preciously Christian. What the pastor has to say he has said in the service at the church or chapel. This at the graveside is a final benediction.

A Benedictory Service

What I do at the graveside is this: After the family is seated and the friends have gathered around, I read Revelation 22:16-17,20.

I Jesus have sent mine angel to testify unto you these things in the churches. I am the root and the offspring of David, and the bright and morning star.

And the Spirit and the bride say, Come. And let him that heareth say, Come. And let him that is athirst come. And whosoever will, let him take the water of life freely.

He which testifieth these things saith, Surely I come quickly. Amen. Even so, come, Lord Jesus.

Then I pray something like this: "Dear Lord Jesus, all that hands could do have we done. Where we leave off do you take up and take care. Watch over this hallowed place in holy remembrance until the trumpet shall sound and the dead shall be raised in glory. Give us back, then, these we have loved and lost just for awhile. Bless the family that waits in earth until that triumphant day when we shall be joined together in heaven. Send us away to our homes and to the work that awaits us in thy love and grace, and in thy dear name, Amen."

A Final "Goodnight, I Will See You in the Morning"

Let me close this chapter with the Scripture verses upon which more tears have fallen and more hearts have been uplifted than any other place in the Bible. It is John 14:1-3,27.

Let not your heart be troubled: ye believe in God, believe also in me.

In my Father's house are many mansions: if it were not so, I would have told you. I go to prepare a place for you.

And if I go and prepare a place for you, I will come again, and receive you unto myself; that where I am, there ye may be also.

Peace I leave with you, my peace I give unto you: not as the world giveth, give I unto you. Let not your heart be troubled, neither let it be afraid.

Let me add the most beautiful of poems, the verses that closed the Christian life and witness of England's poet laureate, Alfred Lord Tennyson:

Crossing the Bar

Sunset and evening star,
    And one clear call for me!
And may there be no moaning of the bar,
    When I put out to sea.

But such a tide as moving seems asleep,
    To full for sound and foam,
When that which drew from out the boundless deep
    Turns again home.

Twilight and evening bell,
   And after that the dark!
And may there be no sadness of farewell,
   When I embark;

For tho' from out our bourne of Time and Place
   The flood may bear me far,
I hope to see my Pilot face to face
   When I have crossed the bar.

—ALFRED LORD TENNYSON

Last of all, let me quote the hymn of blind Fanny J. Crosby that was sung at my own father's memorial service. How it moved my heart to a renewed faith in Jesus when I heard it at that solemn hour!

Safe in the Arms of Jesus

Safe in the arms of Jesus,
Safe on His gentle breast,
There by His love o'ershaded,
Sweetly my soul shall rest.

Hark! 'tis the voice of angels,
Borne in a song to me,
Over the fields of glory,
Over the jasper sea.

Safe in the arms of Jesus,
Safe from corroding care,
Safe from the world's temptations,
Sin cannot harm me there.

Free from the blight of sorrow,
Free from my doubts and fears;
Only a few more trials,
Only a few more tears!

Jesus, my heart's dear refuge,
Jesus has died for me;
Firm on the Rock of Ages,
Ever my trust shall be.

Here let me wait with patience,
Wait till the night is o'er;
Wait till I see the morning
Break on the golden shore.

Safe in the arms of Jesus,
Safe on His gentle breast,
There by His love o'ershaded,
Sweetly my soul shall rest.

—FANNY J. CROSBY

18

The Pastor Facing
Discouragement and Failure

The Universality of Troubles and Problems

A long time ago old Job cried in his despair: "My sighing cometh before I eat, and my roarings are poured out like the waters. For the thing which I greatly feared is come upon me, and that which I was afraid of is come unto me. . . . Trouble came" (Job 3:24-26). "Yet man is born unto trouble, as the sparks fly upward" (5:7). "Man that is born of a woman is of few days, and full of trouble" (14:1).

Let no pastor persuade himself that he will escape these days and times of trial. Kings and presidents and prime ministers and corporate executives and great men and mighty men confront awesome troubles just the same as prophets and apostles and missionaries and preachers. No one is exempt, not even Moses or Elijah or Peter or Paul. Least of all, therefore, should the pastor think to escape problems and trials, especially since he lives so close to the people.

Problems Pastors Face

The pastor can be openly, brutally fired. One Wednesday night at our church, at the mid-week prayer meeting, was a family of seven—a man, his wife, and five small, stair-step children. After the service he introduced himself to me. He had been the pastor of a church in a nearby county, had been on a vacation with his family, and when he returned the day before it was to learn that the previous Sunday the church, upon the recommendation of the

329

deacons, had voted the pulpit vacant. He had been fired with no previous intimation of such an action. He came to me with many tears and in deepest desperation. With five little children what could he do and where could he turn? this dedicated, saintly, God-called man.

The pastor can fall into deepest depression and discouragement brought about by his own inner response to the quality and success (or lack of it) in his ministry.

He can become disillusioned by his own unrealized goals. None of his dreams have come true.

He can be immeasurably hurt by unfriendly, unwarranted criticism.

He can fall into despair over the apathy, indifference, and lack of cooperation on the part of his congregation.

He can feel frustrated by having to do so many little, lesser jobs that take him away from the main assignment of studying, preaching, teaching, and soul-winning. He has little time for study and visiting the lost.

He can feel the utter futility of his life's work and life-style if he has a family and the children grow up seeing their father only in the pulpit or in the church office. If there is trouble with a teenager in the home such a confiscation of time by the work can be devastating.

And world without end, the small financial compensation by the church for the needs of the pastor sometimes takes many pastors completely out of the ministry.

When a statistic was reported that one out of ten men who enter the ministry quit the work somewhere along the way, a survey was made to find the reasons why. The replies in order of reasons given were these: inadequate salary, overly heavy work load, fishbowl living, opposition to pastoral leadership. Other reasons given were discouragement because of unconcerned church membership, family problems, loss of faith, lack of personal satisfaction, lack of security.

Truly, truly, the problems in the ministry are legion: social isolation, excessive demands on the part of the people, financial strains, administrative pressures, professional competition, psychological tensions, feelings of inadequacy, anxiety, anger, and ten thousand other demonic devices to destroy the effective work of the pastor.

Marcus Dods, a young minister who later became a great preacher and the author of many marvelous books, wrote in his diary, "No day passes without strong temptation to give up the work."

Change of Pastorates: Solution to Problems?

In many, many instances, there are evils in a change of field of service that is not of the Lord. A pastor will give many reasons for wanting to leave his church, but the reasons are not acceptable before God.

One reason a preacher will leave is because he does not want to study. The congregation tires of him so he goes to another field and there he just turns over the barrel and preaches his sermons until they run out, then he goes to yet another field. This is a tragedy, because the preacher ought to study and to be fresh in his message and stay in one church field all of his life (or until *God* sends him to another pastorate). It is a great loss for the preacher to go to another place where he loses all of the friendships and relationships that he has cultivated slowly over a long period of time. The confidence and love of a congregation which a true minister acquires constitute a tremendous element in his power. There are few ministers who widen their range of original investigation after their first pastorate. In the first pastorate, they push out into new fields and they give themselves to deeply intellectual and spiritual growth.

Sometimes the preacher will leave because of mental depression. A sedentary, studious life often induces abnormal nervous conditions and the hypochondriac misinterprets the feelings of the people and underestimates the results of his ministry. A change is consequently resolved upon but developments show that it does not necessarily help him.

Again, the preacher may want to leave because of loss of popularity. This is often due to real defects in the character and work of the pastor and the remedy is not in a change of field but in the preacher himself. He has failed to cultivate executive, pastoral, and spiritual powers. He ought to do better in himself, then he will not want to change. He will only find in a change another example of his own failure.

But the loss of his popularity in the church does not necessarily mean that he has failed before God. Trials such as loss of popularity among some people enter more or less into every minister's lot, but the trial may be sent as a discipline designed to develop through faith and patience a nobler character and a higher power in the preacher. The pastoral tie ought not be disrupted. Maybe God intends a blessing.

Sometimes preachers leave because of ambition for a distinguished position. There is an unhallowed ambition which, unsatisfied with advancement through natural growth, is ever restlessly seeking some more conspicuous pulpit. This is tragic in the ministry.

Sometimes the pastor wants to leave because of multiplying, unsolvable difficulties in the church. He ought to remember, however, that there are no churches without their difficulties. The pastor ought to resist the expectation that another field will be easier and more salubrious than the one in which he now labors. Under no conditions should the preacher leave unless there is a great, compelling reason for his going. Hardships, difficulties, and trials are not among those reasons.

However, we cannot deny that there are valid reasons why a pastor ought to leave his church.

One reason can be that the preacher grows in himself and as a young man he becomes better able to serve the Lord. A greater field of opportunity seeks him out and he feels it the will of God that he go.

Sometimes there are necessities of health that cause the minister to change to a climate that would be more favorable.

Sometimes the church is so small it cannot support the pastor, and he has opportunity to go to a church that can support him. Being careful and prayerful not to go to a place just because of a larger salary, he ought to go because of his family and the greater freedom he will possess in devoting his entire time and talents to the gospel ministry.

Sometimes there are uncontrollable influences in the church arrayed against the pastor and he has no other choice but to continue his ministry in another place. It is far better for the pastor to sense and to see this developing situation and resign rather than to be fired. If he resigns, he can leave in goodwill and be graciously introduced to pulpit committees and church leaders who are looking for a pastor or a worker in some other corner of the vineyard of the Lord.

But all these decisions should be made in the will and mind of the Lord. Fundamentally and ultimately, the pastor ought to accept trials and tribulations in his church. A change of place will only change the form of the trial. He should face these difficulties where he is and not seek to run away from them. It was Jesus our Savior who said, "In the world ye shall have tribulation: but be of good cheer; I have overcome the world" (John 16:33).

The Pastor Triumphing Over Trouble

Above all and everything else, the pastor needs always to remember that he is not alone in his work. If God has called him, God's Spirit will be with him and help him. Lay it all before the Lord; tell him about it; seek his face and divine wisdom. He has answers we never thought of and ways of solution we never dreamed of. Pray and pray and pray. God will answer and answer. Always the pastor's greatest resource is God.

David was most discouraged when the people forgot his service for them and threatened to kill him. To counter this discouragement, he "encouraged himself in the Lord his God" (1 Sam. 30:6).

"This poor man cried, and the Lord heard him, and saved him out of all his troubles. Many are the afflictions of the righteous: but the Lord delivereth him out of them all. The Lord redeemeth the soul of his servants: and none of them that trust in him shall be desolate" (Ps. 34:6,19,22).

Many of the preacher's problems he brings on himself. Too often poor judgment, indiscretion, blind ambition, thirst for power, dishonesty, personality clashes, plain pigheadedness, etc., take their toll and severely weaken the union so that both church and pastor are frustrated, with anger manifesting itself upon unhappy occasions.

False ambition can eat him up. Never court high places or personal recognition and advancement. We never find the Savior on the pinnacle of the Temple but once, and guess who accompanied him there? Let others seek the chief seats in the synagogue and be escorted to the head of the table and "politic" for election in ecclesiastical circles. *You* do God's work in the calling wherein he has called you and leave the results to him.

Jealousy and envy can consume the heart out of a pastor. It can literally burn him up. Instead of being resentful upon the fame or success of another man, praise God for him, pray for him, rejoice in his accomplishments. A London pastor said that when young Spurgeon came to London he was chagrined and mortified by the vast throngs that came to hear the youth while his own following was so small. He said that he then began to pray for the rising young preacher, and it was not long before he felt that every triumph won by Spurgeon he had a part in it himself. That is great!

Do not be jealous of your predecessor. Embalm him in honey, not in vinegar. The people will love and admire you for it. Speak good words about him. The people who loved him will love you.

Avoid human, man-made stress. The devil is in it, not God. Paul wrote, "Be careful for nothing; but in every thing by prayer and supplication with thanksgiving let your requests be made known unto God" (Phil. 4:6). There are many men who live a quiet and calm life in the midst of frustrating circumstances that would drive most of us up the wall. Humanly speaking, the reason is they have come to trust in the Lord in the same way that they have come to terms with their own inner responses and drives. This will answer any problem of stress.

Avoid that nervous, emotional breakdown. It is man-made, self-made. Ministers used to be the best of all insurance risks. That is no longer true. Life expectancy for the pastor is slipping and casualties from heart attacks and nervous breakdowns are depressingly frequent.

Exercise! God never made a man to sit behind a desk in an office chair every day all day long. A completely sedentary life will cripple every muscle and bone and nerve and fiber in the human anatomy. God made those muscles and joints and sinews to *move.* Move them! Every day the pastor ought to walk or jog or do calisthenics or play a brief game of handball, volleyball, anything. The essential ingredient is its regularity. A half hour's activity each day is much more productive than an afternoon's golf session once a week. Do something strenuous *every day.* Your body and mind and heart will respond beautifully.

Eat right. Follow a balanced diet. A sickly man with a poor stomach, prone to catch every virus that comes along, is half-defeated before he enters the arena to fight the Lord's battles.

There is stress in the pastorate, an everlasting avalance of it every day. But God gives us wisdom to triumph over it all.

How the pastor meets criticism will largely determine his effectiveness in leading a congregation to greater heights of service for the Lord. It would be a rare public figure, indeed, who did not become acquainted with unfriendly and caustic criticism, be he politician, policeman, or preacher. Any man who stands up and out to be seen is vulnerable to all sorts of rock-throwing. What should the reaction of the pastor be?

He can be very sensitive to the unkind words. He can be belligerently hasty in combating what others say about him. He can confront the critic with blustering speech and wear iron, hobnailed shoes as he stomps on the toes of those who dare reproach him. He can make bitter enemies both of the person who said the corrosive sentence and the friends and families who listen to the searing words. But he that spits against the wind spits in his own face. There is no need to scare off a fly with a club when a feather will turn the trick. There are far better ways to react than through bitter reprisal. After all, the minister's work is to break hard hearts and to mend broken ones. His job is not to hurt but to heal, not to war but to witness. We can attract far more beautiful flying butterflies with molasses than with vinegar.

First of all, why not pray about the whole matter? Pray for the persons involved, pray about the situation that caused the criticism, pray for a worthy and Christ-honoring solution. Out of the intercession may come the conclusion that it is best just to ignore it. Maybe the critic was "just talking." People like to talk.

Second, why not consider carefully the criticism if it is worthy calling to mine? Maybe it is the pastor who is wrong. Ask yourself: "Is God speaking to me through this unfavorable word? Is this criticism true? Is it partly true?'' Consider the man who said the words. Is he a man of good judgment? Of noble character?

If I had my ministry to live over again, here is one place where I would utterly and absolutely change. Because a man questions the programs offered by the pastor in a deacon's meeting or in the discussions of a church committee, does not mean that he is the pastor's enemy. After all, wisdom will not die with the pastor (so Job would say in Job 12:2). It could be that another man's observation and suggestions have real merit in them. Listen. Do not be offended. Work out together a better solution or a finer method of approach.

Anyway and finally, the pastor is to exemplify the epitome of Christian witness. If he is not a follower of the Lord, who is? And it was the Lord who said:

Ye have heard that it hath been said, An eye for an eye, and a tooth for a tooth:

But I say unto you, That ye resist not evil: but whosoever shall smite thee on thy right cheek, turn to him the other also.

And if any man will sue thee at the law, and take away thy coat, let him have thy cloak also.

And whosoever shall compel thee to go a mile, go with him twain . . . .

Ye have heard that it hath been said, Thou shalt love thy neighbour, and hate thine enemy.

But I say unto you, Love your enemies, bless them that curse you, do good to them that hate you, and pray for them which despitefully use you, and persecute you;

That ye may be the children of your Father which is in heaven: for he maketh his sun to rise on the evil and on the good, and sendeth rain on the just and on the unjust.

For if ye love them which love you, what reward have ye? do not even the publicans the same?

And if ye salute your brethren only, what do ye more than others? do not even the publicans so?

Be ye therefore perfect, even as your Father which is in heaven is perfect (Matt. 5:38-41, 43-48).

It was the wisest king who ever reigned who said, ''A soft answer turneth away wrath: but grievous words stir up anger'' (Prov. 15:1).

The same King Solomon added, "By long forbearing is a prince persuaded, and a soft tongue breaketh the bone" (Prov. 25:15). We would say that a gentle spirit and a gracious answer kill one's critic with kindness. The ways of a righteous man make even his enemies to praise him. Let the pastor be like that righteous man.

Too often the pastor takes advantage of his pulpit to scold the congregation for nonattendance, for a poor financial response, for a shortage of volunteers, and for any other thing that disappoints him or frustrates him. Always this is a vast mistake. Instead of pouncing on the people with lethal strokes who did come to the worship service, why not show appreciation for those who did come, and why not prayerfully and astutely tackle the problem with all the wisdom and vigor God has given you? T. DeWitt Talmadge one time said: "On stormy days the scolding preacher berates the people who are in church for the neglect of those who have stayed at home. He expects to bring up flowers of Christian character under the blow of a northeast storm. Now, there are times when ministers ought to be indignant and denunciatory; but learn this, young men, you can never scold people out of their sins, nor scold them into regularity of church attendance, nor scold them into heaven. You cannot scold your church up, although you can very easily scold it down. It takes honey to catch flies and men. Never go fishing with a crab apple for bait."

The great Brooklyn preacher-pastor then went on to suggest the cure for the irate clergyman: "In order to avoid this keep your digestion good. You want not only a sanctified heart but a sound liver. Eat no lobster salad Saturday night. Take gymnastics; split wood; ride horseback; row a boat; keep the pores open with a cold water bath and a coarse towel. It is a shame for a minister to wash only his fingers and the tip of his nose. Get good, sound, robust health, and it will be almost impossible for you to scold."

Three things are seen in that exhortation that Talmadge thinks will help the unhappy preacher. One, he speaks of a sanctified heart. That ought to cure many pastoral anxieties. If the man is called of God to preach, he ought to have the love of Jesus in his heart. Two, he suggests proper eating habits. Any doctor will commend such a program for the preacher. It will surprise the pulpiteer what a difference will appear in his preaching when he changes from feeling physically ill to feeling physically strong. Three, Talmadge outlines a schedule of vigorous, rail-splitting exercise. My brother, that ought to cure any man's predisposition to be despondent, dejected, and depressed!

One fruit of the Spirit is patience (sometimes called "longsuffering," Gal. 5:22). How the pastor needs it in working with people! It sometimes requires all the Christian fortitude that a pastor can command to bring this virtue to bear upon a prayed-for project, but the kind and loving waiting pays off in real dividends. When I came to the church here in Dallas, west of the Mississippi River, another went to be under shepherd of a like kind of church east of the river. Both churches were controlled and run by older men (the average age of the deacons in Dallas when I came was over sixty-five, nearer seventy). Over there he was impatient, lost the older men, lost the wealthy families, finally he became so unhappy he lost the church. Today it is a shell, hardly existing. In Dallas we prayed and waited, waited and prayed, worked and longed for the blessing of God. It took me six years just to budge the congregation forward a little bit. But it paid off. We kept the church together, kept the older men with the younger men, kept the old-timers with the new-timers, and the day arrived when the church grew prodigiously. O God, how I thank thee!

It is wonderful when the pastor can accept discouragements, disappointments, and disheartening, dispiriting providences as challenges to be prayed through, worked over, and used as stepping stones to a higher ground of achievement. Any dejecting development is the gauntlet thrown down before the wisdom and ingenuity of the pastoral leadership. Why not accept it in the Spirit of the Lord and turn the trouble into triumph by the power of him who split the Red Sea, made rivers of waters gush from the solid rock, poured fire down from heaven upon the altar of Elijah, raised Jesus from among the dead, and has all authority in heaven and in earth?

Each fall we have a young preacher-graduate of Spurgeon's College in London to come spend a year working with us in our church. After the year's experience in learning how we do things here in America, he returns to a pastorate in England. Our first intern was Rodney Sawtell. His first letter to me, after going home to his assigned church near London, said this: "From a preacher's viewpoint I have once again had to face empty pews. What a depressing sight! The other day I was told of a Baptist Union committee which had collected certain statistics regarding our Baptist work and fed them into a computer. The machine's forecast was that by the year AD 2000 no Baptist churches would be left in Great Britain! What a dismal prospect! And yet *what a challenge* as we go forward in God's strength." Look at that last sentence, "What a challenge!" If there were no sickness, the doctors would be out of a job. If there were no bank failures and frauds, the inspectors would be superfluous. If there were no sinners, the preachers would be just so much excess baggage. If there were no dead churches, there would be no need for the evangelist and the revivalist. Believe me, we need them all! There is a challenge to be met, a war to be won, a lost world to save, churches to be built, children to be taught, and God has called us to do it. Every difficulty and hardship and discouragement carries with it a supreme challenge.

Pastor, stay with it! I asked Preacher Halleck one time what he did with his opposition. He replied: "I just outlive 'em!" He stayed as pastor of the First Church in Norman, Oklahoma, forty-eight years! Do not give up. Victory will come. One of the deacons in our church (Boone Powell) has built one of the great Baptist hospitals in the world, Baylor Medical Center. I was talking to him one day about problems and he said: "Any big problem can be broken down into little problems. Having thus broken it down, solve the little problems one at a time and finally the whole is solved." Take one task at a time. Do it well, then go to the next. Victory is inevitable.

The Pastor Who Is Victim of Circumstances

It is not possible for me to close this chapter without a word of deepest sympathy for those pastors who are the victims of circumstances, of bodily illnesses or cruel providences over which they have no control. A young preacher in my class at the seminary was told by his wife the night he received his degree that she was divorcing him, that she refused to be a preacher's wife, and that she was returning home. My heart bled for him. It ruined his ministry, which was so promising.

Illnesses of mind and body can decimate a pastor's life. Even the incomparable Charles Haddon Spurgeon fell into deepest depression of spirit. He frequently referred to the affliction in his sermons. In one of them he says, "I am the subject of depressions of spirit so fearful that I hope none of you ever get to such extremes of wretchedness as I go to." He died in the very prime of his life. Only God knows the reason for such sorrow and trial. Maybe it was that "in the great trial of affliction" his burdened heart brought untold comfort to the multitude of people to whom he preached. Paul said that it was "lest be exalted above measure" (2 Cor. 12:7) that there was given him a thorn in the flesh. When he besought the Lord to take it from him, the Lord answered, "My grace is sufficient for thee: for my strength is made perfect in weakness" (v. 9). Paul then wrote of his affliction: "And in all things I have kept myself from being burdensome unto you, and so will I keep myself. As the truth of Christ is in me, no man shall stop me of this boasting in the regions of Achaia" (11:9-10).

It may be thus with the godly pastor who bears a heavy burden: God's strength is made perfect in his weakness. Just help us, Lord, for we lean upon thy kind arm.

19

The Pastor in His Personal Life

The Power of Personal Example

The greatest, finest, noblest sermon any pastor ever delivers is that of his own example. Ralph Waldo Emerson said it like this, "What you are speaks so loud, I cannot hear what you say." No man can preach above the crying voice of his own life's example. To be powerfully and movingly effective, he must incarnate in his own flesh and body the spiritual principles he advocates. People can *see* a sermon far easier than they can *hear* one. The gospel according to you is the gospel most of them will follow, not the one in a delivered message or a written book. A good example is worth ten thousand wordy addresses and expostulations. Let the pastor be truly the man of God and the whole world can but be moved by his noble life, even his enemies.

The Holy Scriptures emphasize that the pastor is to lead a personal life that constitutes a worthy example for the people. It is not "Do as I say" but much more nearly "Do as I do." Paul did not hesitate, and that without egotism, to urge his converts to follow him in the example of his own life. He wrote to the Corinthians, "Be ye followers of me, even as I also am of Christ" (1 Cor. 11:1). He wrote to the people who were at Philippi: "Those things which ye have both learned, and received, and heard, and seen in me, do: and the God of peace shall be with you" (Phil. 4:9). He wrote to the church of the Thessalonians, "Ye are witnesses, and God also, how holily and justly and unblameably we behaved ourselves among you that believe" (1 Thess. 2:10). He exhorted his son in the ministry, Timothy, with these words, "Let no man despise thy youth; but be thou an example of the believers, in word, in conversation, in charity, in spirit, in faith, in purity" (1 Tim. 4:12).

The preacher is the preacher not only in the pulpit but more powerfully, dynamically, effectively so in his daily walk before the eyes of the people.

Phillips Brooks said, "And first among the elements of power which make success, I must put the supreme importance of character, of personal uprightness, and purity impressing themselves upon the men who witness them." Quintilian said that the good speaker must be a good man. Saint Francis of Assisi made the same point when he said, "No use to go anywhere to preach unless we preach while we go."

Message Backed by a Life

What the pastor pleads for in the pulpit he must first demonstrate in his own personal, private life. If he preaches on prayer, he must first pray. If he preaches on love, he must first be loving. If he preaches on soul-winning, he must be a soul-winner. Whatever the subject, he must first let the people see that he follows in his own life the virtues for which he pleads in others. Otherwise, his words and his invitations are sounding brass and clanging cymbal.

In the days of the great pastor, George W. Truett, there was in the church here in Dallas a faithful deacon named H. Z. Duke. He was a tither and so believed in being a good steward of the Lord that he went from church to church pleading for the people to be honest and true to God, and God would in turn bless them. Remembering the fame of this successful businessman, I was deeply moved by this story of his appeal to a preacher to lead his people in a commitment to Christ that would result in their tithing all that came into their hands. This is the story as told by that preacher, a county missionary whose name was Brother Kuykendal.

Some years ago when I was county missionary in this county the famous Baptist businessman, H. Z. Duke, who founded the Duke and Ayers Nickel Stores over a wide area, came to this county and spoke about tithing. Speaking as a Christian layman he urged the men and women to try God and see if he would not make good his promises to bless them in material things when they gave tithes and offerings to his cause.

After Mr. Duke had spoken in one community, I took him in my buggy to another community. Mr. Duke said to me, "Brother Kuykendal, do you believe in tithing?"

"I certainly do," I said. "I believe in tithing and I preach it myself."

Sadly I had to answer, "No, I do not. I believe in tithing, but I cannot practice it. You see, I have thirteen children at home. Every meal, fifteen of us sit down at the table. I receive only $125 a month—$1,500 a year—as salary. I have to maintain my own horse and buggy for constant traveling. It is just impossible to take care of all the needs of a family of fifteen out of $125 a month and have money left to tithe. So I believe in tithing and I preach it—but I cannot practice it."

Mr. Duke was a very kindly man. He said, "Brother Kuykendal, would you like to tithe? Would you tithe if I would back you up financially so you could be sure you would not lose by it?"

"Nothing would please me more," I said.

Mr. Duke made me the following proposition: "I want you to set out to give God at least $12.50 every month, as soon as you get your salary. Then as you feel led, you may give more. I promise you that if you need help, I will give it. Simply write me a letter and say, 'Brother Duke, I am giving a tithe, but I miss the money. I need it for my family. I have given this year so much.' I promise you that I will send you a check by return mail. Are you willing to try tithing on that basis?"

I hesitated a moment, deeply moved. Brother Duke said, "I have thirty-two stores. I have plenty of money to make good my promise. I will be glad to do it. Will you trust me and start tithing on my simple promise that I will make good any amount you have given, any time that you find you miss it and need it? Will you trust me about it?"

I gladly accepted his offer. I said, "Yes, Brother Duke, I have long wanted to tithe, but I felt I simply could not do it. Now, thank God, I can tithe and I will be glad to. And I will not feel like a hypocrite when I tell others they ought to tithe."

So I started tithing for the first time in my life. Every month I took the first one tenth of my salary and gave it to the Lord's cause. Later, as I felt led, I gave more. In the back of my mind I always had this thought: Mr. Duke promised me that he would make it up any time I need it. He will send me the money if I simply ask him for it.

But a strange thing happened. It seemed our money went farther than before. I would preach in some country community, and somebody would tie a crate of chickens on the back of my buggy. Somebody would put a ham under the seat, or a godly woman would put some home-canned fruit in my buggy.

A neighbor farmer said, "Brother Kuykendal, God has blessed me so that I cannot get all my corn in the crib this year. I have a big wagonload extra that I cannot keep. May I put it in your crib for your buggy horse?"

Another neighbor drove over with a great wagonload of hay for the cow. It was very strange, but that year we had no doctor bills. The children's clothes seemed not to wear out so badly. It was a happy, happy time. I never did have to call on Mr. H. Z. Duke to make up the money I had given to the Lord in tithes.

Then one day, when the year was about gone and the test was about over, I suddenly realized with shame that I had believed what H. Z. Duke said. He promised to make good anything I lacked because of tithing, and I believed him. But my heavenly Father had made the same promise, and I had not believed him!

I had taken the word of a man when I did not take the promise of God! I had proven God's promises and found that he took care of me and my big family on a small salary. I found that $112.50 per month took care of our family better, with God's blessings, than $125 did without being under the covenant of blessing which he has made with those who seek first his kingdom and who tithe.

Now I have tithed for many years. My salary has been increased year after year. We have always had enough. We have never been shamed. The greatest spiritual blessing of my life, aside from my salvation, has been in learning to trust God about daily needs for my home and a big family.

It is ever thus with the pastor. If he will be in himself what he seeks to cultivate in others, the battle is already half won. If he will himself do before the people what he appeals for them to do, then response is already half favorable. He is a powerful, persuasive pulpiteer who preaches by his example as well as by his words.

The Pastor's Inward Strength

1. The first and foremost of all the inward strengths of the pastor is the conviction, deep as life itself, that God has called him to the ministry. If this persuasion is unshakeable, all other elements of the pastor's life will fall into beautiful order and place.

There is no doubt but that the Bible presents the minister as a God-called man. In the Old Testament no prophet dared intrude into the sacred office of himself. God had to call him (Deut. 18:20; Jer. 23:30; Isa. 6; Jer. 1:4-10).

Ministers in the New Testament are always spoken of as designated by God (Acts 20:28; Col. 4:17). Paul and Barnabas were separated unto the work whereunto the Holy Spirit called them (Acts 13:2). The ministry constitutes a special gift from Christ to the church (Eph. 4:11-12). The gifts for these offices are bestowed by God and the men are sent forth to the work by God himself in answer to the prayers of the people (Rom. 12:6-7; Luke 10:1-3).

The ministers of Christ are called "ambassadors for Christ" (2 Cor. 5:20); that is, they come speaking in his name. They are stewards of God entrusted with the gospel for men. One of the strong words in the Bible concerning the call to the ministry is found written by Paul in 1 Corinthians 9:16-17:

For though I preach the gospel, I have nothing to glory of: for necessity is laid upon me; yea, woe is unto me, if I preach not the gospel!

For if I do this thing willingly, I have a reward: but if against my will, a dispensation of the gospel is committed unto me.

There must always be in the life of the pastor an abiding impression of duty to preach the gospel!

To the gospel ministry there will always be an inward call the pastor cannot quench. There is a fixed and earnest desire for the work on the part of the pastor himself (1 Tim. 3:1). This desire comes from God above. It is a quenchless enthusiasm for the work, as he proclaims God's message for the saving of men (Acts 20:24). Then, of course, there is the call of the church, the outward call. This is expressed in the conviction of the church that results in a persuasion that the man has the qualifications for being a minister of the gospel. If the only one who believes that he is called to the ministry is the man himself, it is a sure sign that he is not called. If a man is called of God to preach, other people will sense it and realize it.

The man who is called of God must have himself personally a deep persuasion and conviction that he is "in Christ." A defect here is fatal—fatal to the minister himself and fatal to the people where God has placed him as an under shepherd.

The man must also have a superior order of piety (1 Tim. 4:12). As we have said, he is to be a model for the people. He is to be sound in the faith (2 Tim. 1:13; Titus 2:1). He must have adequate mental capacity and training in scriptural knowledge (2 Tim. 2:15). He must be apt to teach (1 Tim. 3:2; 2 Tim. 2:2; 2 Tim. 2:24-25). Acts 14:1 says "[Paul and Barnabas] so spake, that a great multitude believed."

He is to be a man of practical wisdom and executive ability. A large part of a pastor's success depends upon his possession of certain practical qualities.

Finally, he must have a good report of them which are without (1 Tim. 3:7; 2 Cor. 4:2; 6:3). The ministry is degraded and slandered by unworthy men, some of whom are guilty of compromise that make even the heathen blush.

Luther wrote in his commentary on Galatians, "Every minister of God's Word should be sure of his calling, that before God and man, he may, with a bold conscience, glory therein, that he preach the Gospel as one that is sent, even as the ambassador of a king glorieth and vaunteth in this, that he cometh not as a private person, but as the King's ambassador."

The famous Christian poet and literary giant, William Cowper, described the God-called man in these poetic lines:

> Would I describe a preacher, such as Paul,
> Were he on earth, would hear, approve, and own—

Paul should himself direct me. I would trace
His master-strokes, and draw from his design.
I would express him simple, grave, sincere;
In doctrine uncorrupt; in language plain,
And plain in manner, decent, solemn, chaste,
And natural in gesture, much impressed
Himself, as conscious of his awful charge,
And anxious mainly that the flock he feeds
May feel it too; affectionate in look
And tender in address, as well becomes
A messenger of grace to guilty men.

—WILLIAM COWPER

If the pastor is thus the true messenger from heaven, and inwardly believes in his divine calling, all the devils in hell and demons on earth cannot stop his effective ministry. He will win souls, build churches, and glorify the name of Christ in his every word and deed.

2. The inward strength of a pastor gained from a worthy wife and a devoted, Godly family is beyond description. It is a living flow of life-healing, soul-encouraging waters. If the pastor has found the companion God has intended for him, he is already building his ministry on solid foundations. It is great to see the pastor's wife be:

A woman who feels that being the wife of a minister will give her the opportunity to do the most effective work she could possibly do for the Lord.

A woman who is willing to become a student of the Bible.

A woman who loves people, finds happiness in visiting with church members, witnesses to the lost, who wants to teach a Sunday School class, is willing to visit the sick several times each week if necessary (many times it is more suitable for a woman to visit another woman in the hospital than it is for the minister himself to visit), will not demand a great deal of time from her husband, is a good housekeeper and desires to be a good wife and mother, makes herself available to as many of the church people as possible, makes the most of her "looks" and is always attractively attired, is a good cook and enjoys entertaining, has an outgoing personality, prays for her husband and his ministry, and can know about problems in the church and keep them to herself.

What a pastor's wife that would be! God multiply her kind in the earth.

Somebody out of the unknown from somewhere wrote these words about the preacher's wife:

The Preacher's Wife

There is one person in our church
Who knows our preacher's life;
Who wept and smiled and prayed with him,
And that's the preacher's wife.

The crowd has seen him in his strength,
When wielding God's sharp sword.
As underneath God's banner folds
He faced the devil's horde.

But deep within her heart she knows
That scarce an hour before
She helped him pray the glory down
Behind the closet door.

She's heard him groaning in his soul,
When bitter raged the strife,
As, hand in hand, she knelt with him—
For she's the preacher's wife!

You tell your tales of prophets brave
Who marched across the world
And changed the course of history
By burning words they hurled.

And I will tell you back of each
Some woman lived her life;
Who wept with him and smiled with him—
She was the preacher's wife!

—AUTHOR UNKNOWN

With a wife like that the pastor is strong in the Lord beyond his own strength. God helps him through her.

3. The ultimate and abiding secret strength of the pastor lies in his daily walk with God. I have heard it said of Martin Luther that

when the responsibilities of his ecclesiastical work became heavy, he could not carry them on without at least four hours a day in prayer. Usually we turn it around, assuming that our many pressing duties make it impossible for us to linger long in the presence of God. But we go further on our knees than by any other way. There are a thousand mistakes we make that would never be made if we took time to pray. There are hasty decisions we follow after, hot and intemperate remarks that we make, false goals that we pursue, and lost souls that we never win, because we have not prayed. All of this beside the poverty of power in our preaching. It is no waste of time for the pastor to spend long hours in prayer. This can be his secret weapon in overcoming every trial and difficulty.

Someone who really knew the Lord and who found all the needed answers in him must have written these lines:

> When you are weary in body and soul,
>   Cumbered with many a care,
> When work is claiming its strength-taking toll,
>   Make it a matter of prayer.
>
> When you're discouraged, distraught, or dismayed
>   Sinking almost in despair,
> Remember, there is One who will come to your aid,
>   If you'll make it a matter of prayer.
>
> And when you are lost in the world's tangled maze,
>   When life seems a hopeless affair,
> Direction will come for all of your ways,
>   If you'll make it a matter of prayer.
>
> —Author Unknown

In every way even God could possibly do has he encouraged us to pray, even to "pray without ceasing" (1 Thess. 5:17). In Jeremiah 33:3 he says:

Call unto me, and I will answer thee, and shew thee great and mighty things, which thou knowest not.

In Luke 11:9-13 our Lord says:

And I say unto you, Ask, and it shall be given you; seek, and ye shall find; knock, and it shall be opened unto you.

For every one that asketh receiveth; and he that seeketh findeth; and to him that knocketh it shall be opened.

If a son shall ask bread of any of you that is a father, will he give him a stone? or if he ask a fish, will he for a fish give him a serpent?

Or if he shall ask an egg, will he offer him a scorpion?

If ye then, being evil, know how to give good gifts unto your children: how much more shall your heavenly Father give the Holy Spirit to them that ask him?

We are encouraged to pray by the example of God's people. Abraham stood long before the Lord, interceding for the lost cities of the plain (Gen. 18:23-33). Moses so pled for his people that he asked to die if they could not be saved (Ex. 32:30-34). Sorrowing Hannah prayed for the gift of a child (1 Sam. 1:10-18). Daniel prayed for the deliverance of Israel in the days of their terrible captivity (Dan. 9:1-19). Our Lord and Savior, the Lord Jesus, was oft in prayer, sometimes praying all night long (Luke 6:12; Mark 1:35). The church prayed for boldness in witness (Acts 4:24-31). In the Revelation the prayer of the saints ever comes up before God (Rev. 8:3-4).

We are encouraged to pray by the stupendous proportion of our assignment. Facing a lost world, who is equal for these things? Who can regenerate even the humblest child who asks for the way to be saved? O Lord, how we need thy saving, delivering, converting presence! Our task sends us to our knees.

And it is the pastor down on his knees that gives him inward, spiritual strength that can be gained in no other way. Pray for the lost, pray for the church, pray for the people, pray for understanding and patience, pray over and about everything that concerns the responsibility and duties of a God-fearing, soul-loving pastor.

Spiritual force comes from within, from the hidden life of God in the soul. It comes from the Holy Spirit (Matt. 10:20). The virtue of an electric wire is not in the wire but in its connection with the generator. The power of the minister is not in the polish of his style or the effectiveness of his illustrations or in his fervor or in the order and arrangement of his discourse, but his power is found in the living connection with God and his capacity to act as a connecting link between God and the human soul. It is God in the soul that is the secret of true pulpit power. So the preacher ought to spend much time alone, there with the Lord by himself. Let him bare his soul before God. Prayer has its mightiest reflex power upon the minister himself. The whole man is elevated, ennobled, and transfused with divine life as he holds communion with God. When Moses had been with God in the mount, his face shone with such a glory that Israel could not stedfastly look upon it. It was when Jesus was praying that he was transfigured (Matt. 17:2). Prayer and meditation are the strength of the pastor. Spiritual truth is revealed only to the spiritual mind (1 Cor. 2:14).

The love of God, the condition of the lost, the saving grace of Christ, these are not matters of cold, barren intellectualism. The atmosphere of prayer will be most sensed in the congregation in the very attitude and tone and voice and gesture of the preacher. Payson on his deathbed said, "Prayer is the first thing, the second thing, and the third thing necessary for a minister." Whitefield spent hours of each day on his knees with God's open Word before him. Jesus spent sometimes the whole night in prayer. At other times he was described as rising up a great while before day to seek communion with his Father.

The preacher ought to give himself to supplication and the appropriation of divine truth in prayer with an open Bible before him. God's only way, so far as we know, of saving and sanctifying the soul is through the truth of God (1 Pet. 1:23; John 17:17), delivering to the people the mind of God as we find it in the Holy Scriptures. The best lives have found the greatest value in those sessions set aside for prayer. So will you.

His Outward Strength

There are many facets of a pastor's life that are openly seen by the people. If these are in beautiful order, the ways and habits of the pastor inspire confidence among the parishioners; if something in the life-style of the pastor is sorely lacking, he ought to go into some other work before the disappointed people force him out of the ministry and into secular work.

What are these outward strengths (or weaknesses) of the pastor? Here are some we name.

1. He ought to present before the people an earnest effort as an able minister of the gospel. A lazy, indifferent pastor is a blot on the good name of the ministry. The janitor may be lazy and the cook may be no-account, but not the preacher. He ought to be the hardest worker of them all. Wise and faithful in dealing with the souls of his people, he ought day and night to be declaring the whole counsel of God (Ezek. 3:17-21; 33:7-9; Acts 20:27).

2. The business relations of the pastor ought to be above reproach. He ought to owe no man anything (Rom. 13:8), that is, he ought to incur no debt that he cannot make ready provision to pay. As a principle of life, he ought not to run into debt. He is to live within his income, whatever that is, and he is to use all care and all proper forms in making business commitments and arrangements. He is to live by the gospel (1 Cor. 9:14), and if that is impossible, he is to supplement his income by honest labor in some other field of endeavor. For the preacher to be a bad risk in the business world is unthinkable.

One corollary that will bless and help the pastor of good business principles and habits is the confidence he thereby engenders in the souls he is seeking to lead. If the pastor is a man of good, common business sense, the ablest men in the church will listen to him at budget time, at church-building time, and program-enlargement time; in fact, his ability to lead the men into any kind of expansion will largely be determined by the amount of confidence the men have in his common-sense, practical leadership. To be a visionary will not do, however prayerful the preacher. He must also find terrestrial feet for his dreams.

3. Let me point out to the pastor a material, business arrangement that will bless him immeasurably as he comes to the close of his ministry. It came to me poignantly in the county seat town of my first pastorate. Pastor of a little congregation of Presbyterians was the sweetest, dearest little man you ever saw, with a wife just as petite and precious. But they were growing old. The men of the church, fearing the responsibility of an old man on their hands, decided to fire him. After all, who wants to support an aged couple? Even family members are reluctant to put up with the poorer elements of their tribe; and many of them even refuse to take care of father, mother, and grandparents. No wonder, there-

fore, that the leaders of this church thought it expedient to dismiss their pastor before he became a financial liability.

When the proposal was announced to the sweet, little preacher, he astonished the visiting committee. He rejoiced! He replied: "My wife and I have a house in Florida. We have a private, personal income with more than enough for all our needs. We have continued in the ministry only because we felt the call of God in the church. But if the church feels that our work is finished, we shall take it as the Lord's will for our lives, move to our home in Florida, and live at ease the rest of our days." Thereupon it was the turn of the men on the dismissal committee to be astonished. They reasoned to one another: "Say, men and brethren, we have made a mistake. We have got this man wrong. He is an asset, not a liability. He is a good businessman, not a mendicant. We need a pastor like that." They so reported to the church, and the church voted unanimously and enthusiastically to keep him!

What human nature is like!

But I never forgot the lesson. I reread Proverbs 6:6-8, a passage of business brilliance in which God's wisest man said that we ought to provide in summer time for the cold of the coming wintertime. The wintertime is coming for the pastor as well as for all other men, and he needs to prepare for it. If the church sees that you are not going to be a liability and a burden, they will have a disposition to keep you without fear.

Save up for old age. Carefully make arrangements with your church pension board for the most generous support they can offer upon the day of your freedom from pastoral duties. You will be glad that you did. The church will be glad, also. And if you even add to that retirement check from the pension board an increase from your own private savings and investments, you and everybody will be all the better for it.

4. All of this means that the good pastor ought to be a good manager. He must never let his emotions, however well-meaning they are, carry him beyond his ability to pay for his likes and loves. A young theolog at the seminary made appeal to one of our businesswomen for financial help. She went to see the student and his wife. The first thing she noticed in the kitchen was a dishwasher. She asked the suppliant where the money for the appli-

ance came from. He replied that he wanted to show his young wife how much he loved her, so he bought the dishwasher on credit with monthly payments. The businesswoman exclaimed, "Any girl ought to be able to wash dishes for two!" I am sure the young preacher truly loves his wife but he certainly does not love his ministry in its business reputation. They both need to pray for and pay for and proceed on a more spiritually profitable and agreed-upon footing.

The pastor needs to be an expert manager in three categories of his life: One, time; he has just so much and no more. Two, money; he will have just so much and no more. Three, energy; he has just so much and no more. It does not glorify God for the pastor to go bankrupt in any of the three.

5. Being a public figure, the pastor must be most careful about allowing himself to be drawn into political controversy. He ought to take part in the civic life of his community and state and nation (Rom. 13:1-7), but his pronouncements ought always to be on the basis of principle and not according to personal, political accommodations. The pastor ought always to respond on the grounds of what is the right, moral, godly thing for the people to do.

Sometimes to distinguish between the personalities involved in a campaign and the moral principles involved is not easy. Some issues are very clearly delineated for the pastor: pornography, drunkenness, homosexuality, gambling, violence, and many like moral issues classified by Paul as "the works of the flesh" (Gal. 5:19-21). But many areas of civic life are sometimes gray in appearance, not black and white. In any event, it is far better for the pastor to stay with moral principles involved in any issue, and keep his personal preferences for personalities to private conversations.

6. The pastor ought to avoid the extremes of being a hail-fellow-well-met with everybody, and at the same time not appearing to be antisocial. There is a golden mean in social relationships.

7. The pastor ought to be a Christian gentleman and he ought to dress like one and look like one. God made him a man before God made him a preacher. Why not look the part of a God-made man, representing the causes of Christ with dignity and with sobriety? One pastor of a large church went to his church in Bermuda

shorts, and so had stated conferences with his people. He said this informality placed him on their level and made his parishioners feel comfortable. On the basis of that actual inanity he is no longer there. There are certain rules of decorum and dress that a good pastor will meticulously observe.

8. Let the pastor always speak without coarseness or indelicacy. He can be gentle, courteous, affable, gregarious, even fun-loving, but he ought always to avoid like the plague the lewd, double intendre, the filthy joke, any questionable word or gesture, or any sentence that would make the purest of his flock blush with shame (Col. 4:5-6). In his amusements and recreations, the pastor ought always to share in programs that are good and right (1 Cor. 10:32-33; Titus 1:8). The pastor's relationships with all his own people and with all people, strangers and everybody, must be above reproach. He is the moral leader, example, and conscience of the community.

9. The personal, anatomical habits of the pastor ought to contribute to his vigorous, good health. Some pastors are born with severe human deficiencies and congenital weaknesses, but the way we live ought not to contribute to them. Rather the opposite; we ought to follow those practices that make us stronger, more robust in appearance, and in effort. If the pastor can be rested and strong in mind and in body before the Lord's Day services, the power by which he preaches in the pulpit will be multiplied. He ought to preserve at all hazards a high tone of physical vigor and a healthful, elastic, enthusiastic response to the opportunity God has given him.

One of the surprises I sustained in a meeting of a foreign mission board was their questioning of candidates. The first one concerned their health, not their spiritual condition or high sense of calling. When I talked to some of the members about that, they replied that it was useless to send a weak, sick emissary to the foreign field—that it was a waste of their time and God's money. It is surely a disappointing development to a church to call a pastor and the first thing anyone knows he turns sick and anemic.

Here are a few things among others that any pastor can do to stay well and to continue his ministry all the years with increasing happiness in the challenge of achieving great things for God.

(1) The first is to eat correctly. If you do not believe you are what you eat, try not eating for several weeks and see what becomes of you. The *you* that anybody sees is what you eat. That means for health place bulk in your diet (bran and vegetables, etc.) and drink lots of water and fruit juices. Forget about the candy and the junk foods. The less sugar you eat the better off you will be.

(2) Exercise every day, not just once in a while or once a week. Follow a routine pattern of physical exertion every day. Do it faithfully and energetically. If you do not have time to exercise, neither do you have time for anything else. Physical effort is most important.

Plain, simple jogging (if the doctor says so) or walking, or bending, or any other calisthenics, or playing an exerting game, any of these things will do. Just *do* it.

(3) Develop good habits of preventive value. I asked my country doctor friend, when I was a country pastor, how he stayed well, visiting all the sick people. I wanted to visit them, also, but I was advised not to, lest I catch their diseases. This occasioned my visit with the country doctor friend. What did he do to stay well? He replied: "I do two things. I wash my hands and I gargle my throat." I have been doing those two things ever since.

(4) Some of our illnesses and distresses are brought on by our own foolishnesses. My doctor said to me: "You ought to wear some kind of sandals when you take a shower after you exercise at the YMCA. It will keep you safe from many possible germs that can attack your feet." Considering his advice, I went to the sales counter and found that a pair of sandals would cost thirty-seven cents. *Thirty-seven cents!* I thought, *I shall just save me that much money.* I picked up warts, beds of warts, over the bottoms of my feet. I went to the doctor. He said, "These warts are caused by a virus. You have picked it up walking on a floor barefooted. Where have you been?" I shamefacedly explained my saving of thirty-seven cents! We can be "pound wise and penny foolish."

(5) Go to the physician and the dentist regularly for checkups. It will be one of the wisest programs you ever followed. They will count it a great privilege to keep the man of God well and strong.

The Advice of a Political Leader

A most successful and greatly honored political leader one time said to me, "Let me give you what I expect in my pastor. If they can be of value to you in your preaching to preachers, then I shall be most grateful." The list is printed here, not because it is infallible, but because it represents what a devout layman thinks about the place and program of a preacher.

1. I want my pastor to love the Lord, the church, me, and my family.

2. I want him to be merciful and compassionate. I need help and encouragement and I look to him for it.

3. He ought to be a good businessman, full of practical wisdom, what many call "smart."

4. I would like for him to be patriotic, to love our country.

5. He ought to support our community. A dead town is not good for a church.

6. He ought to be tolerant.

7. Let him leave preaching on economics and politics to someone else. Most preachers are not economic wizards.

8. He needs to know where the money comes from, but preach as little on money as he possibly can.

9. He ought to strive to give the people a purpose in life, to motivate people for good.

10. He ought to *really preach*. Preach on the grace of God, on pardon and forgiveness, on faith, on assurance, on God's love and mercy, on how to be saved. He ought to feed the sheep.

Any experienced pastor, looking over this list of ten things the politician wanted his pastor to do, would add to, change, and reemphasize some of them. But from a layman's point of view, the list is worth considering by any pastor.

20

Do's and Don'ts for the Pastor

The Do's for the Pastor

In His Personal Life

1. Do make every effort to maintain close ties with your family. Spend quality time with them. Keep your wife and children as a first priority.

2. Do make sure, in the first place, that you marry a godly, consecrated woman, one who will be a good pastor's wife.

3. Have special days and times to spend with your wife and children.

4. Take time to pray, to be alone with God. Keep your mornings for God. Tell the people the arrangement so other lesser things can be done at later hours. Take everything to God in prayer. "Pray without ceasing" (1 Thess. 5:17).

5. Commit each day to the Lord. Take a spiritual inventory of yourself each day. Are you growing in grace and in the knowledge of the Lord?

6. Be a splendid example of Christian living for all to see. Contribute more than a tithe to the Lord.

7. Be scrupulous and ethical in all your business dealings. Keep good financial records. Pay bills promptly.

8. Be truthful and dependable.

9. Be punctual in all your engagements.

10. Always seek to keep a positive attitude. Never allow your-

self to become a negative, defeatist person. Always look for the positive side of a problem.

11. Keep your mind open to new ideas, but be slow to follow cheap fads.

12. Show enthusiasm and alertness.

13. Keep well and strong physically. It make the difference between victory and defeat in your ministry.

14. Have regular physical checkups.

15. Check to see that your breath is fresh. Halitosis in the preacher is offensive beyond description.

16. Take a little time off each week to recuperate and recharge your mental, emotional, and spiritual strength.

17. Dress appropriately *all* the time, on Sundays and during the days of the week as well. Be clean, neat, immaculate, and in style. Church members want to be proud of their pastor in the way he looks.

18. Dress in fashion, not with wild and loud colors and styles.

19. When it is appropriate, feel free to dress in a casual manner.

20. In being well-groomed, keep your shoes shined, your socks matched in color with your shoes, your shirt and all linens clean, your hair cut and combed, your fingernails cut and buffed, your car clean, and your study in order.

21. The best garment to put on every day is a wide, wonderful smile. The world needs it!

22. Balance your study with your pastoral responsibilities;, especially take time to study.

23. Give yourself sufficient time for sermon preparation.

24. Strive to be a student all the days of your life.

25. Read the biographies of great men both in secular, as well as ecclesiastical history.

26. Study the classics of literature, but above all, constantly study the Bible. A way to do this is to be constantly preaching through a book of the Bible.

27. Have a reading plan. Become familiar with great literature, with the stories of great art and artists and of music and musicians. As a result sermons and addresses can be enriched and strengthened.

In His Preaching Ministry

1. Preach the Word. This is what God says we ought to do (1 Tim. 3:16 to 4:2).

2. Preach as Paul did: First, the doctrinal truth of God, then the practical appeal based upon the revealed truth. Our pragmatic appeal ought always to come out of our doctrinal thesis.

3. Preach the truth of the Scriptures whether it is popular or not. Criticism will come no matter what is preached. If it is mere criticism from man, it does not matter.

4. Let the reprimand for error or unfaithfulness never be from God. Always work and preach as pleasing to our heavenly Father.

5. Never waver from the truth of the Scriptures. Preach it with zeal and with conviction. Do not settle for mediocrity; be the mightiest preacher you can.

6. Be true to your convictions, to your Lord, to yourself. Do not compromise yourself. A denominational executive said to me after I was elected president of the Southern Baptist Convention: "Criswell, do not try to placate the liberals. They are not going to like you no matter what you do." I learned how true was that admonition. If I had a liberal hair in my head, I would pull it out.

7. Give first priority in your ministry to soul-winning and sermon preparation.

8. Preach for a verdict. Drive for decisions. Make the message itself a strong appeal for the Lord. Do the work of an evangelist.

9. Use beautiful diction and grammar. Be careful in your choice of words and in your pronunciation of words. They are the vehicles with which you are carrying your message.

10. Preach expositionally most of the time.

11. Take advantage of special days. Use them for the emphasis the occasion brings, as mother, or country, or our blessings from God, or the dead, or the resurrection. Special days can be great springboards if we turn them to the preaching of the truth of God.

12. The preacher is to be "apt to teach" (1 Tim. 3:2). This is one of the qualifications of his calling. Teach in your sermons. The people need to be instructed in the way of the Lord.

13. Use appropriate illustrations in your sermons. They brighten a sermon with light. They are windows of heaven

through which pour the wisdom and understanding of God. Most of them should come out of personal experience. If the preacher works with his people, he will have a daily assortment of interesting illustrations for the truth of his message.

14. Make Christ Jesus the center of your preaching. If you would have the Holy Spirit with you, glorify the Lord Jesus. That is the work and assignment of the Holy Spirit (John 16:13-14).

15. Always have a humble spirit. Clothe yourself with humility as you would with a garment.

16. Urge the congregation to pray for you as you preach. Encourage them to study their Bibles and to bring them to the worship services of the church.

17. Display public respect and love for the Bible in the manner in which it is held. We try to teach children to care for their Bibles. When one stands before them and rolls his Bible or folds it back or slings it about in the air, that is contradictory to the reverential respect which ought to be so beautifully displayed.

18. Let the sermon always move toward a known and stated objective. If you aim at nothing, you are sure to hit it!

The Pastor and Church Services

1. The physical appearance of the church ought to be in keeping with the respect we hold in our hearts for the house of God. It ought ever to be as clean, as comfortable, as beautiful, and as inviting as we can make it.

2. Let the people Sunday by Sunday place flowers in the church in honor of and in memory of loved ones.

3. Keep all the musical instruments in tune.

4. Have something going on as people arrive in the sanctuary, at least an organ playing familiar hymns.

5. Have a platform of personnel that look nice, pay attention, and who love the Lord, magnificently so.

6. Let the pastor be available after the service to meet visitors. This "makes friends and influences people."

7. Let every service be a praise service. O come, let us magnify the Lord together, let us exalt his holy name! (Ps. 34:3).

The Pastor Ministering to People

1. Pray for and be concerned for the welfare of your flock.

2. Be sensitive to their feelings, griefs, sorrows.

3. Be an empathetic listener.

4. Be available to share your time with others. Help as much as possible to face and to meet the needs of the families in the church.

5. Be patient with the failures and weaknesses of others.

6. Visit every family in the congregation if possible. Acknowledge the presence of little children. Call them by name if possible.

7. The most important thing next to leading a lost soul to Christ that a pastor can do for his people is to love them individually.

8. Respect the confidentiality the church people pour into the ears of the pastor. Pray for them in all their problems, telling God all about it, not anyone else.

9. Write letters of recognition and appreciation.

10. Always compliment and encourage others. Look for the good in them. Help bury the bad.

11. Listen to the members of the congregation. Many times they just need someone *to listen.*

12. Minister compassionately and nonprofessionally to the ill and the bereaved. Be there in their sorrow, not because you are paid to do so, but because you want to do so.

13. Be a good shepherd. Take time to visit the sick in the hospital; it may mean everything to one in deepest despair.

14. In counseling with women at the church, be sure your secretary or other personnel is close by. In a visit in a home, take your wife or a godly layman with you.

15. When death comes to a family member, be sure to visit in the home of the sorrowing.

16. Ask God to keep you in loving sympathy and sensitivity to those who need you.

17. Watch your temper! A pastor can undo in five seconds the progress and respect he has worked fifty years to achieve by berating a staff member, a church member, or anyone else. "He that is slow to wrath is of great understanding: but he that is hasty of

spirit exalteth folly. . . . A soft answer turneth away wrath: but grievous words stir up anger'' (Prov. 14:29; 15:1).

18. When an article appears in the newspaper featuring the accomplishments and achievements of one of your church members or colleagues, cut out the article and send it to him with a warm letter of appreciation. Such a thoughtful gesture will mean more than you could know to the person who sees that you take time for them in such a personal way.

His Soul-winning Ministry

1. Let the pastor be the leader in every soul-winning effort. He should never ask the people to do something he himself does not do.

2. Keep a program going in the church that finds prospects for the people to visit. This can be through a census, through information gained from church visitors, and in several others ways. But use them all zealously.

3. Call people on the telephone. That is an excellent way to contact prospects.

4. Train all the people in the congregation in soul-winning and in discipling.

5. Be consistent and persistent in your soul-winning efforts, not by fits and spasms, but as a matter of lifelong dedication.

6. Let the pastor visit with other staff members and with other laymen in his church as often as possible.

7. Keep evangelism foremost in the program of the church.

8. Visitation must be considered by the pastor as the most important activity in the church, insofar as weekday activities are concerned.

9. The people must be led to visit regularly. If we go, the lost will come.

10. It is wonderful for the pastor to visit his people, to know them by families, to call them by their names.

11. Let the pastor always magnify the invitation time at the public services. Let the people be in prayerful attention, remaining for the entire time of appeal.

12. Establish a policy about the reception of children for baptism. Set a time period for their instruction in church member-

ship, and an age for their baptism. I personally have a rule that the child is not to be baptized before he is nine years old.

13. Let the pastor be sure to visit with every child and his family before the child is baptized.

14. New converts and new members should be received into and by the church individually and with every cordiality. Make each person feel special (he is!). This creates a spirit of warmth and fellowship in the life of the church.

His Administration and Organizational Work

1. Let the pastor pray that God will help him to be a good church administrator. He needs all the wisdom of a corporate executive.

2. Plan a great program for the church. Dream dreams for the good of the people and believe that with God's help you can bring the dream to a reality.

3. Develop a balanced program to meet all the needs of the people and the kingdom of our Lord, remembering that the Sunday School is the greatest instrument we have for reaching people.

4. Know the Sunday School personnel and their work. Visit with them in their work whenever and wherever possible.

5. Expect excellence from both the staff and the leadership of the church. Delegate responsibilities to staff members and to lay leadership, and rely upon them to do the work well. When authority is delegated, stand by the one to whom the work is assigned, especially when confronted by disgruntled members. Give the chosen leader freedom to function.

6. Brag on everyone. People love praise. Praise your staff and leaders publicly. Encourage them to do more for Jesus.

7. Let the pastor stay in touch with all church activities in some way. Let him be aware of every area of church life and know what is going on.

8. Let the pastor work and choose and commend without partiality. It is easy to show partiality to people of means—people of leadership ability—people with much talent—people with charming personalities, but there are many others who need to be recognized.

9. Build a strong Sunday School. The Sunday School is the

backbone of the church. As the Sunday School grows, so the church grows. It needs to be well-staffed by trained leadership. A constant training program is needed. Weekly times of praying and studying and preparing are necessary.

The pastor must be an avid supporter of the Sunday School and say so often, as he is many times dependent upon the Sunday School to see a program through. In the majority of our churches, most of the lost people are won to the Lord out of the Sunday School departments.

10. Let the pastor particularly take advantage of and major on the experience of the age group fifty-one through sixty-four. This is a time of attainment, financially and socially, to a great degree. Many are professional people and have risen to prominence in their fields. Most of them have grown spiritually and have been active in church life. Not only can they contribute to the leadership need but can be a tremendous asset to the financial program of the church.

11. Involve all the people you can in service opportunities. Disciple believers. Train them for places of leadership in the church. Organize them into a soul-winning circles. Keep it going throughout the years.

12. Plan and pursue the plans made for outreach ministries. Let us build our work far beyond the four walls of the sanctuary.

13. Attempt to meet with the staff leadership of the church regularly. Meet with them often on an individual basis. Let a splendid report in a spirit of love characterize the relationship between the pastor and his leadership.

14. Surround yourself with people who love the Lord and his work.

15. Use deacons and deacon committees to help you in your ministry, especially in the administration of the church.

16. Spend time with the men whom God has sent your way. Disciple these men; make of them true servants of Christ. Pour your very life into them.

17. Pray always and by name for these men who are elected to the fellowship of deacons, work on the appointed committees, and all who teach and train in the church organization.

18. Express gratitude and appreciation for your workers. Many

people give of themselves, their talents, their time for service to the Lord. God will bless, but it surely is encouraging to them for others to express gratitude and appreciation.

19. Establish goals in writing for each area and division and department in the church and review progress toward the goals on a regular basis.

20. Maintain straight and strict business practices and procedures in every function of the church. No question should ever be raised about the integrity of our financial program.

21. Have a library or media center in the church and encourage the members to use the materials. Their lives can be enriched. Teachers can improve their teaching if they will find and use suitable materials. God speaks through the printed page, too.

22. Establish definite, appropriate, respectable codes of conduct and dress for those participating in the regular work and service of the church.

23. Involve as many leaders as possible in planning the program for the church. This will greatly heighten and deepen their interest.

24. Do not hesitate to spend any amount of time discussing methods on how to improve the administration practices of the church with your capable laymen.

25. Recognize the value of preschool (Cradle Roll, Nursery, Beginners) in the overall church program.

26. Encourage men to teach children. How can a child who does not have a Christian father desire to relate to our heavenly Father unless we provide a relationship with Christian men?

27. Encourage capable people to teach in children's areas.

28. Compliment leadership with children. Usually they are forgotten.

29. Lead the church adequately to provide for the needs of the children in the yearly budget.

30. Have classes for all ages in preparation for baptism and church membership.

31. Remember that the women of the church can be a vast resource of help if they are cultivated in a positive manner.

32. Before any problem, always ask yourself this question: How would Jesus handle this situation?

His Missionary Leadership

1. Be mission-minded and mission hearted. As goes the pastor, so goes the church. When the pastor is concerned with the needs of people and leads his members to help meet those needs in the name of the Lord, his people will follow.

2. Cultivate a missionary spirit in the church. This has to be found in the pastor himself and then in the devoted effort on the part of the church to support the missionary message. Giving should be presented not as a duty, but as an exalted privilege whose reward is in itself (Acts 20:35).

3. Encourage mission education for all ages. Support the missionary enterprises sponsored by the church.

4. Be concerned about the Great Commission of our Lord (Matt. 28:18-20; Acts 1:8). Let the pastor lead the church to do all three; disciple, baptize, and teach all nations.

5. The pastor should be familiar with the mission education program which WMU and Brotherhood provide for the total church.

6. The pastor should promote missions through the pulpit in sermons and natural ways which show his concern and familiarity with missions. Missions should not always be a project, but promoted as a vital part of the church program.

7. The mission education staff should be a part of the church staff which outlines and purposes the organized life of the church.

8. Provide situations (prayer service, special mission emphasis in evening worship services, etc.) in which missions will be taught.

9. Provide opportunities for members of the church to share in large group experiences in lay missions.

10. Encourage youth mission teams to work within the church, in the city, and in areas away from home. Give youth an opportunity to share experiences.

11. Encourage mission support by praying for the missionaries, by inviting missionaries to share in the church program, and by featuring the special times of weeks of prayer, by setting goals of giving.

12. The pastor should encourage retired members to participate in mission teams in the missionary associate program and in the Christian Service Corps.

13. Have a basic understanding of the importance of mission education to preschool children and youth age levels.

14. Learn the name and age level of each organization.

15. Learn the goals of the organizations.

16. Plan to attend one or more meetings, retreats, or parties held by each group during the year.

17. Take an active part in recognition services.

18. Recognize special achievements by the groups at the Sunday and/or Wednesday night services.

19. Endorse these organizations through the pulpit as well as in the church bulletin.

20. Call attention to special events sponsored by the organizations.

21. Support "Weeks of Prayer."

22. Ask missionaries to speak in the church services.

23. Express gratitude both publicly and privately for the volunteer leadership of the organizations.

His Ministries Beyond the Church

1. There are many denominational responsibilities placed upon the pastor beyond his local church: associational, statewide, Convention-wide, worldwide, educational, missionary boards, committees, conferences. Help all you can.

2. In every way possible be a leader in the community. Take advantage of opportunities to help in worthwhile community projects.

3. Cultivate friendship with other faithful ministers.

4. With regard to our relationship with other denominations, no church ought to isolate itself. It ought not to stand aloof from the Christian community. There ought to be friendly relations developed with Christians of differing denominational views. We ought to be charitable in our judgment of each other and we ought to abstain from language that might reflect on the motives of those who differ with us. There are many ways that we can be helpful and encouraging to people who also call on the name of the Lord. A church will ordinarily develop more effectively its own gifts and its own spiritual power by working with others and

especially with those of a common denominator, such as our own denomination.

The German pastor, Martin Niemöller, was one of the outstanding Protestant scholars in Europe during World War II. In writing about the political and religious persecution of the Jews in Nazi Germany, he stated: "In Germany, the Nazis came for the Communists, and I did not speak up because I was not a Communist. Then they came for the Jews, and I did not speak up because I was not a Jew. Then they came for the Trade Unionists, and I did not speak up because I was not a Trade Unionist. Then they came for the Catholics, and I was a Protestant so I did not speak up. Then they came for me—but by that time there was no one to speak up for anyone."

5. In our relationship with our successor after we have left the church pastorate, faithfully follow the strictest ministerial ethics. The new pastor is now God's man for the people. Pray for his work; do not hinder him.

Return for a wedding or for a funeral or for a service *only* at the invitation of the present pastor. Without his word of consent, do not enter into the pastoral life of the people.

The "Don'ts" for the Pastor

Personally

1. Don't compromise the Word of God. Preach it as it is in the power of the Holy Spirit.

2. Don't make apologies for the truth of God.

3. Don't do anything that violates your sense of God's will.

4. Don't be put in a corner or frightened by deacons, trustees, or influential members. Don't be overly influenced by a certain few in the church.

5. Don't forget your friends.

6. Don't allow money to influence which church you accept to pastor.

7. Don't lose sight of your vision for winning souls.

8. Don't make important decisions quickly. Seek the Lord and wise counsel.

9. Don't drain yourself physically and emotionally. You be-

come weak in the pulpit if you do.

10. Don't be afraid to admit you were wrong and ask for forgiveness.

11. Don't expect a thank-you.

12. Don't get discouraged by circumstances.

13. Don't become a negative thinker.

14. Don't come to the point where you think you have all the answers. Do not pretend you have the solution to every situation.

15. Don't come to the point where you tell God how blessed he is to have you as his minister.

16. Don't forget your family.

17. Don't neglect the sick; don't turn aside from your hospital ministry. Many times this can be an evangelistic opportunity to reach a whole family.

18. Don't forget to pray in every visit. People are more blessed by our intercessions than by our human arguments and observations.

19. Don't be careless and unreliable.

20. Don't resent constructive criticism.

21. Don't blame others for your failures.

22. Don't seek honors which come from men. The pastor stands or falls before God and not men.

23. Don't betray confidences shared with you.

24. Don't become materialistic in your life-style.

25. Don't let yourself fall into professionalism—ministering outwardly because you are paid to do it but losing the inward love that would make you want to help.

26. Don't become a "marrying-parson."

27. Don't become discouraged by the failures of others.

28. Don't give the devil an opportunity to destroy your ministry. Watch your times of counseling, especially with women.

29. Don't become overly concerned with material gain.

30. Don't let personal problems "show." Don't lose your temper—always be in control of yourself. You are the spiritual leader. Don't speak negatively about one member to another. Don't be upset about trivial matters; your time is too precious. Don't be disturbed with opposition or criticism. Stand tall; every leader experiences it. It may be used constructively.

31. Watch the temptation to be prideful in what you are able to do. Do not thank yourself for any victory won. Thank God. Praise him for every victory.

Organizationally

1. Don't become detached from your staff and from your leadership.

2. Don't reprimand staff or leaders publicly. Do it privately, and then with love and grace.

3. Don't criticize more than you commend.

4. Don't become so dictatorial that you lord it over God's people and God's heritage.

5. Don't show favorites, either in staff or in church leadership or in church membership.

6. Don't praise people when they don't deserve it.

7. Don't be "an apple polisher," a sycophant.

8. Don't become so involved in outside affairs until you don't have time for your own flock. If God called you to shepherd the flock, then faithfully do it.

9. Don't feel that you have to make every visit yourself. Train others and use others to help you in your visitation program.

10. Don't be pulled away from the tremendous emphasis that ought to be placed on the Sunday School. A great Sunday School will pay dividends in every area of the kingdom of God.

11. Don't underpay your staff. There is a saying, "You get what you pay for."

12. Don't violate the chain of command established in the structure of the church. Don't let people go over the heads of staff members to reach the pastor. Work *through* the organization and *with* the leaders.

13. Don't show undue consideration to one division, department, leader, or member. It takes a lot of diplomacy and tact, prayer and wisdom, to prove your love for each alike.

14. Don't magnify little problems.

15. Don't forget that you are a servant.

16. Don't isolate yourself from community activities and areas of community concern.

In the Pulpit

1. Don't preach the same sermons over and over again.

2. Don't neglect to prepare the sermon carefully and prayerfully. Don't let anything interfere with study and preparation time.

3. Don't underestimate the ability of your people to learn. If you teach the Word as you preach, they will learn enormously.

4. Don't speak above the level of the understanding of the congregation.

5. Don't be away from the pulpit too much. Sometimes a few times is too much.

6. Don't preach from notes if at all possible.

7. Don't ramble all over the place. Have a definite thought, expressed in a definite message, reaching toward a definite goal. Organize the sermon well. Let it move logically from point to point.

8. Don't be pompous in the pulpit. In every way before God show deep humility and deference.

9. Don't try to shine as a master magician in things spiritual. It is God who works the miracles. Give all the thought, honor, message, results, glory, praise to him. Magnify the Lord Jesus, not yourself.

10. Don't forget to share the public services with all others possible, both on the pulpit platform and through audience participation. Don't seek to do everything yourself.

11. Don't try to be somebody else. Be yourself.

12. Don't forget with thanksgiving in everything to praise the Lord. Let the public worship have that ring, tone, and atmosphere.

13. Don't forget the lost. Preach to them. Don't forget the hurt in heart. They are always present. Comfort and strengthen them. Don't forget the young. They are our hope for tomorrow. Don't forget the old. They built the foundation upon which we stand. Keep them all in your heart, in your prayers, and in your sermons.

14. Don't forget to take a handkerchief with you into the pulpit. Check your pocket to see that you have it.

15. Don't be pedantic, wearing out further the same old time-

worn clichés, trite, stereotyped, and exhausted expressions.

16. Avoid distracting gestures.

17. Avoid facial expressions that do not match the point you are emphasizing.

18. Don't be pseudointellectual.

19. Don't accept Saturday night engagements, especially late hour ones. Get ready for the morrow.

20. Don't be afraid of the unusual service. Instead of an empty church on holidays, take advantage of the situation to pack the house with a dramatic production, a musical program, or a thousand others things that involve the interest of many people.

21. Don't let the hungry sheep come to church services and go away hungry and unfed.

22. Don't tell a joke relating to the Lord and to the Holy Spirit in the pulpit, or anywhere else.

23. Don't embarrass others in public.

24. Don't take advantage of your people in the pulpit.

25. Don't preach in your public prayers.

26. Do not be afraid to stand up for the truth.

Spurgeon was keenly aware of the various theological controversies raging in the religious world. He was not afraid to do battle with the foe. He introduced a monthly paper, *The Sword and the Trowel.* The title was adapted from Nehemiah's rebuilding program of the walls of the Jerusalem. The sword indicated his battle with the enemy, while the trowel pictured the broken breeches in the wall of the religious world.

27. Do not be discouraged by personal handicaps. We all have them. God's strength is perfected and honored in the inherent weaknesses of humans.

> Moses could not speak.
> Jeremiah was afraid.
> Peter was sinful and volatile.
> Paul had a thorn in the flesh.
> Wesley was diminutive.
> Moody was uneducated.

Whitefield was afflicted with asthma
(he died with an attack of it
after preaching a sermon).

It is God "Who maketh . . . his ministers a flame of fire"
(Heb. 1:7).

Evangelistically

1. Don't get discouraged; you will eventually win somebody.
2. Don't talk about irrelevant things; keep your prospect face-to-face with Jesus Christ.
3. Don't argue or show irritations; God is love.
4. Don't monopolize the conversation; let the lost man talk of his background, experiences, and problems.
5. Don't talk at first about the church; Christ has a better reputation than your church.
6. Don't ask questions that get no for an answer; get yes, yes, yes, until you get yes for Christ.
7. Don't feel compelled to answer all excuses; witness for Christ.
8. Don't be sidetracked into a social visit or be content to give an invitation to attend preaching; press for a decision for Christ.
9. Don't fail to have a prayer of consecration after one makes a decision to trust Christ.
10. Don't fail to follow through and to follow up. If at first you don't succeed, try, try, and try again.
11. Don't hesitate to press the appeal for Christ at the conclusion of every sermon and service.
12. Don't "be weary in well-doing." In due season you will reap if you faint not. God sometimes seems to want to see if we are really committed to the task of soul-winning.
13. Don't fail to praise God for every soul won.
14. Don't leave the new convert to be swallowed up by the unbelieving world. Keep him in the fold, teaching, training, encouraging in every possible way.

15. Don't baptize small children below the age of nine.

16. Don't ignore the poor, the needy, the unlovely. Sometimes they will respond the most readily to the gospel message of salvation.

21

The Reward of a Work Well Done

This Final Chapter an Epilogue

This final chapter closing the book is more like an epilogue than a further discussion. We have followed through the many-faceted ministries of the pastor and, even though so much of his work is done in tears, yet the reward of rejoicing is ever near and ever present truly, "They that sow in tears shall reap in joy. He that goeth forth and weepeth, bearing precious seed, shall doubtless come again with rejoicing, bringing his sheaves with him" (Ps. 126:5-6). It is as my great predecessor, Dr. George W. Truett, one time said to a small group of young preachers: "When I was young I had my heart set on being a lawyer. But God called me to be a preacher. Now after these long years in the ministry with all their heartache and tears, even though I once wanted to be a lawyer, yet if I had a thousand lives to live, I would give them all to be a preacher of the Gospel of the Lord Jesus Christ." He moved my soul as I heard him say that. After these years, now numbering over half a century, I feel the same. If I had ten thousand lives to live, I could wish that every one of them could be devoted in some way to the extension of the kingdom of Christ."

The Blessed Privilege of Being a Pastor

There ought to be in the pastor an habitual looking above for the rewards of his work (1 Tim. 4:8). The recompenses of the faithful pastor are from God and are of special magnitude and blessing. These rewards come in part in the present life. A faithful

377

minister finds them alike in a clear conscience and a sense of the approval of God upon his work and the blessed results that follow from it.

He may be sorrowful in some of his ministries, but always rejoicing in his heart. Consider the martyrs who sang while they were executed. Henry Martyn said: "I do not wish for any heaven on earth besides that of preaching the precious Gospel of Jesus Christ to immortal souls. I wish for no service but the service of God in laboring for souls on earth and to do his will in heaven."

Dr. Doddridge said, "I esteem the ministry the most desirable employment on earth and find a delight in it and advantages from it which I think hardly any other employment on earth could give me." Rutherford said, "There is nothing out of heaven next to Christ dearer to me than my ministry." Brown said. "Now after forty years of preaching Christ, I think I would rather beg my bread all the laboring days of the week for an opportunity of publishing the Gospel on the Lord's Day than without such a privilege to enjoy the richest possessions on earth."

The conscious presence of Christ, the blessed privilege of declaring to guilty men God's rich and free mercy, the delight in the work of saving souls and of ministering comfort and strength anh hope to the sorrowing, the weak and the despairing, the joy of communion with saints, all of these enter into the minister's experience and give to his work even on earth an unspeakably rich reward.

The Scriptures speak of these heavenly remembrances so beautifully:

And they that be wise shall shine as the brightness of the firmament; and they that turn many to righteousness as the stars for ever and ever (Dan. 12:3).

Then shall the righteous shine forth as the sun in the kingdom of their Father. Who hath ears to hear, let him hear (Matt. 13:43).

And he that reapeth receiveth wages, and gathereth fruit unto life eternal: that both he that soweth and he that reapeth may rejoice together (John 4:36).

For our light affliction, which is but for a moment, worketh for us a far more exceeding and eternal weight of glory (2 Cor. 4:17).

For what is our hope, or joy, or crown of rejoicing? Are not even ye in the presence of our Lord Jesus Christ at his coming? (1 Thess. 2:19)

Henceforth there is laid up for me a crown of righteousness, which the Lord, the righteous judge, shall give me at that day: and not to me only, but unto all them also that love his appearing (2 Tim. 4:8).

Blessed is the man that endureth temptation: for when he is tried, he shall receive the crown of life, which the Lord hath promised to them that love him (Jas. 1:12).

All of these scriptural words offer a composite of John Bunyan's description of a faithful minister in *The Pilgrim's Progress*. He had eyes lifted up to heaven, the best of books in his hand, the law of truth was written upon his lips, the world was behind his back, he stood as if he pleaded with men, and a crown of gold did hang over his head.

The Pastor's Crown

In 2 Corinthians 5:10 the apostle Paul speaks of our standing before the *BEMA*, the judgment seat of Christ where we shall receive our final rewards. In ancient Grecian games the athletes (runners, wrestlers, javelin and discus throwers all,) assembled before the judge's stand, an elevated platform on which the umpire sat, to receive the rewards of their excellence. The winner received a crown of laurel leaves. Some received no reward at all; they did not prevail.

We are encouraged in the Holy Scriptures to be faithful in our work unto death to be true to the faith even though it costs us our lives. If we are thus faithful, our Lord will bestow upon us a crown of life (Rev. 2:10).

There are five crowns of reward described for us in the New Testament, and all of them are possible for certain worthy pastors, four of them within reach of every pastor.

1. The first of them is the martyr's crown, the crown of life. It is mentioned twice. In James 1:12 we read: "Blessed is the man that endureth temptation: for when he is tried, he shall receive the crown of life, which the Lord hath promised to them that love him."

And in Revelation 2:10 we read: "Fear none of those things

380 CRISWELL'S GUIDEBOOK FOR PASTORS

which thou shalt suffer: behold, the devil shall cast some of you into prison, that ye may be tried; and ye shall have tribulation ten days: be thou faithful unto death, and I will give them a crown of life."

Every age has known ministers who have laid down their lives for the faith, and our life is no different. Fellow Christians are being martyred all over the earth, these who have "loved not their lives unto the death" (Rev. 12:11).

2. The second is the soul-winner's crown. There is the crown of rejoicing spoken of by Paul in Philippians 4:1. "Therefore, my brethren dearly beloved and longed for, my joy and crown, so stand fast in the Lord, my dearly beloved." And by the same apostle in 1 Thessalonians 2:19-20. "For what is our hope, or joy, or crown of rejoicing? Are not even ye in the presence of our Lord Jesus Christ at his coming? For ye are our glory and joy." Those we have brought to Jesus will be our everlasting rejoicing when Jesus comes for his own.

Things that happened to me in the early, beginning days of my ministry made a far deeper and indelible impression on me than things that happen to me now. In my first little country pastorate, while a student in school, I drove over the roughest road to a most out-of-the-way place to lead a boy sixteen years of age to the Lord (he was just two years younger than I). I baptized him in a river, rejoicing in my convert.

A few months later, when I drove out to my little church, I was told at the first farm home I visited that the lad was dying and was calling for me. He had a tragic case of pneumonia, which in the days before antibiotics almost always proved fatal. I went to the home but I was too late. The youth had sunk into a deep coma and could not be aroused to let him know that I was there. In a few minutes the doctor turned to us and said, "The boy is dead."

With tears of sorrow I asked the mother and the father why he so wanted me to come. They replied: "We do not know for certain. The doctor had told him and us that he could not live. He knew he was going to die. It was not that you pray that he live. He told each one of us good-bye and that he would meet us in heaven. But he would not tell us what he wanted to say to you."

Often through the many years have I thought about the lad.

What did he want to say to me? I think it was this: "Pastor, I want to thank you for driving over those rough roads to this out-of-the-way place to win me to Jesus. I shall be in heaven soon all because of you."

What a reward! "I am here in heaven all because of you." This is the soul-winner's crown.

3. The third is the crown of righteousness, described by Paul in 2 Timothy 4:8: "Henceforth there is laid up for me a crown of righteousness, which the Lord, the righteous judge, shall give me at that day; and not to me only, but unto all them also that love his appearing." To the wicked and to the unsaved, the coming of the Lord is a terrible thought. It means this eternal judgment of damnation. But to the righteous, to these who love the Lord Jesus, the appearing of your Savior is joy unspeakable.

4. The fourth crown is the victor's crown, given to those who subdue the carnal passions of the body. It is described by Paul.

Know ye not that they which run in a race run all, but one receiveth the prize? So run, that ye may obtain.

And every man that striveth for the mastery is temperate in all things. Now they do it to obtain a corruptible crown; but we an incorruptible.

I therefore so run, not as uncertainly so fight I, not as one that beateth the air:

But I keep under my body, and bring it unto subjection: lest that by any means, when I have preached to others, I myself should be a castaway (1 Cor. 9:24-27).

Paul says this is an "incorruptible" crown. Free from the compromises and degradation of the corrupting flesh, the believer in Christ can live in his grace and power a beautiful and sanctified life. The Christian who refuses worldly pleasures and amusements, turns aside from fleshly lusts and carnal desires, will not be ashamed at our Lord's coming. Thus writes the sainted apostle John in 1 John 2:28-29:

And now, little children, abide in him; that, when he shall appear, we may have confidence and not be ashamed before him at his coming.

If ye know that he is righteous, ye know that every one that doeth righteousness is born of him.

He receives the victor's crown.

5. The fifth crown is the pastor's crown. This is the reward reserved especially for him. God sets the faithful pastor apart from all others of his people to be singled out for signal and unusual recognition. This crown is described by Simon Peter in 1 Peter 5:1-4. It is given by the chief Shepherd when he shall appear. Oh, what a day, what an hour, what a moment for the faithful pastor! "God having reserved some better thing for us" (Heb. 11:40).

The Pastor's Reward

The rich reward of the pastor could never be expressed in terms of monetary stipends and salaries. He is paid in the coin of heaven, a rich compensation hallowed in this life and forever sanctified in heaven. The love and affection of his people is worth more than all the gold and silver in the world.

Here is a letter written to and about me on my thirty-fifth anniversary as under shepherd of the church here in Dallas. The church member who wrote it blessed my soul more than all the tributes given me on that memorial day. I speak of it here and publish it here to show how rich are the rewards of the pastor who will pour his life into the people of his congregation.

There are many God-called pastors serving churches all over the world. Within these walls, however, the very word, *Pastor,* has a hallowed meaning. Among other meaningful associations, it reminds us of the warmth, the dignity, and the faithfulness of the dear pastor who has served as under shepherd of this flock for thirty-five years. Both he and his predecessor, Dr. Truett, have been addressed by their people as simply "Pastor," and when we speak of the pastor or pray for him, he is always the "Pastor."

What makes the pastor of the First Baptist Church unique? That is an unanswerable question for the pastor has a many-faceted personality. He is sophisticated, learned, a citizen of the world, and as uncomplicated as cornbread and buttermilk. He is equally comfortable preaching before a large convocation anywhere in the world or to a handful of people under a brush arbor; and his enthusiasm and zeal for the Lord is not diminished by one circumstance or the other.

The Bible tells us that Christ loved the church and gave Himself for it. Christ truly loves this church and guards its pulpit zealously.

What makes the pastor's ministry so significant in our lives as church members?

First, he is simply Our Pastor, God's divinely chosen under shepherd of this flock, and as our pastor he touches our lives again and again.

If you came to this church confessing Christ as your Savior, he welcomed you into the kingdom and into the church with great, exuberant joy, and he reverently baptized you.

Only in heaven is recorded the names of those to whom he has preached, for when he has prayed and by personal witness led to a saving knowledge of Jesus Christ.

If you have long membership here, he knows your parents, your children, and perhaps even your grandchildren and other members of your family.

He shares our successes, our triumphs, our broken dreams, broken hearts, and broken lives.

If you have had a serious illness, more than likely he visited you in the hospital.

He performed your marriage ceremony.

He rejoiced with you when your children were born, and as they grew, again and again, with great tenderness the pastor pointed the way to salvation; and as a parent how could one ever forget the preciousness of the pastor's visit and prayer with each child as he approached baptism.

The pastor shares laughter and play with us and our children.

If you have ever found yourself in deep trouble, he was available to you for counsel and help; for he lives down where his people live. Following the example of our Savior, he is touched by our infirmities.

If death has knocked at your door, he wept with you as he buried your dead.

Whoever you are, he has made a difference in your life; and whoever you are, he has prayed for you.

We are especially privileged to be members of this choir

384 CRISWELL'S GUIDEBOOK FOR PASTORS

serving in this church; for the pastor loves and supports the choir and its leadership in a mighty way.

I love to hear him preach. He is an example in preparation, both intellectually and spiritually. But when he preaches, rather than his having prepared himself to preach *his* message, it would appear rather that the Holy Spirit has prepared him to deliver God's message. But God has a scholarly and tireless messenger. As a listener, I never cease to be amazed at his fingertip knowledge of history, geography, literature, science, politics and the arts . . . his vigorous proclamation of the gospel of Christ, the verity of the message, the timeliness of the message, his enthusiasm, his originality and his faithfulness to the Scriptures are a constant blessing.

His encouragement to the choir is without compare. But it is honest encouragement. We are very sensitive to his response to our music, and if we do not do good, he communicates that to us. However we do, he keeps us always reaching to do better for God.

His example in preparation is such that I cannot make casual or presumptuous preparation to sing. I must make ready vocally, intellectually, and spiritually. . . .

There is nothing negative or in between about the pastor. Always he sounds a positive note. Always he leads us forward, outward, and upward. A writer for a Dallas newspaper once commented that one of the things he liked about the pastor of the First Baptist Church was that he didn't mumble when he talked. If he has something to say, he says it out loud and clear.

Pastor, we thank you for your preaching, for the glory of the message, for its strength and power, for rightly dividing the word of truth to the saving of our souls and the changing of our lives, as we yield ourselves to discipleship.

Thank you for all that you do for our children, for our families.

Thank you for loving good music.

Thank you for loving our music, and for encouraging us to sing yet a sweeter note, a more heavenly refrain.

Thank you for the richness of the music leadership through these years.

Thank you for praying for us.
Thank you for being to us our Beloved Pastor.

I am not at all worthy of this tribute, but that a member of the church of our Lord could write such words to me makes the toil and effort of the work worth it all a thousand times over again.

Thus Paul closed his life and ministry with the holy words of 2 Timothy 4:6-8, looking forward to the crown of righteousness:

For I am now ready to be offered, and the time of my departure is at hand.

I have fought a good fight, I have finished my course, I have kept the faith:

Henceforth there is laid up for me a crown of righteousness, which the Lord, the righteous judge, shall give me at that day: and not to me only, but unto all them also that love his appearing.

And thus the author of Hebrews would encourage us to be faithful in the race God hath set before us:

Wherefore seeing we also are compassed about with so great a cloud of witnesses, let us lay aside every weight, and the sin which doth so easily beset us, and let us run with patience the race that is set before us,

Looking unto Jesus the author and finisher of our faith; who for the joy that was set before him endured the cross, despising the shame, and is set down at the right hand of the throne of God (Heb. 12:1-2).

Now the God of peace, that brought again from the dead our Lord Jesus, that great shepherd of the sheep, through the blood of the everlasting covenant,

Make you perfect in every good work to do his will, working in you that which is well-pleasing in his sight, through Jesus Christ; to whom be glory for ever and ever. Amen (Heb. 13:20-21).